THE BEATLES AND IRELAND

CW00541943

THE BEATLES AND IRELAND

MICHAEL LYNCH AND DAMIAN SMYTH

Foreword by Tom Dunne

The Collins Press

Published in 2008 by
The Collins Press
West Link Park
Doughcloyne
Wilton
Cork

© Michael Lynch and Damian Smyth 2008

Michael Lynch and Damian Smyth have asserted their moral right to be identified as the authors of this work.

All rights reserved. The material in this publication is protected by copyright law. Except as may be permitted by law, no part of the material may be reproduced (including by storage in a retrieval system) or transmitted in any form or by any means, adapted, rented or lent without the written permission of the copyright owners. Applications for permissions should be addressed to the publisher.

British Library Cataloguing in Publication Data

Lynch, Michael

The Beatles and Ireland
1. Beatles 2. Beatles – Homes and haunts – Ireland
3. Musical landmarks – Ireland
I. Title II. Smyth, Damian

782.4 2 166 0922

ISBN-13: 9781905172788

Design and typesetting by Anú Design, Tara
Typeset in Garamond 11pt
Printed in Malta by Gutenberg Press Ltd

Mixed Sources
Product group from well-managed forests, and other controlled sources
www.fsc.org Cert no. TT-CoC-002424
© 1996 Forest Stewardship Council

The paper used for this book is FSC-certified and totally chlorine-free. FSC (the Forest Stewardship Council) is an international network to promote responsible management of the world's forests.

Contents

Preface

The story of the Beatles has been told so often over the years, it is no exaggeration to suggest that almost everything the group ever did or said – collectively and individually – has been recorded. Bookshelves groan under the weight of tomes that explore the minutiae of the group's musical, cultural and historical legacy. Yet in all those volumes there is one chapter of the group's career that has been

mpL

1 Soho Square · London W1D 3BQ

1 March 2005

Michel Lynch
County Laois
Ireland

Dear Michael

Thank you for your recent letter to Paul McCartney to which he has, in his absence, asked me to reply.

Although Paul was flattered to be asked, unfortunately he is unable to provide you with a forward to your proposed book. Paul is inundated with countless projects at the moment and therefore he is not considering any additional requests at this time.

Paul would nevertheless like to thank you for considering his involvement and wishes you every success with the book.

Yours sincerely

Jessica Wells

Letter from MPL on behalf of Paul McCartney.

overlooked – the story of their Irish heritage and connections with Ireland.

When the Beatles first played in Dublin at the Adelphi Cinema in November 1963, Paul McCartney announced that it was 'great to be home'. Certainly the reception the group received in Dublin at the height of Beatlemania was the same as they experienced in every other country they visited. The only difference was that three-quarters of the group – John, Paul and George – could truly be said to be returning to the country of their forefathers. Then, at a civil rights march in New York in 1972, John proclaimed his Irish roots declaring, 'My name is Lennon and you can guess the rest', before going on to remind the crowd that in England Liverpool is called the 'capital of Ireland'. Later, he famously bought an island off the coast of Co Mayo. In more recent times, Paul chose Castle Leslie in Co Monaghan as the venue for his marriage to Heather Mills.

We are Beatles fans with an Irish pedigree and, as for so many other people, the band has provided a soundtrack to our lives. Damian's first musical memory was of seeing the Dave Clark Five on television performing their 1964 hit, 'Bits and Pieces'. Wings' 1973 album, *Band on the Run*, stands out as a particular favourite and it was the album that ignited his lifelong fascination with the work of the Beatles and their various solo incarnations. In 1994, to commemorate the 25th anniversary of the Beatles' last public performance on the roof of their Apple offices in London, he staged a reconstruction of the event on the roof of Dublin radio station, Anna Livia FM, with renowned Irish Beatles tribute band, the Quarrymen. The performance was broadcast live.

His work has frequently brought him into contact with people who have Beatles connections, including former Wings guitarists, Denny Laine and Henry McCullough, the Beatles' personal assistant, Alistair Taylor, early Beatles promoter, Allan Williams, and John Lennon's first wife, Cynthia. He has also met and interviewed Yoko Ono, and David Bowie on the subject of George Harrison. Last, but not least, he met Paul McCartney at Castle Leslie on the day before his wedding to Heather Mills in 2002. Damian lives in Dublin with his wife and their two daughters.

Michael's first musical inspirations were of the 1980s variety, such as Wham! and Prefab Sprout, but the first concert he went to was Paul Simon in Dublin in 1987. Since then, he has attended gigs in Madrid, Hamburg, London, Liverpool, Copenhagen and Bratislava, and even admits to attending a Eurovision Song Contest in Kiev. Along the road he has encountered Paddy McAloon and David

Bowie amongst many others, spoken to Stevie Wonder on the phone, and appeared onstage at Bon Jovi and Madonna gigs. But he describes his meeting with Paul McCartney as the musical highlight of his life. Michael lives in his native Laois with his wife and their two children.

There are many, many stories to tell of the Beatles in Ireland and there are many Irish people to tell of meeting and working with the group over the years. In this book we've just tried to include as many of these stories as possible.

Damian Smyth and Michael Lynch
Dublin and Co Laois, July 2008

Acknowledgements

We would like to thank our families, who have put up with the long hours, mountains of paperwork and never-ending talk of the Beatles, all required to complete this project.

We would also like to offer our sincere thanks to the following people for their insight and material which, no matter how small or incidental, has made this book possible: our editor, Adrian Smyth, who smoothed out the rough edges, improved the overall quality and brought his expertise to this body of work. Pete Brennan, President of Beatles Ireland (the band's Irish fan club), who deserves special credit for all his input into the early research of the Beatles and their associations with Ireland, and for the material and interviews he provided; Mark Welsh, for his unstinting help and enthusiasm during the course of our research over the last three years; Derek Clarke and everyone else associated with Beatles Ireland and its website. Thanks also to: Bill Harry, Jorie Gracen, Keith Badman, Freda Kelly, the late Harry Lush, Tommy Nolan, John Healy, Sandra Grant, Declan Meehan, Gael Linn, Ken Ronan, the late Frank Hall, Sean Newman, Tony French, Richard and Maureen Hall, Scott Maher, Fran King, Rob McKinney, Donovan, the late Alistair Taylor, Liam Kelly, Tom Dunne, Dave Fanning, Dick Doyle and Daniela Bindl at IRMA, John Pinder and Philippa Hayes at ChartTrack, John Lynch Snr, Paddy Barron, Samantha Leslie, Pete Murphy and all at EMI Ireland, Martin Daly, Richard Evans, Ken Martin, Rachel Grimes, Dave McAleer, Jenny Headen, Patsy Rogers, Martin McAloon, Harry Prytherch and Richie Taylor. Lew Baxter, Hilary Maklin, Laura Meehan, Ann Marie Kelly, Larry Gogan, Ian Dempsey, Daithi Ó Dufaigh, Gerry Murphy, Geoff Rhind, Ed and Betty Ryan, Tony Foran, Andy Halpin, Paul McLoone, Gay Byrne, Jutta Bobbenkamp, Andrew Basquille, Eamonn Carr, Alan Corr, Ryan Tubridy and Ronan Collins. And of course anyone else we may have forgotten, but you know who you are.

If you would like to contact the authors with regards to corrections, copyright, omissions or anything regarding this book, please e-mail us at:
www.thebeatlesandireland@yahoo.ie

Photographs

Pictures are supplied or reproduced with kind permission of the following: *Amharc Eireann*, the Gael Linn Newsreel; the Beatles Ireland website and Pete Brennan; Bill Bernstein; Maxime Botella; the French family collection; Richard Hall; the *Evening Herald*; Pat Hill; the *Irish Independent*; Michael Lynch; Maxwell Picture Agency; the *The Mayo News*, Mirror Group Newspapers; the National Library of Ireland; Eileen Reid; Terry Saunders; Damian Smyth; the *Irish Sun*; Trinity Mirror plc; and Ulster Television. To those anonymous hands who took photographs that we have not credited, our apologies and please contact us with a view to acknowledgement in subsequent editions of this book.

Foreword

I met Paul McCartney at one of his shows in Barcelona in early 2003. Afterwards I phoned my sister. She gasped: 'Thomas Dunne, of Donard Road in Drimnagh, Dublin, Ireland, has just met Paul McCartney of the Beatles!' Her words evoked an image of a snotty-nosed urchin from a housing estate in Dublin. And that urchin had just met a Beatle!

This book manages to do for Ireland what my sister's words did for me. It puts in brilliant perspective what it was like for Ireland to meet the Beatles, making the various experiences of the Irish people who met them as real, tangible, personal and heartfelt as if it was happening today.

Considering the vast tomes that have been written about the Beatles it seems incredible that to date no account has been given of their numerous Irish connections – the almost mythical Adelphi concert, the Irish heritage of Paul, John and George, the fact that Paul got married here and John bought an island – this book sets that record straight.

When we think of the Beatles we tend to think of flights landing at JFK, exotic trips to India, crowds screaming at Shea Stadium and interviews with Ed Sullivan. It is important to remember there were also landings at Shannon, holidays in Dromoland Castle, hysterical girls in the Adelphi and interviews with Frank Hall.

Fans will see evidence of how Irish the Beatles were everywhere, not just in their music but also, and particularly, in their wit. This book goes some way to explaining a bit about that and the part Ireland subsequently played in their lives. All chronicled in glorious, loving, minute detail.

When I was myself lucky enough to interview Paul, the song 'All You Need is Love' went through my mind. Having seen the audience reaction to his shows and the unfathomable depth of emotion that was directed towards the stage, and knowing what faced him later that night in Dublin, I wondered just exactly how much love can you really use?

'Well,' said Paul, 'You need all you can get, mate. I think we all do.' I couldn't help but agree. Well guess what, Paul, John, George and Ringo? Here's some more! Enjoy!

Tom Dunne

The Beatles in Dublin in November 1963. (*Evening Herald*)

1

The Beatles' Irish Family Tree

John Lennon

Lennon, Ó Lionáin, Ó Leannáin: Found overall in Ulster, in the south-east of the Republic, east Galway–Mayo. The derivation may be from *leann* (cloak), or *leannán* (lover, paramour).

The Lennon name is the anglicised version of the Irish, O'Leannain, and is commonly found in Cork, Fermanagh and Galway. John's grandfather, John (Jack) Lennon, was born in Dublin in 1858 and, like many men of his time, emigrated to seek better prospects. He found work as a freight clerk in Liverpool but earned his living, for the most part, as a minstrel singer, taking after his own father who was a singer in Ireland. Jack married Dubliner Mary Anne 'Polly' Maguire in 1915 in Liverpool.

Amongst their children was Alfred (John's father), born at 27 Copperfield Street, Toxteth Park, on 14 December 1912. In later life Alfred was employed as a ship's steward and also earned extra money as a singer. On 3 December 1938, Alfred married 24-year-old cinema attendant, Julia Stanley, at Liverpool Registry Office. Their son, John Winston Lennon, was named after his grandfather, John, and the British wartime leader, Winston Churchill, and was born in Liverpool

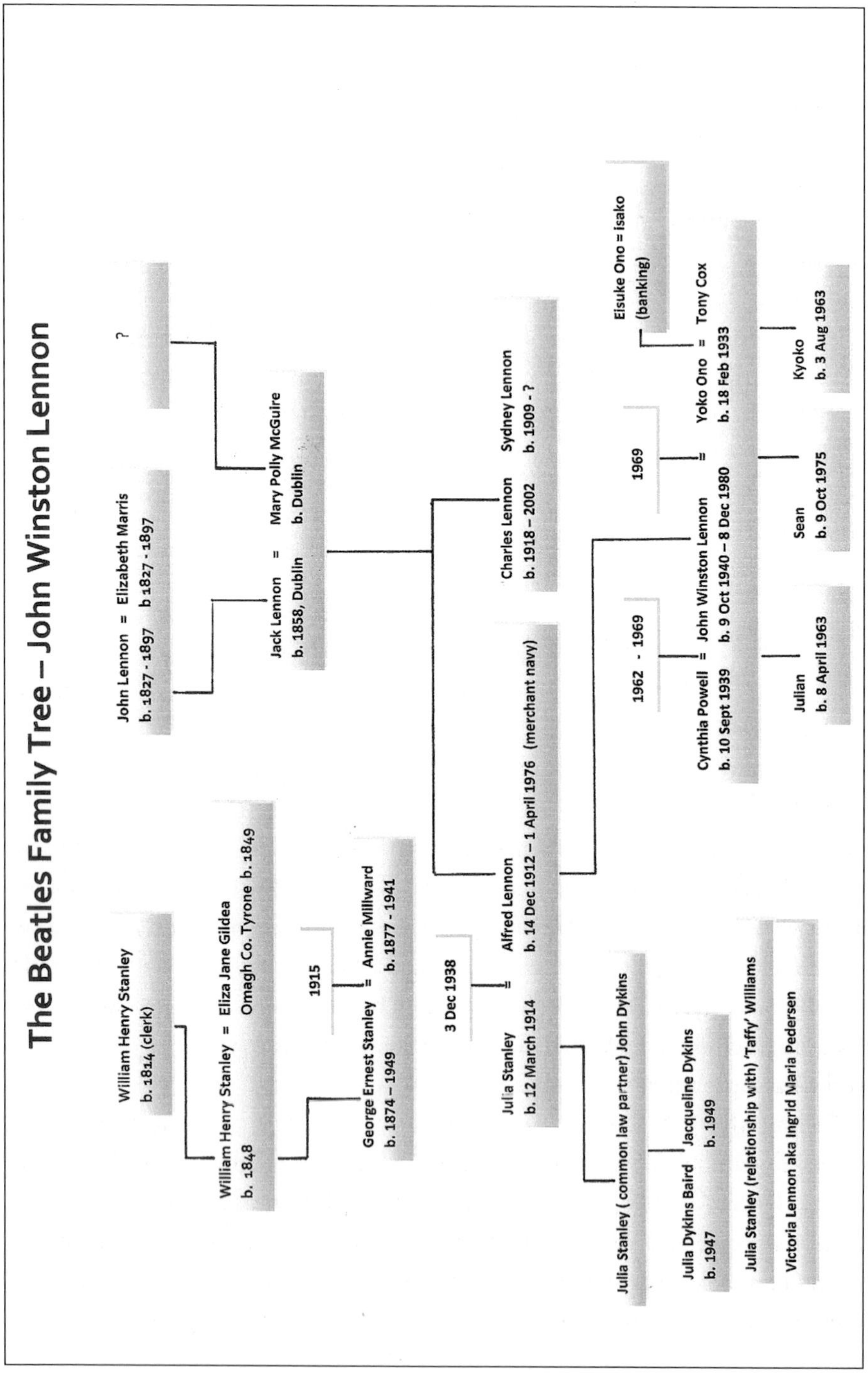
The Beatles Family Tree – John Winston Lennon
William Henry Stanley
b. 1814 (clerk)
John Lennon = Elizabeth Marris
b. 1827 - 1897 b 1827 - 1897
?
William Henry Stanley = Eliza Jane Gildea
b. 1848 Omagh Co. Tyrone b. 1849
Jack Lennon = Mary Polly McGuire
b. 1858, Dublin b. Dublin
1915
George Ernest Stanley = Annie Millward
b. 1874 – 1949 b. 1877 - 1941
3 Dec 1938
Julia Stanley = Alfred Lennon
b. 12 March 1914 b. 14 Dec 1912 – 1 April 1976 (merchant navy)
Charles Lennon
b. 1918 – 2002
Sydney Lennon
b. 1909 - ?
1962 - 1969
Cynthia Powell = John Winston Lennon
b. 10 Sept 1939 b. 9 Oct 1940 – 8 Dec 1980
1969
= Yoko Ono = Tony Cox
b. 18 Feb 1933
Eisuke Ono = Isako
(banking)
Julian
b. 8 April 1963
Sean
b. 9 Oct 1975
Kyoko
b. 3 Aug 1963
Julia Stanley (common law partner) John Dykins
Julia Dykins Baird
b. 1947
Jacqueline Dykins
b. 1949
Julia Stanley (relationship with) 'Taffy' Williams
Victoria Lennon aka Ingrid Maria Pedersen

Maternity Hospital on 9 October 1940. During the war, Alfred became estranged from his family. John Lennon never knew either of his Irish grandparents and his mother's family, the Stanleys, who eventually raised him, were of Welsh extraction.

George Ernest Stanley, Julia's father, was born in 1874 in Everton. He was a musician and previously a sailor in the Merchant Navy. He married Annie Millward in November 1906. Julia's grandfather, William Henry Stanley, was born in 1848 in Birmingham and he was to marry Eliza Jane Gildea. Gildea is an Irish name meaning 'servant of God' and came into the family with John's great-great-grandfather, Charles Gildea, who was possibly an immigrant from Ireland.

In later years Lennon became increasingly interested in his Irish ancestry. On 9 October 1975, John became a father for the second time, when Yoko gave birth to their son, Sean Taro Ono Lennon. John gave his second son the name Sean, the Gaelic version of his own name.

Paul Mc Cartney

McCartney: Found in Belfast, mid-Ulster, Derry, North Antrim, Louth, Monaghan.

Irish Roots

Paul's maternal grandfather, Owen Mohan, was born in 1880 in Tullynamalrow in Co Monaghan, the son of a farmer also named Owen. He emigrated to Glasgow at the age of twelve. When he was 25 he moved to Liverpool and a year later he married a Glaswegian of Irish descent, named Mary Theresa Danher. His bride was the daughter of John Danher, an ironmonger and chandler of Aigburth Road in Liverpool and Jane Baines of Minto Street, Toxteth Park. Jane's father worked as a gas fitter.

In 1919 Mary Theresa died during childbirth, along with her infant daughter, Owen's fourth child. After this, Owen took his three children, Wilf, Mary and Bill, back to Ireland where he attempted to farm. Two years later Owen met and married his second wife, Rose. Unfortunately his farming endeavours were not successful and so he brought his family back to Liverpool where he eventually found work as a coal merchant.

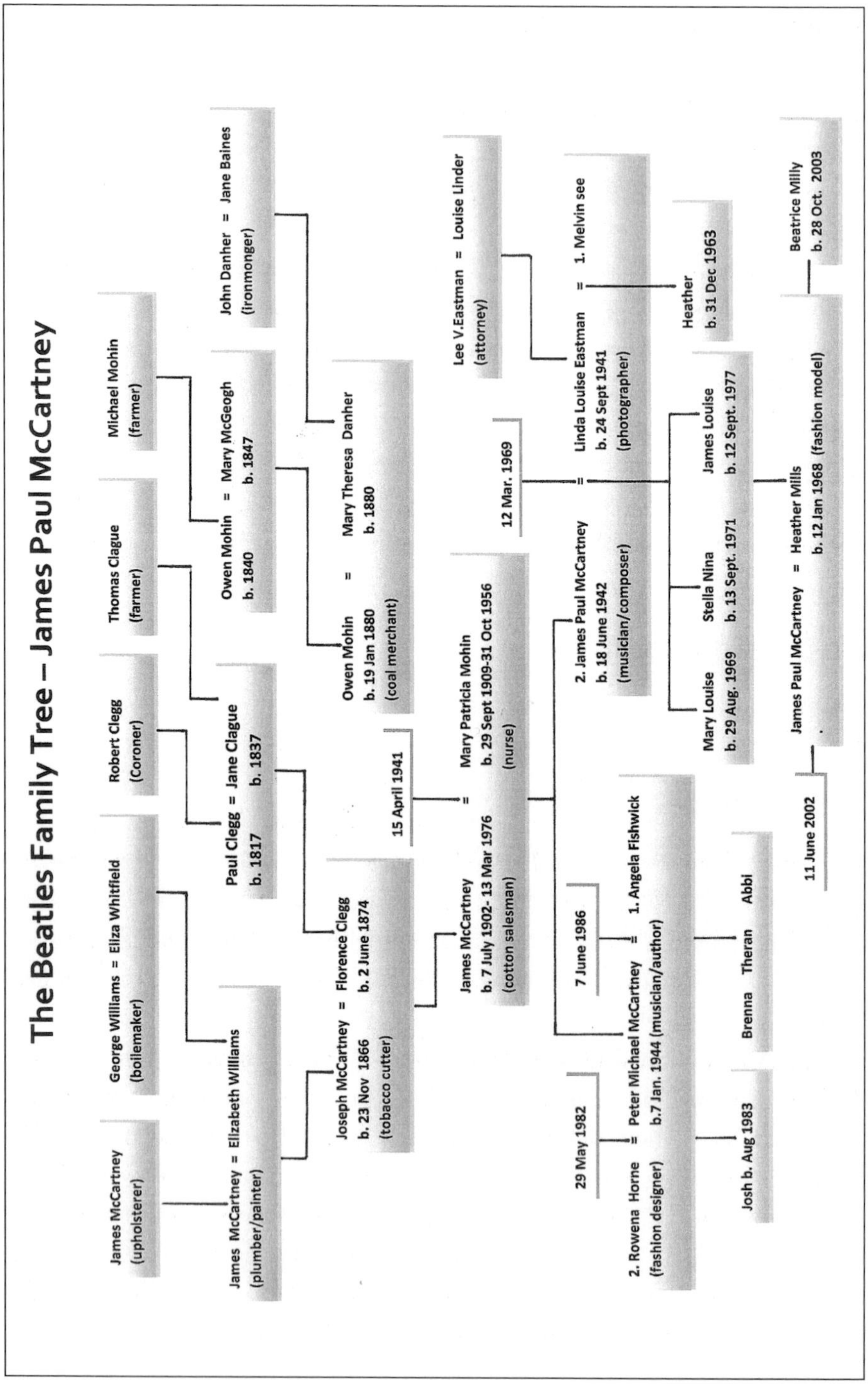
The Beatles Family Tree – James Paul McCartney
James McCartney
(upholsterer)
George Williams = Eliza Whitfield
(boilermaker)
Robert Clegg
(Coroner)
Thomas Clague
(farmer)
Michael Mohin
(farmer)
James McCartney = Elizabeth Williams
(plumber/painter)
Paul Clegg = Jane Clague
b. 1817 b. 1837
Owen Mohin = Mary McGeogh
b. 1840 b. 1847
John Danher = Jane Baines
(ironmonger)
Joseph McCartney = Florence Clegg
b. 23 Nov 1866 b. 2 June 1874
(tobacco cutter)
Owen Mohin = Mary Theresa Danher
b. 19 Jan 1880 b. 1880
(coal merchant)
15 April 1941
James McCartney = Mary Patricia Mohin
b. 7 July 1902- 13 Mar 1976 b. 29 Sept 1909-31 Oct 1956
(cotton salesman) (nurse)
Lee V.Eastman = Louise Linder
(attorney)
12 Mar. 1969
29 May 1982
7 June 1986
2. Rowena Horne = Peter Michael McCartney = 1. Angela Fishwick
(fashion designer) b.7 Jan. 1944 (musician/author)
2. James Paul McCartney
b. 18 June 1942
(musician/composer)
Linda Louise Eastman = 1. Melvin see
b. 24 Sept 1941
(photographer)
Heather
b. 31 Dec 1963
Josh b. Aug 1983
Brenna Theran Abbi
Mary Louise
b. 29 Aug. 1969
Stella Nina
b. 13 Sept. 1971
James Louise
b. 12 Sept. 1977
11 June 2002
James Paul McCartney = Heather Mills
b. 12 Jan 1968 (fashion model)
Beatrice Milly
b. 28 Oct. 2003

Paul's mother and father

It seems that Owen's daughter, Mary Patricia (later to become Paul's mother), did not get along with her new Irish mother, and so she went to live with her aunts. At the age of fourteen she began a nursing career, first at Alderhey Hospital and then at Walton Hospital. By the age of 24 she had become a ward sister.

Mary met her future husband, James (Jim) McCartney, during a German air raid on Liverpool and they were married on 15 April 1941 at St Swithin's Roman Catholic Chapel in Gill Moss. At the time of their marriage Jim was a cotton salesman living at Scargreen Avenue, Fazakerley. During the war he also worked in Napier's Aircraft factory and was a volunteer fireman at night.

Some sources claim that Paul's paternal grandfather, James McCartney (a plumber and carpenter), was actually born in Ireland; others suggest that it was Paul's great-grandfather, also James McCartney, who was the first of the family to leave Ireland. Both of these men were Roman Catholics, but Paul's father, Jim, was raised in the Church of England and grew up without having any specific knowledge of his Irish background, other than knowing that the McCartneys were of Irish origin. During their adolescent years, Mary, who was a devout Catholic, raised her two sons to be aware of their Irish heritage.

On 18 June 1942 James Paul was born at 107 Rice Lane, Walton Park. Two years later, their second son, Peter Michael, was born. When Paul was fifteen, his mother came home one afternoon from a hospital appointment having been diagnosed as being in the late stages of breast cancer. She died within weeks. To help ease the sorrow of the sudden loss of his mother, Jim bought Paul a guitar.

The design of Sir Paul McCartney's coat of arms, granted in June 2001, not only incorporates his musical career, but also incorporates his Liverpudlian roots – the crest shows a Liver bird holding a guitar in its claw. The time he spent with fellow band members John Lennon, George Harrison and Ringo Starr is represented by the four curved emblems on the shield resembling beetles' backs, while the two black circles shown on the shield symbolise records and CDs. The motto *Ecce Cor Meum* means 'Behold My Heart', the title of the oratorio Sir Paul wrote during his first wife, Linda's, illness.

George Harrison

Harrison. Found in Ulster, Connacht, North Leinster

Of all the Beatles, George Harrison can truly claim to have the strongest Irish roots. His family tree can be traced back to the thirteenth century when his ancestors, who were Norman knights from France, settled in southern Ireland at the time of William the Conqueror. Given the name 'Ffrench' by their peasant subjects, these knights owned all the land that could be seen from the tower of their Norman castle in Co Wexford, 60 miles south of Dublin.

During the time of Oliver Cromwell the family refused to renounce their Catholic beliefs and, as a result, were stripped of their property and thrown into a life of poverty, toiling on the land and continuing to do so for the next 300 years. Records show that as recently as 50 years before George Harrison began his musical career, his Irish forebears still lived a humble peasant life on a tiny farm at Corah, Co Wexford.

Clockwise from left: George, his mother Louise and brother Pete in O' Connell Street, Dublin, in the 1950s; George's grandfather during his time with the Liverpool City Police Force (*French family collection*); George's great-grandparents, James (centre) and Ellen French (second left), enjoying a bite to eat on their two-acre farm in Co Wexford. (*French family collection*)

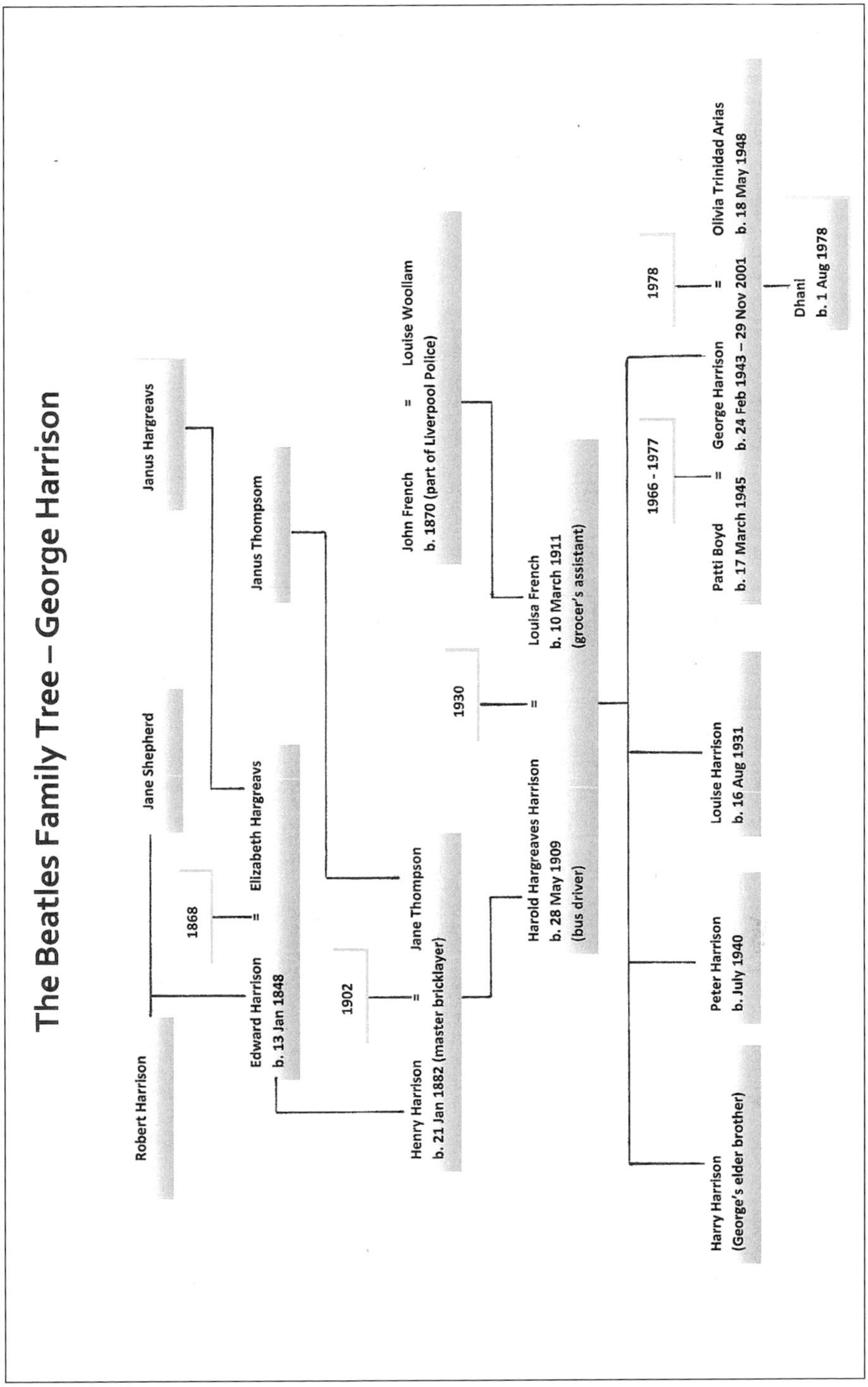
The Beatles Family Tree – George Harrison
Robert Harrison
Jane Shepherd
Janus Hargreavs
1868
Edward Harrison
b. 13 Jan 1848
=
Elizabeth Hargreavs
Janus Thompsom
1902
Henry Harrison
b. 21 Jan 1882 (master bricklayer)
=
Jane Thompson
John French
b. 1870 (part of Liverpool Police)
=
Louise Woollam
1930
Harold Hargreaves Harrison
b. 28 May 1909
(bus driver)
=
Louisa French
b. 10 March 1911
(grocer's assistant)
Harry Harrison
(George's elder brother)
Peter Harrison
b. July 1940
Louise Harrison
b. 16 Aug 1931
1966 - 1977
Patti Boyd
b. 17 March 1945
=
George Harrison
b. 24 Feb 1943 – 29 Nov 2001
1978
=
Olivia Trinidad Arias
b. 18 May 1948
Dhani
b. 1 Aug 1978

A Harrison family snapshot: George (centre back), with his Irish cousins and parents either side of his aunt and uncle, John and Doris French, on holiday in Portrane, County Dublin, in the late 1940s. *(French family collection)*

George's great-grandfather, James Darby Ffrench, was born in 1825 and he married Ellen (née Whelan), born in 1831. The two struggled all their lives to produce enough to feed and clothe their five children and meet a monthly rent of 14*s* 6*d* for their two-acre farm. When they died within two months of each other in 1906, James was 81 and his wife was 75.

Their children, who by now had dropped the extra 'f' from their name, struggled on with the farm for four more years. When Elizabeth, the eldest daughter, died in 1911, the surviving siblings sold the smallholding and divided the proceeds. One of the remaining children, John, born in 1870, emigrated to Liverpool where he signed up with the city's police force. He was sacked, along with the rest of his colleagues, during a bitter union dispute that became known as The Liverpool Lock-out, in which policemen were banned from entering their own stations.

Following a brief spell as a carriage driver, he found employment as a street-lamp lighter and moved to a small terraced house, 9 Albert Grove, Wavertree, where his wife bore seven children. One of their children, Louise, met her husband-to-be, Harold Hargreaves Harrison, when she was a teenager working as a grocer's assistant and he was a steward in the Merchant Navy. After being laid off by the Navy, Harold signed on the dole before finding regular work as a bus driver.

Harold Harrison married Louise in 1930 and they moved to a tiny two-up, two-down, in 12 Arnold Grove. They had four children, Louise (born 1931), Harold (1934), Peter (1940) and George (1943). When their youngest son was six, the family moved from Wavertree to a spacious, modern council house at 25 Upton Green, Speke.

Despite not being the most academic of children, George passed a scholarship exam to attend the Liverpool Institute, the city's top grammar school. It was while he was on the bus to school one morning that he met a fellow pupil of the

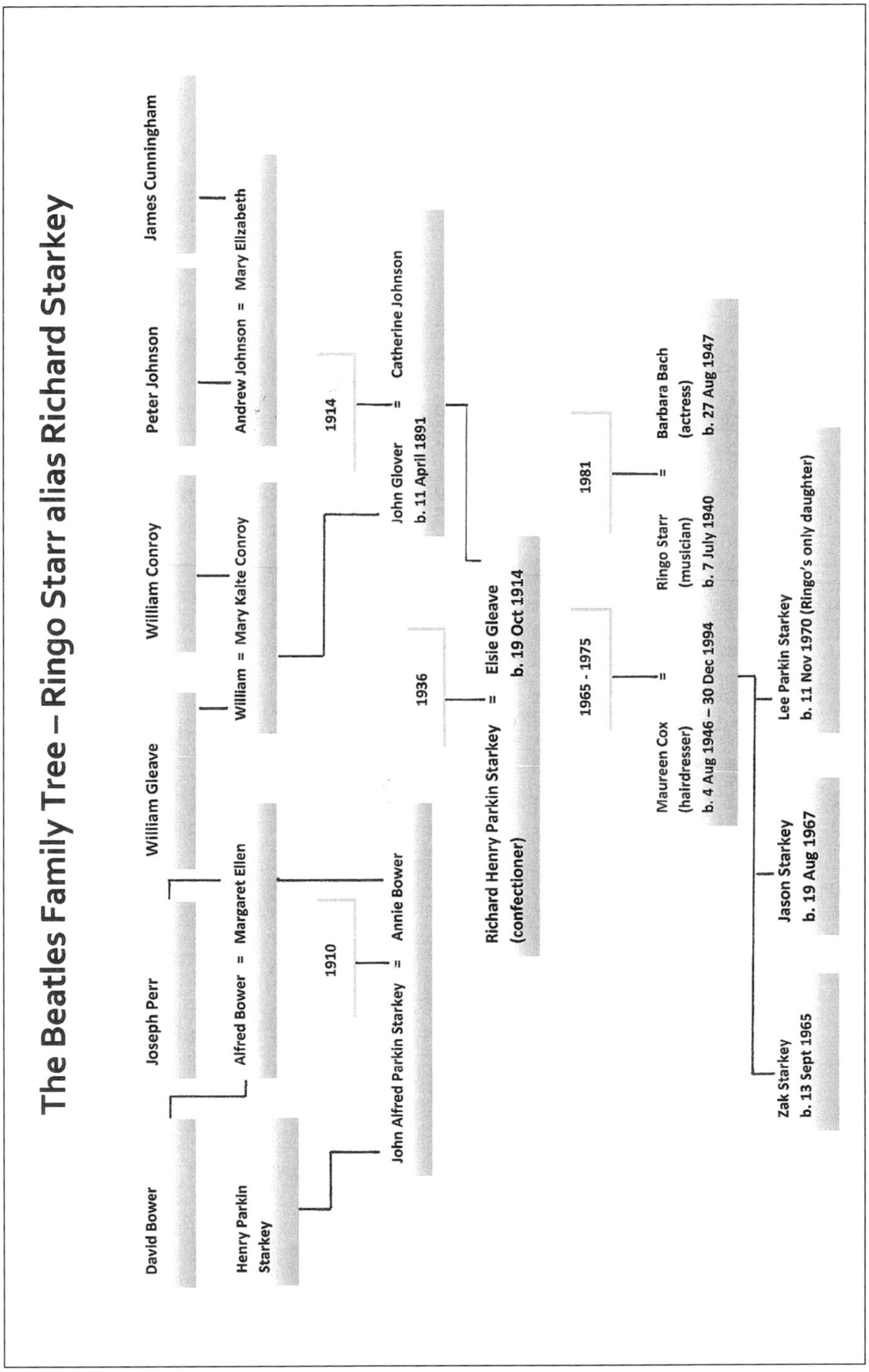
The Beatles Family Tree – Ringo Starr alias Richard Starkey
David Bower
Joseph Perr
William Gleave
William Conroy
Peter Johnson
James Cunningham
Henry Parkin Starkey
Alfred Bower = Margaret Ellen
William = Mary Kalte Conroy
Andrew Johnson = Mary Elizabeth
1910
John Alfred Parkin Starkey = Annie Bower
1914
John Glover b. 11 April 1891 = Catherine Johnson
1936
Richard Henry Parkin Starkey (confectioner) = Elsie Gleave b. 19 Oct 1914
1965 - 1975
Maureen Cox (hairdresser) b. 4 Aug 1946 – 30 Dec 1994 =
Ringo Starr (musician) b. 7 July 1940
1981
= Barbara Bach (actress) b. 27 Aug 1947
Zak Starkey b. 13 Sept 1965
Jason Starkey b. 19 Aug 1967
Lee Parkin Starkey b. 11 Nov 1970 (Ringo's only daughter)

Institute, Paul McCartney. Paul invited him to join a band called the Quarrymen, formed by a third pupil of the same grammar school, John Lennon.

Ringo Starr

(Starkey. Old English word meaning 'stiff', 'dry', 'severe', 'unyielding'. Fairly rare, but occasional in Dublin and Co Down.

Some press reports in England at the height of Beatlemania suggested that Ringo Starr, the Beatles' drummer, also claimed Irish heritage. However, in his 1992 biography, *Ringo Starr: Straight Man or Joker?*, Alan Clayson describes Ringo as the only Beatle without Irish blood. An examination of his family tree, while not absolutely ruling it out, would seem to suggest that he is the Beatle with the least claim to any Irish ancestry.

Ringo Starr was born Richard Parkin Starkey at 9 Madryn Street, Liverpool, on 7 July 1940. His parents were Richard Henry Parkin Starkey, a confectioner, and Elsie Gleave. The only glimmer of an Irish connection might be found on Elsie's side of the family. Ringo's great-great-grandmother, Mary Kate Conroy, was the daughter of William Conroy from Toxteth. Conroy is a name commonly found in Galway, Laois and Dublin and so it would seem that Ringo may well have Irish roots on his mother's side of the family.

2

The Beatles in Dublin and Belfast, November 1963 and October 1964

The Beatles' autumn tour of Britain and Ireland (which ran from 1 November – 13 December 1963) commenced immediately after the group returned from Sweden.

The prestige tours in Britain at the time were run by major London-based promoters. Early in 1963, the group was booked to appear on a second short Scottish tour by the Cana Variety Agency. The agency had secured the group at the bargain price of £42 per show. In February 1963, Drogheda promoter Gerry Murphy had sent a letter to the Beatles' manager, Brian Epstein, inquiring about the possibility of having the group appear at a venue in Drogheda town, Co Louth. Epstein replied, 'The Beatles are available for some dates in March and April for a fee of £1,000.' Unfortunately, Beatles fans in Ireland would not see the group until November of that year, as Murphy's budget would not cover the group's trip to Ireland.

Brian Epstein was determined to place his protégés on a theatre tour and he contacted Arthur Howes, who booked them as support on the bill of the Helen Shapiro tour, commencing in February 1963. Later in the year they were booked to play Dublin and Belfast as the main act and by the time the tour arrived in

Break A Leg

Gerry "Murph" Murphy

NEMS ENTERPRISES LTD
DIRECTORS: B. AND C. J. EPSTEIN

12-14 WHITECHAPEL, LIVERPOOL, 1 TELEPHONE ROYAL 7895

BE/BA:

14th February 1963

Dear Sir,

Thank you for your letter of the 8th instant with regard to the BEATLES. The BEATLES are available for one week May 11th - 17th for which their fee would £1,000. I would require payment of this in advance. With many thanks for your enquiry.

Yours sincerely,
Brian Epstein.

1, Hill Street,
Dundalk,
Co. Louth,
Eire.

Dublin on 7 November 1963, Beatlemania in the city was already well established.

Everywhere they had appeared in recent months, the group had been smuggled in and out of concert venues in operations resembling army exercises. Once inside a theatre, they could do nothing but remain cooped-up in dingy dressing rooms. The Irish leg of the tour was to follow the same format as that of the British, so nobody expected anything to be any different when the band travelled to Dublin to make their first appearance in Ireland.

There were reports that two of the Beatles would travel by B&I Ferries from Liverpool to Dublin and that the other two would travel by Aer Lingus in a bid to avoid an over-enthusiastic welcome from their Irish fans. In the end, however, all four Beatles, along with the support programme, travelled together from London on the day of the concert.

Dublin, 7 November 1963

At Dublin Airport a crowd of about 400 fans waited for the group to arrive. George's mother, Louise, was also there to meet her son, having come over to Dublin to visit her numerous relations.

Just after 12 noon, the specially charted Aer Lingus Viscount aircraft landed and taxied to the main terminal to off-load its musical cargo. After a few minutes, John, Paul, George and Ringo came down the steps of the aircraft. The waiting crowd went wild with excitement. The Irish media were on the ramp to greet the group, eager to get interviews.

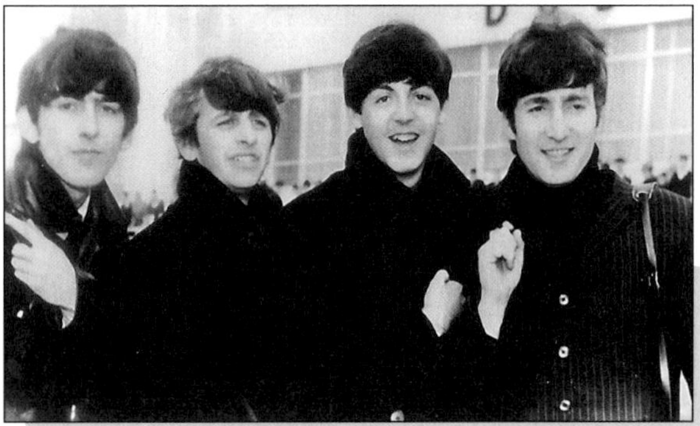

A never-before-published photograph of the Beatles just after their arrival at Dublin Airport, 7 November 1963. *(Terry Saunders)*

RTÉ reporter Frank Hall and cameraman Jacky Merryman were on hand to conduct an interview for the RTÉ news-magazine television programme, *In Town*, which was transmitted that evening. The following is a transcript of the interview:

Frank Hall: Tell me first of all, is the haircut an act by accident or design?

John: Accident.

Frank Hall: You didn't have time to get your hair cut in the first place?

John: No, it just happened, you know. Ringo's was by design because he joined later.

Ringo: Yeah, I designed it. [*Laughter*]

Frank Hall: How often do you get your hair cut, by the way?

John: Uh, well we don't. We try not to mention that.

Paul: It's a dirty word.

Frank Hall: The 'Liverpool sound' is a bit of a puzzle to some of us older people, especially in Ireland. Could you define it for me?

George: It's a puzzle to us, too.

Paul: It's not really a 'Liverpool sound', you know.

John: There's no such thing.

Paul: It just so happens that the new groups that have come out all happen to have come from Liverpool, so people sort of generalise a bit and say, 'Aha! The "Liverpool sound"!' But really, you know, if you listen to the groups, they're all quite different. It's not all one big sound that's coming out.

Frank Hall: Well, it's no use saying, 'Are you surprised by your success?' because quite clearly you're not a bit surprised.

Paul: Oh, we are!

John: We are surprised, but you're just sort of, you know, so surprised that it doesn't even register.

Paul: We look surprised everyday!

[*Frank Hall laughs out loud.*]

Paul: We look off our heads.

Frank Hall: About your Irish backgrounds … ?

Paul: Yeah, I think we've all got a bit.

Frank Hall: [To John] I think I saw you being greeted by somebody outside?

John: No, no, that was George.

George: That was me! Well actually, it was my mother. [*Laughter*] She came over here, you know, because she's got hundreds of cousins and relatives over here, and then she hadn't seen us for weeks anyway, 'cos we've been away. So she's come to see the show and to see her cousins. And one of the cousins was here with her.

Frank Hall: Your mother has to come to Ireland to see you?

George: Yeah! [*Laughs*]

Frank Hall: Well, this in a way kind of typifies the kind of extraordinary upset that must occur in your private lives. Do you all get home at all?

George: Oh, yeah. Sometimes you get home for a whole week. But sometimes you don't get home for months on end.

Paul: It's normally about one day in, say, three weeks.

George: [*Jokingly*] A new idea, telephones, helps a bit, you know.

Frank Hall: God bless Graham Bell.

Paul: Yeah.

George: Freddie Bell. [*Laughter*]

Frank Hall: Does the continuous living together and working together cause any temperamental stress on you?

Paul: No, actually it's quite lucky because we've been …

Beatles: [*Singing together*] … We've been together now for 40 yeeeears!

Paul: You know, we've all been mates for quite a long time, so we don't get on each other's nerves as much as we could. [*Cue mock fighting*]

Paul: We're quite friendly.

Frank Hall: [*Laughing*] Yeah, so I see. So far as I can see, the greater portion of your public seems to be female. To what do you attribute this extraordinary success? A lot of people here would be very interested to know this.

Ringo: You can't make it out, you know.

John: We're male, aren't we? [*Laughter*]

John: It'd be a bit funny if they were all fellas. [*Effeminate voice*] 'Oh! Get away!'

Ringo: It's very nice, you know. We don't know why. If we knew we'd be 'made', more or less. You'd just go and get about six groups like us who are attractive to women.

Paul: What's he talking about? [*Laughter*]

Frank Hall: It's bigger than the four of you!

Beatles: Yeees …

After the short interview, the group was driven to the Gresham Hotel for lunch with the concert venue manager, Harry Lush. At the Gresham, RTÉ had set up a second interview with them. This time it was the turn of Paul Russell and

Adelphi Manger Harry Lush (left) and Michael Nerney, seen here posing with the Beatles. (*Evening Herald*)

cameraman Bill Robinson, who were hoping to capture the group for the RTÉ television programme, *The Showband Show*. A stills photographer was also present.

For one 14-year-old schoolboy from Dublin, the Beatles' visit to the capital was to leave him with a lasting memory and four autographs. His parents had forbidden Ken Ronan from attending that night's concert in the Adelphi, so the intrepid Ken and his mate had bunked off school in the hope of seeing the Fab Four. He finally tracked them down at Dublin's Gresham Hotel and walked through the door to find the Beatles lounging around in the foyer. Ronan recalls:

> We walked straight in past the porter and our jaws just dropped. The four of them were just sitting there waiting to be picked up. They weren't a bit stand-offish and they were quite willing to sign the paper I grabbed that was lying nearby. I asked them where they were going and they said they were going to see George Harrison's cousins in Drumcondra.

By then, some of the members of the hotel staff had seen what was happening and the teenagers were ushered out.

Hours after arriving at the Gresham, the Beatles were to get their first taste of Irish Beatlemania when they held a press conference at the Adelphi in the late afternoon. The press conference turned out to be a most haphazard affair. Even before entering the boardroom of the Adelphi some teenagers, mostly girls, spotted the group stepping from their chauffeur-driven car and rushed forward, following the group into the concert venue. Eventually, the screaming teenagers were ejected and it became possible for the Irish journalists to do their work.

Paul McCartney declared that someone told him he could get an Irish McCartney tartan, and he asked the assembled audience, 'Did you ever hear the like?' Ringo was asked about his hobbies, which he listed as 'girls, drums and cars'. He said he found it difficult to write his name because of the two rings on his right hand – one the size of a small apple. He went on to say he was at a complete loss as to what made the Beatles tick.

The last word went to Paul McCartney. When one journalist asked how long their success would last, he replied, 'It could end tomorrow, but I hope it won't.'

Also in attendance at the press conference was the Liverpool playwright Alun Owen. Owen had previously met George Harrison in Liverpool's Blue Angel Club, but first encountered all four of the Beatles in October 1963. Brian Epstein wrote to him, apparently at the suggestion of Paul McCartney, and then subsequently met him after a performance of one of his plays in Liverpool.

Owen's play of the time, *A Little Winter Love*, was one of the highlights of the Dublin Theatre Festival and so he had travelled over with the band. He had also begun writing the script for *A Hard Day's Night* whilst in Dublin. When Owen was asked about being approached to write the screenplay for the Beatles' first feature film he replied, 'The Beatles are a great bunch of lads, why not? We all come from the same area of Liverpool.'

One young Irish reporter at the press conference was Donal McCann – who was later to become one of Ireland's most renowned actors. In an RTÉ interview in 1993 he spoke about the day he met and interviewed the Beatles:

> I was about to finish my shift and was getting ready to go home, having completed my copy-boy duties at the paper for the day, hoping in some way to get a ticket to see the Beatles. As I was doing so, the person who was to go to the Beatles' press conference to do the atmosphere piece rang in sick. Around this time I was sort of ingratiating myself with Sean McCann, the feature editor. So after the phone had been put down, Sean McCann had a quick look around the office and suggested that I go! At this point I got a great compliment from the late Conor 'News' O'Brien, the editor in charge, when he said, 'He has too much fucking imagination!'
>
> I was finally given the Club Orange bottle cap to wear on my lapel, which was the thing that opened the door to the press conference. I went from the office, with printer's ink, which they still used then, around my face, I was kind of dirty. John Lennon didn't believe for one moment that I was a journalist. I asked him if he believed in God, and he didn't reply immediately. He conferred with Alun Owen, and came back to me saying, 'I have my reservations.'

> There were a lot of girls and young people on Abbey Street. They knew the Beatles were in the Adelphi, because the curtains were drawn in the boardroom in the upper part of the building. I found it very satisfying to go up and tweak the curtains every now and then, knowing that the large crowd would scream, because they thought they had got a glimpse of one of the Fab Four. It was me, the dull one, acting the maggot.

Writing about the concert in the next day's *Evening Press*, McCann described the feeling in the auditorium, 'The atmosphere was hot and sharp; full of powder and perfume and a frightening excitement.'

One Beatles fan managed to gatecrash the Adelphi press conference. She was a 16-year-old girl by the name of Margaret Graham who took it upon herself to go to the side door of the Adelphi, and try her luck. After a few moments she summoned the courage to knock on the door. Margaret recalls:

> I told the guy on the door a complete lie, which was that I was from the national syndicate of papers, and was trying to get the viewpoint for the young fans. And, my God, they let me in! So up I went into the conference room, I remember it was very small. There were about 25 to 30 people in the room and three of them were the Beatles. There was John, Paul, Ringo but no George. [Harrison, having spent some of the afternoon seeking and finding his Irish cousins, returned to the Adelphi in time to meet the press.] I must admit I didn't mind too much as he wasn't at the top of my list. I went straight over to Paul McCartney, and told him the lie I had told the doorman. He also bought the lie! I went on to tell him that I had been to the Cavern with a group I was very involved with at the time. It was hopeless, I became instantly sixteen again and went all weak at the knees and I said to him, 'I'm not a journalist, I just love you!' He was very nice and we talked for about ten minutes. Just before I left the Adelphi, Paul asked me where I would be sitting at the show. He later dedicated the song 'Till There Was You' to me.

Tommy Nolan was on duty at the Adelphi as lighting operator for both Beatles concerts and was party to a brief, and less than cordial, chat backstage prior to that evening's first performance.

He had made his way to the men's toilet and was in the cubicle when there was a sharp knock on the door, followed by, 'Hurry up in there', in a very Liverpudlian accent. Tommy replied, 'When I'm ready.' On opening the lavatory door the owner of the Liverpudlian accent said, 'Do you know who I am? I'm John Lennon.' Nolan answered, 'I don't give a f**k who you are', to which Lennon replied, 'I could get you thrown out of here.' To which Tommy responded, 'I'm the sparks, if I get thrown out, there'll be no show.' Tommy continues, 'I met the rest of them. They were all really nice guys and when I saw John later, I was up here [in the balcony] looking down, and he looked up at me and we both smiled and there were no hard feelings, nothing like that.'

Tony Foran was a trainee projectionist at the Adelphi that night:

> What I remember most of all is that I was only fifteen years of age. I was employed around July but wasn't to start until September. I got word that the Beatles were coming on 7 November and I was asked to be in Abbey Street around 10 or 11am on that morning.
>
> I remember getting the bus into the Adelphi in Abbey Street and at that time the whole place was closed off. There were people from the corner of O'Connell Street right down Abbey Street. I came into the cinema and I hadn't a whole lot to do and I got in touch with the chief projectionist here at the time, a guy called Mick O'Toole, and he had a second projectionist called Bill Kenny, both deceased.
>
> There was a Frank Kelly who left, Paddy Grace, and a Brian Coyle, who was the apprentice. Now the projectionists' responsibilities were just the spotlights and I had to make my way up to the projection room. There were no rehearsals.
>
> Really and truly, there was nothing to do all day, just make sure the lights were working. We had to get rid of the screen, by raising it up. It was 50 feet high. We had to raise it up again, push the speakers back out of the way to clear the stage, which we did, but all the time Abbey Street was a hive of activity.
>
> There were girls outside screaming, the police were outside trying to control the crowd and I don't think the Beatles had even arrived at this stage. I didn't realise the importance of it, but I knew it was something special.

Three lucky Irish fans meet their idols on stage at the Adelphi, Dublin, in 1963. (*Evening Herald*)

Harry [the Adelphi manager] went with his party and met the Beatles at the airport and brought them back. Harry had a way of putting everyone at ease and he made the staff feel that way on the day in question. On those days we were the most important people, not the people who came to perform on stage.

We had two shows, the 6.30pm show and the 9pm show. I remember people getting in touch with us from the stage, the stage lighting etc, and telling us to stand by, that the stage show was starting. I can't remember the support acts but they came on and that was very hard to hear.

There was an incident in either the first or second show and either John Lennon or George Harrison were playing a solo on the guitar and we couldn't hear the cue and Paul McCartney was pointing to us to move the spotlight onto them, and that was actually written about in the papers.

All we could hear was screaming and there were two girls that Mick O'Toole must have known because he let them stand in the projection room and they were screaming and pulling their hair out. If you can imagine the Beatles on stage, two elderly gentlemen are doing the spotlights, and these girls screaming and shouting!

We had no sound in the projection room and we couldn't hear what was going on. We had a little walkie-talkie. We had cues for different colours, different people, so there were two spotlights. Mick O'Toole would be on one, Bill Kenny on the other.

I'd be just up there looking on, getting the colour. If there had to be a colour changed from pink to blue, that'd be my job with the other guys. They could have requested pink or blue or magenta for the slow songs but that was like all stage shows.

What I remember most about them was the noise, just the noise. I remember speaking to ushers about it. The ushers in those days were all big men. You had to be over 6 feet to be an usher. I often remember Jack O'Kelly saying that during the break between shows, they [the

Autographs of Paul and Ringo as obtained by an Irish fan at the Dublin gig.

Beatles] were actually up in their dressing rooms writing songs. They never wasted a minute, and I remember them saying they were lovely people, lovely guys, but these guys were there to protect them.

There was Jack O'Kelly and Jim Hyland and they were two big men, big ushers, with Tom Mann, and John Ward was the head usher, and they all said the same. As soon as they finished, they had their cup of tea or coffee up in their dressing room and they were writing more songs.

The Adelphi seated 2,300 and another 300–400 standing (I don't know how they got in), and a lot of press also. Everything was well organised and done professionally. The second show again was over very quickly. Just screaming and noise. I think they only played for about 30 minutes.

Again, it was all over before you could say 'boo!' It was a day you could never experience and forget. I've never experienced a day like it. I've worked on many a stage show and had I known then what I know now, I would have taken notes and got autographs.

Dublin teenager, Sandra Grant, was also at the show. She recalls:

I queued outside Eason's from 8am that morning and got my tickets at 2pm. They cost *6s 3d* and the other tickets were *8s 6d* and *10s 6d*. I met George Harrison's aunt by accident upstairs in the Adelphi Cinema whilst waiting to go into the second show. I just happened to start chatting to her by accident and she told me that she was George's aunt and couldn't believe the excitement that the show was creating.

She took some Polaroid photographs from her handbag showing George at home with his parents in Liverpool. At that point I asked her to get me his autograph after the show if she could, and she told me that she worked in Macy's store in Georges Street and I said that I would be over first thing the following morning.

We went to the show and my friend got me their autographs afterwards. She got Paul and Ringo after the show, as John had nipped to the toilet. Next morning I arrived over to Macy's at 9am as they were opening and made straight over to her. As she saw me approach, she opened a drawer underneath the counter and produced a publicity still of the Beatles

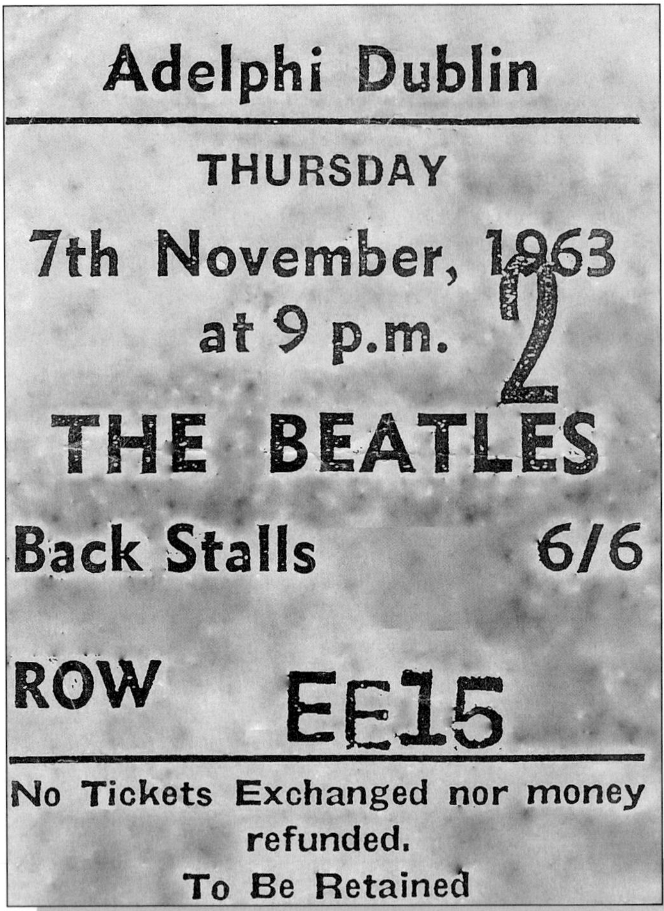

Adelphi Dublin

THURSDAY

7th November, 1963

at 9 p.m.

2

THE BEATLES

Back Stalls 6/6

ROW EE15

No Tickets Exchanged nor money refunded.

To Be Retained

Andy Halpin's ticket for the Beatles' second Dublin show.

and, to my delight, George had signed it. I couldn't believe my good luck and how good she was to remember to obtain it for me with all the excitement of the Harrison family get-together after the show.

Andy Halpin also attended the second concert. According to Andy:

I bought the tickets about two to three weeks before the gig, about 10 or 11am on a Saturday morning. We only had to queue for about one to two hours for the 9pm show and the tickets cost *6s 6d*. We went down around 8pm and there was pandemonium. Thousands of people on the streets, and the people coming out of the earlier show were just hanging around waiting to see what was happening.

We got in and the thing I remember most was the noise, the absolute noise. I couldn't hear a thing. We were more than halfway back. It was the noise more than anything else I remember. I've been at shows since but I've never experienced that noise.

I remember them coming on, and there was a blue curtain as a backdrop and they had the silver-grey suits with the collars. Everyone seemed to enjoy it. Just the fact of seeing them, without hearing them, satisfied a lot of people.

Catherine Hansard (mother of Glen Hansard of Academy Award and The Frames fame) met the Beatles that night. According to Glen: 'When the Beatles played the Adelphi, my mother and her friend climbed up a drainpipe there, got into a room and hid under a table. Then the four lads came in. It was their dressing room and they didn't know and basically, Ringo caught my mother under the table with her friend and called security and they were thrown out. They couldn't believe it.'

The Beatles held a press conference at the Adelphi that was not televised. Outside, Frank Hall attempted to interview the screaming, hysterical fans, about their 'undying love' for their heroes, and their favourite Beatle, all filmed by cameraman Jacky Merryman.

Hall: Listen, what are you doing down here?

First Female Fan: To see the Beatles of course!

Hall: I know you are, but what is particularly good about them?

First Female Fan: They're great: their hairstyles, their coats, their leather jackets are fabulous, they're a sensation.

[*The guard in charge then tells Frank Hall to move back.*]

Hall: [To a second female fan] What are you doing here?

Second Female Fan: I'm just waiting for Paul McCartney to come!

Hall: Yeah! What is it about these fellows that has you down here, being tortured? What are you doing here?

Second Female Fan: I think they're marvellous.

Hall: Sure, they're only lads, they're only schoolboys!

Second Female Fan: They're terrific!

[*The guard in charge now moves in to break up the crowd and Hall and his cameraman move into the Adelphi to continue their interview with some of the fans.*]

Hall: [To third female fan] Can I ask you, so what time did you take up your position here today?

Third Female Fan: About quarter past one, yeah!

Hall: What is it about these fellows that brings you out at this hour of the day?

Third Female Fan: I don't know. They're just gorgeous! [*Laughs*]

Hall: Well now, be a bit more explicit. I mean, is it their singing? Or is it their hair or what?

Third Female Fan: It's their singing, their hair and their jackets!

Hall: And is that all?

Third Female Fan: No … everything! I don't know! It's the way they sing and everything!

Hall: What about you? [To fourth female fan]

Fourth Female Fan: I like the way they sing.

Hall: What way do they sing? I've never heard them.

Fourth Female Fan: They have a great beat!

Hall: Like what? I mean give us a sort of indication.

Fourth Female Fan: Like 'She Loves You'.

Hall: Yeah, and you love them?

Fourth Female Fan: Yeah!

[*Hall now moves to some more fans inside the Adelphi.*]

Hall: What about you ladies?

Fifth Female Fan: I just like them!

Hall: You just like them! You're not mad about them?

Fifth Female Fan: No, not mad about them

Hall: So you have no right to be here at all?

Sixth Female Fan: Well, I like them, I'm mad about them!

Hall: [To the girl next in line] What about you?

Seventh Female Fan: I don't like them!

Hall: So what are you doing here?

Seventh Female Fan: We are here getting tickets for next week for Helen Shapiro!

[*Frank Hall laughs out loud.*]

Hall: Very good! Well that's it, what ever it is. My sympathies are with the girl who is booking for Helen Shapiro! And this is good night, and, for all I know, it is a goodbye.

When he spoke to Pete Brennan (President of Beatles Ireland, the Irish Beatles fan club) in February 1994, a year before his death, Frank remembered the events of that day only too well:

> They were damn hard to interview. They were a bunch of young … I was too hard on them. They were too young to be famous. I didn't like John Lennon particularly. He was cheeky. Above all I disliked Ringo Starr. Nothing against the guy personally but he was the worst drummer I'd ever heard in my life. They must have been loyal because anybody else would have dropped that guy, and he couldn't sing either.
>
> We got the interview done anyway and they wanted crowd reaction, so I went down to Abbey Street, and I will never forget, it was dreadful. We were standing outside the Adelphi Cinema and it was like a lunatic asylum. It was almost impossible to move. We got in through the back door on Princess Street, but we thought we'd go and do it on the street. We thought the crowd might fall back a bit. Out we went and it was like a posse. We thought they were going to hang us. It was dreadful, and finally a Superintendent guard came over and said, 'If you don't get the hell out of here, I'm going to charge you with disturbing the peace', so we wondered what we were going to do, so a few of us, myself and the assistant manager of the Adelphi, the late Michael Nerney, formed a 'snatch party'.
>
> We opened the door of the Adelphi, reached out and pulled [some fans] in, one by one. So we lined them up – and this is what I want to make absolutely clear – I just lined them up as they came in. And there they were and, I might as well tell you, it was like talking to the cat. 'Oh, they're lovely', 'Oh, Ringo's lovely' … but finally I came to this

> girl, very nice, respectable. I'm not saying the others weren't respectable, but she didn't look the Beatles type.
>
> The rest of them were wild about the Beatles, but she was fairly cool, and I said, 'Are you a Beatles Fan?' And she said, 'Certainly not! I'm here to book for Helen Shapiro.' But I want to make it perfectly clear. Everyone said [afterwards], 'You did that on purpose.' I did not do it on purpose. It was just that I was astonished as anybody else.

Hours before the show started, guards had been deployed in the streets around the Adelphi Cinema. Motorists were warned not to park their vehicles in the locality and most business firms had shuttered their windows. Dublin journalist Liam Kelly gave an eyewitness account of the scenes that were to emerge both inside and outside the Adelphi:

> It's a pity some enterprising disc company didn't arrange to make a live recording of the night's first memorable show. It was an all-stops-out affair, with an audience to match the mood. Liverpool's attractive Vernon Girls contributed 'Ain't Gonna Kiss Ya', and a somewhat faster, but no less imaginative, treatment of 'Be My Baby' than that of the Ronettes' original. A deftly executed version of the plaintive 'Passing Strangers' was succeeded by 'Funny All Over' and their current single, 'Tomorrow Is Another Day'. The Brook Brothers opened with Neil Sedaka's former hit 'You Gotta Learn Your Rhythm And Blues'. 'Warpaint', the number most associated with them, and the duo's thoughtful interpretation of a country-flavoured 'Seven Daffodils' proved outstanding.
>
> A seven-piece outfit, Peter Jay and The Jaywalkers, launched into 'Do You Love Me?' to thunderous applause. Apart from their closing number, 'Can Can 62', which spotlighted the group's skilful drummer, they registered heavily with a slick medley of titles popularised by the Temperance Seven, Acker Bilk, Russ Conway, The Shadows and other British notables.
>
> The Kestrels had personality, poise and a compelling, pulsating style, especially evident during 'There's A Place' and the infectious 'Green Green'. If audience reaction is any criterion, the artists involved in this spectacular presentation are assured of greatly increased record sales

The Beatles performing at the Adelphi Dublin on 7 November 1963.
(Courtesy of 'Amharc Eireann' The Gael Linn Newsreel, produced weekly and shown in cinemas nationwide from 1959 to 1964)

and a wonderful reception whenever they choose to return to Dublin.

Frank Berry, Canada's 'Madman of Magic', an unobtrusive yet invaluable compère, led the crowds in chanting, 'We want the Beatles', until the curtains parted to the strains of the Liverpudlians' 'I Saw Her Standing There', embellished by handclapping, cameras clicking and a couple of thousand voices singing along. A powerful delivery of 'From Me To You' helped to build the tension.

'All My Loving' provided a useful preview of their second LP. After Ringo Starr's feverish version of 'Boys', the pace stacked for the sentimental 'Till There Was You', from Meredith Wilson's 'The Music Man', a rather unexpected, though welcome, choice.

Their Gold Disc award winner, 'She Loves You', was virtually obscured by unrestrained cheering (come to think of it, who heard more than a dozen words from the Beatles?). The attendants managed to keep the huge audience under control, although, for a time, many left their seats on the balcony to twist in the aisles. But in the final five minutes, hundreds rushed from their seats and ran to the stage. The attendants were powerless and were crushed. An aggressive teenager snatched a torch from one of the ushers and threw it onto the stage. Papers and programmes were also thrown. Many more stood on their seats, clapping and stamping their feet. The din was deafening and seldom could the artists be heard at all.

At the stage, the curtain dropped altogether and the safety curtain

> was brought down also as a precaution. Amazing scenes were witnessed after the first show as 2,000 people emerged into the street, where hundreds were waiting to gain admission to the second show and hundreds more were standing, cheering and screaming. In the crush, young women and children fared worse. For a considerable time the crowds refused to move. Gardai then commenced to push the crowd back towards O'Connell Street.
>
> An unruly section of the crowd created a tense scene for minutes as they resisted and tried to overturn parked cars in Middle Abbey Street. They were forced to within a few yards of the junction of O'Connell Street, where they kept up continuous shouting and made several attempts to break through the Garda cordon. One particularly ugly incident developed when several of the crowd pushed a parked car on to the roadway knocking down several of the teenagers.

Shortly before the group's second show came to end, just before 11pm, scuffles erupted for a second time in Middle Abbey Street and, at one point, at least a dozen young men were taken into custody in squad cars and a Black Maria.

While this was going on, the Beatles were safe and were unaware of the disturbances they had caused. A cinema management spokesman said, 'We will

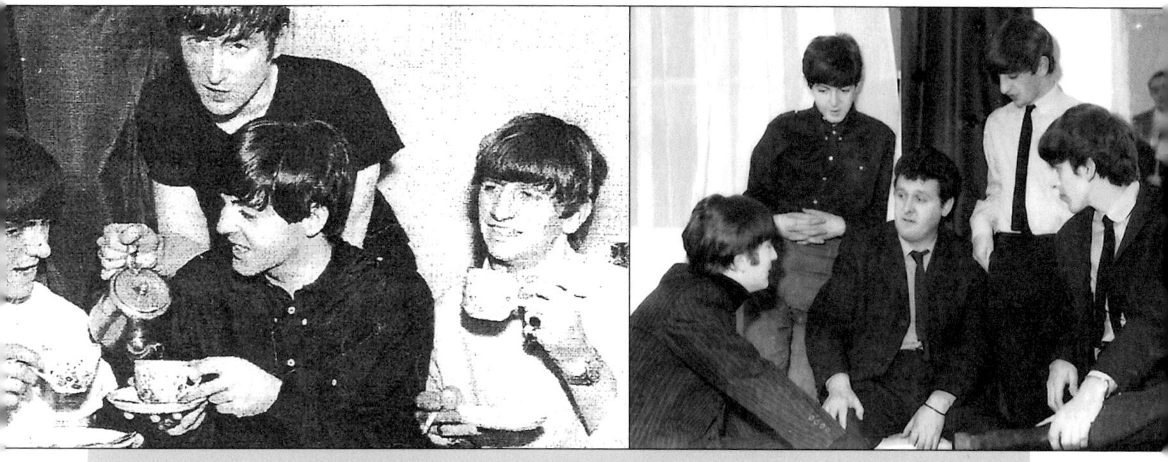

From left to right: The Beatles taking a tea-break between shows at the Adelphi Cinema, Dublin (*Maxwell Picture Agency*); The playwright Alun Owen with the Beatles in Dublin on 7 November 1963. This was his groundwork for writing the script to the film *A Hard Day's Night.* (*Evening Herald*)

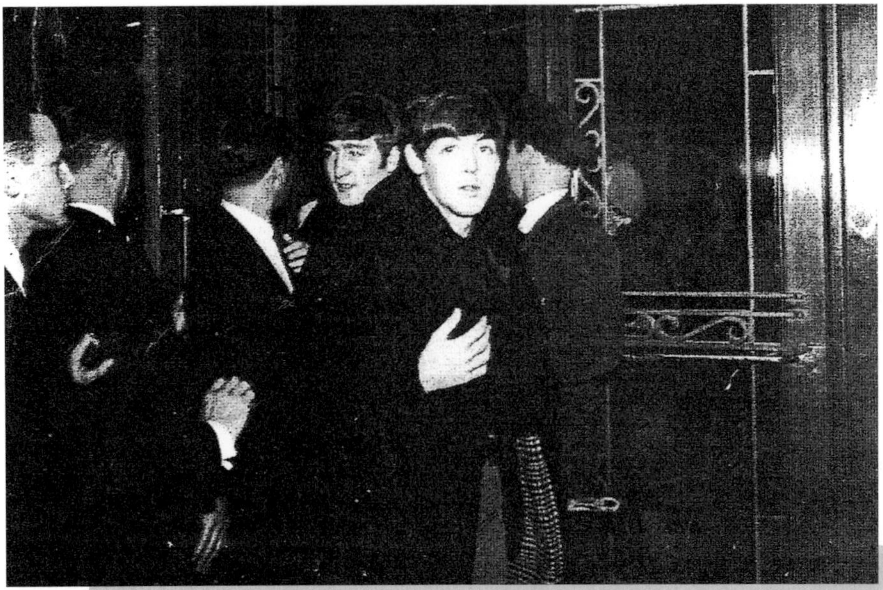

Paul and John passing through the doors of the Adelphi cinema, 7 November 1963. (*Maxwell Picture Agency*)

keep them here all night if necessary.' As it turned out, it wasn't necessary. Not only had the crowds broken up with only a few die-hards remaining by midnight, but the band had been whisked to the safety of their hotel in an *Evening Herald* delivery van.

Speaking to Pete Brennan in March 1994, John Healy of the *Irish Independent* takes up the story:

> I was in the newsroom working, and I heard commotion on the street. I looked out the window and the place was packed. A lot of people stayed outside. We were wondering how to get them out after the concert, as it was choc-a-bloc. There was a guy who worked for the *Herald* and he wrote for the young people, named Billy Ratcliffe.
>
> Billy was monitoring everything and he organised a circulation van. It had *Evening Herald* on one side and *Irish Independent* on the other. He had the van at the back of the Adelphi because the circulation department was out in Princess Street, which was next door to the back door of the Adelphi.

When the concert was over, the van was backed up. Quietly the four Beatles slipped out the back door, into the van, and we had seats made of papers. Michael Nerney, the assistant manager of the Adelphi was there. He organised the rear exit, masterminding everything. It was done very quickly, very fast.

I was sent down to write, to see the exit, see the escape. I'd got word of it for the *Independent*, and Liam Kelly was sent for the *Herald* and we'd a photographer with us, Jack Murphy.

Jack took a picture of the four Beatles sitting in the van. They were very frightened. They knew if they didn't get out this way, they'd be torn to bits, and they were frightened. They were pale actually coming out. They didn't have an awful lot to say. They [had just suddenly] realised 'Let's get out of here fast', so the doors were closed by their road manager. He slapped the side of the van and said, 'You're off' ... It didn't take us long to get there. Three minutes from Princess Street up to the Gresham.

In the van were the four Beatles, myself, Liam Kelly, and the driver. Paul was sitting with his back to the driver. We didn't even see him. We

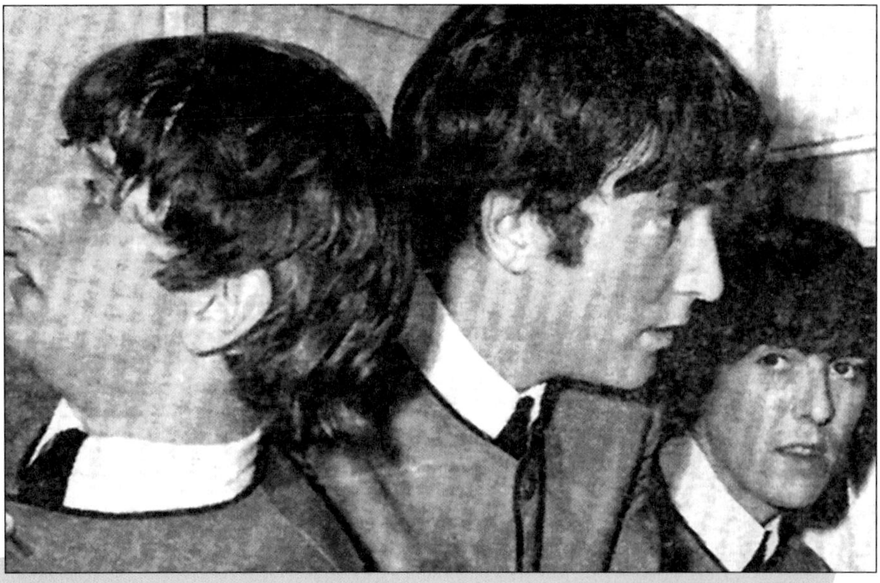

Ringo, John and George pictured inside the *Evening Herald* newspaper delivery van as they make a swift exit from the concert venue to their nearby Dublin hotel. (*Evening Herald*)

The crowd scenes outside the Adelphi during the Beatles' concerts there. (*Evening Herald*)

were driven to the back door of the Gresham, the doors were opened and we were rushed in. There was somebody waiting and they rushed us through the kitchens and the staff and chefs were saying, 'Who's that?' Young people would know them, but the mature people working in the kitchen, they wouldn't know them.

They went straight through and said nothing. Then we went into the foyer. They said they were surprised with the reception they got, they were delighted with it, and I think they were a bit scared. I didn't

> go any further. The only regret I have is that Jack Murphy didn't take the full picture, with me in it. So we went as far as the lift, the four of them got into it and up they went. I didn't go any further. I went back and wrote my story.

Liam Kelly recalls the secret getaway in an interview with Pete Brennan in 1994:

> I don't know who came up with the idea, but we decided we could probably get them out in the back of one of our vans. It was dispatched to park outside the back door of the Adelphi Cinema.
>
> Shortly before the concert ended, myself and Jack Murphy, the photographer, climbed into the back of the van. We didn't know exactly what was going to happen. It was just an ordinary van with newspapers

Jack Flanagan, who drove the *Evening Herald* van is pictured here after completing his mission. (*Evening Herald*)

in the back and we were sitting on these. Suddenly the concert ended, there was a tap on the van and in came the Beatles, the four of them just ran into the van.

On the short trip to the Gresham they just said, 'We knew we'd get a good reception, but we didn't think we'd get this reception, unbelievable reaction.' We got out of the van and I said to the Beatles, 'Come on lads, we're going up', so we went through the kitchens, much to the amazement of all the staff who couldn't believe it was the Beatles. We went through so quietly they didn't realise what was happening.

We went through the Aberdeen Room, which was the main area at the bottom, got into the lift and went up. We were told what room they were in, so there was just the four Beatles, myself, and the photographer, Jack Murphy.

I said, 'I know lads you're all uptight and everything, but I just want to have a chat with you and a few pictures', and they said, 'No problem', and they sat on the bed and they jumped around, and they were all chatting. They were like a bunch of kids at the time, and I started talking to them individually, and I found John Lennon one of the nicest fellas, though people said he was very dour, but he was great. I'd a long chat

Eileen Reid and The Cadets meet the Beatles at the Gresham Hotel, Dublin, after their Adelphi concert on 7 November 1963. (*Eileen Reid/Irish Independent*)

> with him and McCartney. The others I can't remember talking to, but that's my memory.

The crowds who had congregated outside the front of the Gresham Hotel in the hope of getting a glimpse of their idols were tricked. Some years later, Alun Owen recalled:

> One of the parlour-maids at the Gresham Hotel fell on her knees before them! She had brought in a tray of coffee and cakes in a nice normal, sensible fashion, walking across the room and setting down the tray. Suddenly, she flung off her cap, dropped to her knees and cried, 'I'm going to pray for you, boys! I'm going to pray for you!' The Beatles weren't shocked, they didn't laugh and they weren't embarrassed. Paul just helped her to her feet and talked to her as if they had been nicely introduced at a party.

Showband singer Eileen Reid of the Cadets takes up the story:

> The Fab Four were staying in the Gresham Hotel in O'Connell Street and our manager, Tom Costelloe, arranged for us to meet them. As I waited in the corridor outside the room where they were resting, accompanied by Tom, Pat and a couple of the Cadets' members, a legion of screaming Beatles fans were outside and would have killed to be in my shoes.
>
> When John Lennon and Paul McCartney came out of their room, we were introduced as a major force in the Irish music scene who dressed in naval uniforms and were noted for our interpretation of Beatles' hits. Paul was very natural and friendly and seemed unaffected by his success. He put his arm around me for the photograph session and gave me a playful squeeze. He was happy with his own good fortune. John Lennon was the opposite, being down in the mouth and with that 'what-am-I-doing-here-with-these-people?' look on his face.
>
> When he heard that we were doing the Beatles' hits on stage, he quickly said it was all right to perform them, but we couldn't record them. He seemed to think someone might take something from him,

> and he was a bit possessive about what he had achieved. The boys in the Cadets didn't like him either, but we were glad of the opportunity to talk to the most famous show business people we would ever meet. Ringo Starr and George Harrison didn't come out of their room, but John and Paul did enough talking for them all.

We leave the final word to Liam Kelly: 'They were a super band, but at this stage I don't think they knew, or they felt, they were going to become "the Beatles".'

Belfast, 8 November 1963

The group left Dublin the next morning, Friday 8 November, at 11.45am, to travel to Belfast by car. They were booked to appear at The Ritz Cinema, in Fisherwick Place. The second leg of the Beatles' tour of Ireland in Belfast was to follow the same format as the previous night's engagement in Dublin. Having made their way from Dublin, along with the rest of the support acts who made up the autumn tour, the Beatles stopped en route, just over the border at a pre-arranged spot, to be interviewed for Ulster Television by reporter Jimmy Robinson. The item was included in that evening's edition of the Ulster News. The opening shot of this clip of the Beatles, which lasted just under one minute, showed George Harrison trying to push John Lennon onto the Dublin–Belfast road just as a white van is passing in the background.

Paul: Look out for the cars [in an Irish accent] that's suicide you know, and that's the answer to the question.

Ringo: It's very nice to be in Ireland.

Reporter: Have you been any way flattered by the response of the teenagers?

Paul: It was marvellous last night. [Referring to the Dublin concert.]

Paul: Yes very flattered and we hope it will be as good tonight.

Reporter: Were you very satisfied?

The Beatles are interviewed by Ulster Television on the Dundalk-to-Newry road, on the way to their Belfast gig on 8 November 1963. *(Ulster Television)*

John: It's marvellous and people are wonderful, they go mad.

George: And six cars were arrested!

Ringo: We were locked in the dressing room when it happened … [Referring to the scuffles after the Dublin concert]. So I said to Paul, 'What's happening?' [Laughter] I love that!

Paul: Shut-up! [To Ringo]

Reporter: Boys, can I introduce you to my barber?

John: Do you know you look like Matt Monroe?

[*Reporter laughs*]

George: Give us, 'From Russia With Love'.

Reporter: Well, thanks boys.

Beatles: Thanks.

On their arrival in Belfast at 2pm, the Beatles went to the BBC regional television

Paul McCartney comes down the steps of the ABC Ritz Cinema with the help of the Royal Ulster Constabulary shortly after their concert on 8 November 1963. *(Photo courtesy of The National Library of Ireland)*

studios at Broadcasting House, where they taped an interview with Sally Ogle for the magazine programme *Six Ten*, the BBC's rival to UTV's *Ulster News*. The Beatles had also been contracted to sing (mime) one song, but this didn't happen.

After the television interviews, it was off to meet the print media at that night's venue. The original plan was to have one of the support acts, Peter Jay and The Jaywalkers, arrive at the front of the Ritz while the Beatles sneaked around the back wearing flat caps. However, the commissioner of the Royal Ulster Constabulary vetoed this, saying, 'The Beatles must be seen, otherwise there will be riots.' The group had to enter the venue after 300 policemen forced a passage through the crowds of screaming fans.

At the press conference in the ABC Cinema, the group was in irrepressible form and soon convinced the dozen or so journalists present that, far from being stereotypical 'beatniks', they were normal young men full of the joys of life.

Paul McCartney talked about the trip by car from Dublin to Belfast: 'We crossed the border without any trouble,' he said, 'The Customs officers asked us had we anything to declare, but we had nothing.'

Paul was amused that one of the Customs officials asked him for his autograph: 'Your fame spreads, you know,' he said laughingly.

George Harrison affirmed that his grandparents were from Ireland: 'I have been here before,' he said with pride. He said he was last in Ireland at the age of eight. He said he had many relatives in Dublin and several other parts of the country.

As the Beatles continued their press conference, outside the venue it was 'Operation Beatlemania'. Police were deployed around the streets of Fisherwick Place. The RUC were, by now, fighting off a very large gathering of fans and, like the previous evening in Dublin, motorists were warned not to park their vehicles in the locality of the venue. The operation was controlled from the Belfast City Commissioner's office, where plans were laid for crush barriers around the concert venue and in Royal Avenue, near the Grand Central Hotel, where the group would stay overnight.

The scenes that greeted the group in Belfast seemed to be much the same as scenes that had greeted them at every other stop on their tour. However the establishment in Belfast had a different view on the behaviour of fans. The Rev Eric Gallagher, preaching in the Grosvenor Hall ten days later, said that the scenes during the Beatles' visit were far more violent than 'the worst specimens of mass hysteria associated with extreme forms of emotional religious revivalism'. Nationalist politician, Patrick Gormley, put down a question at Stormont asking if the Home Affairs Minister, Bill Craig, had considered mobilising the B Specials for the visit. Another nationalist, Eddie Richardson, tongue firmly in cheek, suggested changing the name of the B Specials to the 'Beatles Force'.

The group's first Belfast appearance would prove to be extra special for Audrey Gowar, the 17-year-old founder of the original Irish Beatles Fan Club. As the group made their way out of the Ritz Cinema, she gave Paul McCartney an appreciative peck on the cheek, an image that was captured by a photographer from *The Daily Mirror* and published in the following day's edition.

Return to Belfast, 2 November 1964

The Beatles decided to include a second visit to Belfast on their autumn tour in mid-October 1964, rather than make an appearance at that year's Royal Variety Performance on 2 November in London. Ringo broke the unwritten showbiz rule by exploding after a reporter suggested that the Beatles' absence from that

The Beatles arrive at Aldergrove Airport, Belfast, for their second Belfast performance on 2 November 1964.

year's Royal bill was due to their fading popularity. 'We were invited!' he fumed. John insisted, 'There was never any intention to snub the Queen. Our tour took in Belfast as a late date, and the invitation to the Royal show came afterwards,' to which Paul added, 'Over 4,000 tickets had been sold for the Belfast show and we couldn't let the kids down.' George added that they were all disappointed at the turn of events.

As the group flew into Aldergrove Airport – an hour later than scheduled, due to fog – a tight security net fell around them and they were immediately whisked off to their hotel. Among some of the earliest Beatles fans to arrive at the airport were Phyllis Toan and Lynda Lyness, both of whom had been waiting since 5am. Many of the teenagers who gathered had made their own posters and banners, 'We Love You Beatles', and 'Welcome Our Golden Boys', but for schoolgirl Marlene Poots and her chums everything went wrong. They waited, wrapped in raincoats, for seven hours in fog and drizzle at Aldergrove for the arrival of the famous four with a carefully painted six-foot 'Welcome' poster. But when the weary girls proudly unfurled the banner, an aircraft blew it to pieces as it took off.

On their arrival in Belfast, the Beatles sent a telegram to Cilla Black who appeared that night on the Royal Variety Performance. It read, 'Hope it's a right Royal rave'.

At the time of the Beatles' second visit to Belfast, Cyril Gracey was working as a driver with the cargo department of the UK airline, British European Airways (BEA). He recalls:

> I had the pleasure of delivering the Beatles' musical instruments to the King's Hall. I also met all four and got their autographs which I gave

> away to a few screaming fans at that time. John Lennon gave me a holdall and I was told to ensure that it [was first] … off the van I was driving … when I reached the King's Hall. After loading, I threw the holdall into the cab, there was a small hole in the bag and a small tin of black paint fell out. He must have used it to touch up chip marks on his or some of the others' equipment. Eager for a souvenir, I kept the little tin, which I still have. To anyone else it's just a tin of paint, but I know it once belonged to John Lennon.

Pandemonium reigned inside the King's Hall. The yells were deafening when the group took the stage, dressed in immaculate black suits. As a few frantic teenage girls stripped off their clothes, others fainted and had to be carried from the hall.

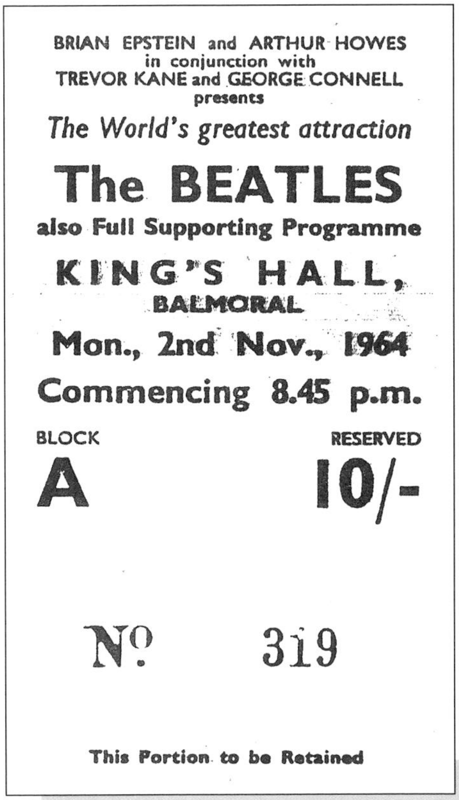
BRIAN EPSTEIN and ARTHUR HOWES
in conjunction with
TREVOR KANE and GEORGE CONNELL
presents
The World's greatest attraction
The BEATLES
also Full Supporting Programme
KING'S HALL,
BALMORAL
Mon., 2nd Nov., 1964
Commencing 8.45 p.m.
BLOCK RESERVED
A 10/-
No. 319
This Portion to be Retained

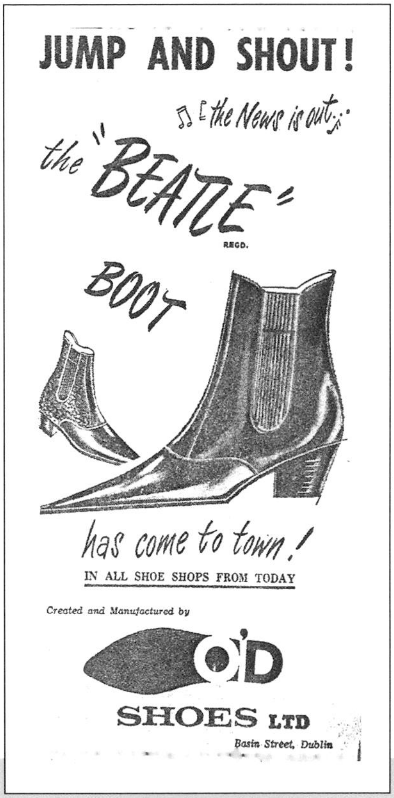

Left to right: ticket stub for the 1964 Belfast concert;
Irish newspaper advert for Beatles Boots in 1963.

It was fantastic, incredible and completely disproved the critics who predicted that the Beatles were finished. The 17,500 fanatical fans gathered in the venue that night composed the biggest crowd then known in the UK for any pop show, yet another record added to the group's long list of achievements. One of the *Belfast Telegraph*'s news reporters filed the following report of the Beatles' second visit to the King's Hall:

> Before the show, dark-haired Margaret proudly showed me the autograph she had obtained at the airport. It was Paul McCartney's and when Paul appeared on stage she went frantic with joy. When the show was over she broke down and wept. As I left the hall she tried to say goodbye, but the words didn't come. She slumped over her seat with tears running down her face. You might have been in the audience, but the chances of hearing the Fab Four sing were extremely slim. The province's teeny-boppers screamed their way through much of the concert as Beatlemania took hold. There were even reports of clothing being thrown on stage, and boys and girls fainting.
>
> The hysterical mayhem started at Aldergrove Airport the previous day as hundreds of fans tried to force the police cordon as the Beatles' plane touched down. There was nothing else talked about for the rest of the day, other than how it might be possible to get a ticket. Teenagers poured in from all over the island, just to be near the Beatles and to taste the euphoria. Northern Ireland had stolen the Beatles from under the Queen's nose, some said, as the same night they could have been at the Royal Variety Command Performance in London. Paul McCartney is reported to have said, 'We couldn't let the Belfast fans down.' The King's Hall audience was the Fab Four's largest ever gig in the United Kingdom, as about 17,400 people invaded the auditorium.

As the 1964 tour approached its end, the American magazine *Newsweek* claimed the Beatles were bored with one-night stands, world tours and, worse still, each other. They declared that, 'They might give up touring and go into TV and films, Elvis-style.' The *Daily Mirror* weighed in on the debate too, by declaring 'Beatlemania days are over, not because the fans have lost interest, but because the Beatles are tired of whistle-stop tours.'

3

The Beatles' Irish Holiday, Easter 1964

Even if it surprised the Beatles (and they often said it did), they took Beatlemania fully in their stride. But for their wives and girlfriends, life in the band's shadow was becoming increasingly difficult. It was not long before even their personal freedom was infringed upon.

On 2 March 1964, the Beatles began filming *A Hard Day's Night*, directed by Richard Lester, with the screenplay written by Alun Owen. As part of the storyline, the Beatles were to meet a group of schoolgirls on a train. One of the girls booked for this role was a young model called Pattie Boyd. Pattie was brought to the attention of the British public when she appeared in a series of television commercials for Smith's Crisps. The commercials were produced by Richard Lester. At the end of the first day's filming, George, smitten with Pattie, asked if she would go out with him that night. She said no. George was not put off. The following week he asked her out again. By the end of the month she'd introduced him to her family and they were a couple, eventually marrying in 1966.

Filming of *A Hard Day's Night* was ongoing, but as the Easter weekend of 1964 loomed, the Beatles felt they were in need of an extended break from the routine of filming. Ringo was about to spend the weekend at Woburn Abbey as the guest of Lord Rudolph Russell and Paul was to remain in London. George had been trying to keep his blossoming relationship with Pattie out of the newspapers, a task that had become virtually impossible. He suggested that John and his wife, Cynthia, join himself and Pattie for an Easter holiday in Ireland.

In her book, *A Twist of Lennon*, published in 1978, Cynthia Lennon gives an informative insight into that Easter weekend spent at Dromoland Castle in Co Clare:

> John and George were to disguise themselves with false moustaches, scarves and hats. A six-seater plane was hired and a suite of rooms was duly booked at Dromoland Castle Hotel.
>
> On arrival at Heathrow Airport the charade began, trying hard not to lose our self-control in the face of the curious public who, when confronted by a pair of Inspector Clouseaus rushing conspicuously through the airport, followed by two equally conspicuous giggling females carrying mounds of hand luggage, stood and stared in disbelief.
>
> Obviously aware of whom they were seeing, but not able to put a finger to their identity, we made it to the six-seater propeller plane without being apprehended and we clambered into, what seemed to me to be, a car with wings. I was really terrified; it was so small and vulnerable. I closed my eyes as we took off, and had them closed for most of the bumpy journey.

After arriving at Shannon Airport, the party of four made the short trip to the seventeenth-century castle, which was later described by Cynthia Lennon as a 'heavenly retreat'. She continues:

> Our suite of rooms had been occupied not long before by President Kennedy, or so we were informed. Pattie and I got on famously. She was a friendly, bubbly character, a great girl full of fun and boundless enthusiasm, very childlike but in no way immature. She always reminded me of a very beautiful flimsy butterfly. I envied her, her figure, her dress sense and her confidence. Whenever fashions changed Pattie was in there first with all the right gear, looking beautiful as ever.
>
> Our first day of freedom and peace from the rat race was enjoyed by one and all. Exploring the hotel and grounds without having to look over our shoulders gave us a sense of false security. At last we

John and George battle it out with swords from a suit of armour found in a hallway in Dromoland Castle, Co Clare, during their Easter weekend break in 1964. (*Mirror Newspapers*)

> thought we had cracked it. The evening meal passed without a hitch and we retired to our respective beds, safe in the knowledge that tomorrow would prove to be just as beautiful and relaxed.

Unfortunately, even the west of Ireland was not out of reach of the world's media and so it was that, on the second day, John, George, Cynthia and Pattie woke up to the press all looking for a Beatles exclusive. Cynthia continues:

> Dawn broke, the phone started ringing, the curtains were drawn, and before we had time to rub the sleep out of our eyes we realised that we were surrounded. That we were in a castle was very apt, but instead of being confronted by the enemy bearing bows and arrows, they were

John gets to grips with croquet as George takes a more relaxed approach to the game. (*Mirror Newspapers*)

> armed with cameras. Holed up in the grounds of the hotel wherever you looked, they pointed their weapons in at us in a very threatening manner.

Following a discussion between John, George and Eric Piper, a *Daily Mirror* photographer, a photo-shoot was hastily set up in the grounds of the castle. Piper managed to out-fox his Fleet Street colleagues to get exclusive pictures of John and George, playfully battling it out with swords acquired from a suit of armour found in the castle's hall. As part of the arrangement, Cynthia and Pattie were not to be photographed, so as not to infringe on their weekend break.

Not to be outdone, RTÉ managed to get a TV camera crew into the grounds of the castle, just as the impromptu photo-call was beginning. The resulting footage was later used as a news item for that day's television news, but has rarely been seen since 1964.

When it came time for the party to leave the castle to return to England, an appeal was made to the management of the castle for assistance in facilitating a discreet departure, which Cynthia describes in her book:

> Only the Irish could have come up with the solution that enabled us to foil our adversaries. It was brilliant in its simplicity. To prevent George and Pattie from being photographed together, we would have to split up. John and George were to go to the airport alone by conventional means, and Pattie and I were to be smuggled out of the hotel, Irish fashion. Everyone entered into the spirit of the operation. Patti and I were to dress up as chambermaids. Black dresses, white frilly caps and aprons, we donned our disguises and stood admiring each other, it was great fun. The idea was for us to carry large bundles of dirty laundry in a large wicker laundry basket down to the staff entrance to the hotel. The staff would keep a lookout for the enemy, while the laundry basket was emptied and the two of us climbed in.
>
> You can imagine we felt like a couple of jack-in-the-boxes as the lid was lowered and secured tightly above us. The plan [in] its original form was for the driver of the laundry van and a member of the staff to carry the basket, with us safely inside, to the vehicle. Once inside he was to have released us for the journey to the airport. Everything went according to plan until we felt ourselves being dumped very roughly into the back of the van, followed by shouts of panic and confusion all around us. Before we knew where we were, the van doors were slammed quickly and resoundingly shut, the engine was put into gear and we were away.
>
> Pattie said, 'Cyn what is happening? Where are we going? We'll suffocate and die in this thing. Shout, Cyn, Shout.' In vain we yelled at the top of our panic-stricken voices. 'Help, help, let us out! Driver you've forgotten to let us out.'
>
> As the van rounded bends and speedily took corners, the basket we were trapped in slid from side to side of the clattering van, no way was

the driver going to hear us, he was too caught up in the excitement of the escapade. Exhausted and hoarse, we gave in with arms, legs, and feet crunched up in the most unlikely positions. We completed the journey feeling like a couple of redundant acrobats from Billy Smart's Circus. In spite of our excruciating discomfort, our ruse proved to be a great success. I don't know how long it took the poor miserable, drenched reporters and photographers to twig that we had flown the coop. At least we weren't in the vicinity to hear the swearing and cursing that must have occurred when they found out we had made fools of them.

4

A Beatle Buys an Irish Island, 1967

Shortly before he died in December 1980, John Lennon had planned to retire to a remote island in Clew Bay, Co Mayo. Late in 1979, Lennon began to investigate how to renew planning permission to build a house on the island, which he had originally bought, uninhabited, from the Westport Harbour Board in 1967. The story of John Lennon and Dorinish started in March that year when he cornered Alistair Taylor, the Beatles' 'Mr Fixit', in Abbey Road's Studio Two.

'I want somewhere to escape to,' Lennon said. 'I want an island.' Alistair laughed. 'What do you fancy, The Isle of Wight, Barbados, or how about the Isle of Dogs?' 'I'm serious,' John said. 'I want somewhere with green grass and running water, somewhere I can take Julian and Cyn. Just one other thing,' John added. 'It must not be more than two hours' flying time from London. You can do it, you're Mr Fixit,' John said with a smile. Alistair, looking at him in disbelief, replied, 'I'll get on to it in the morning.'

Mr Fixit Buys an Island

Alistair rang estate agents and land dealers but had no success. If he had said that he was making enquiries for a Beatle he would have been inundated with offers

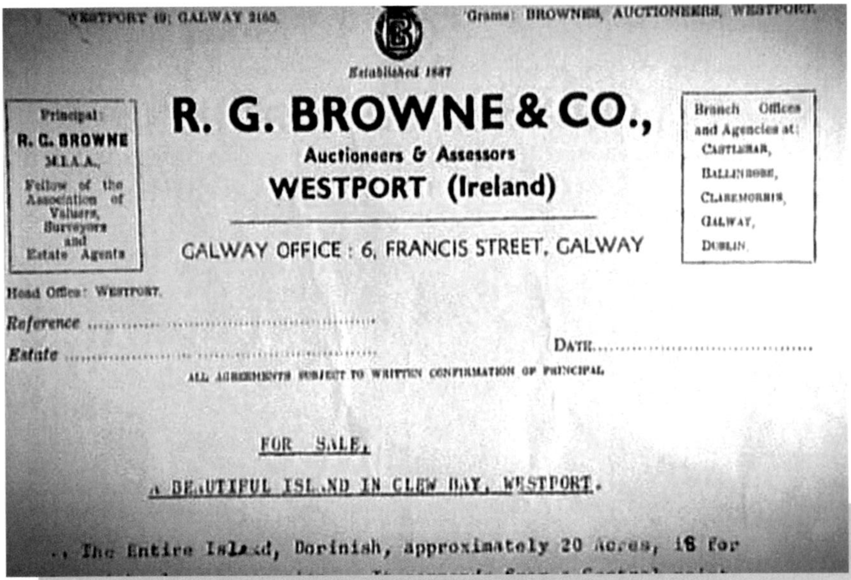

WESTPORT 19; GALWAY 2165. Grams: BROWNES, AUCTIONEERS, WESTPORT.

Established 1887

Principal:
R. G. BROWNE
M.I.A.A.,
Fellow of the Association of Valuers, Surveyors and Estate Agents

R. G. BROWNE & CO.,

Auctioneers & Assessors
WESTPORT (Ireland)

GALWAY OFFICE : 6, FRANCIS STREET, GALWAY

Branch Offices and Agencies at:
CASTLEBAR,
BALLINROBE,
CLAREMORRIS,
GALWAY,
DUBLIN.

Head Office: WESTPORT.

Reference ....

Estate .... DATE..

ALL AGREEMENTS SUBJECT TO WRITTEN CONFIRMATION OF PRINCIPAL

FOR SALE,

A BEAUTIFUL ISLAND IN CLEW BAY, WESTPORT.

.. The Entire Island, Dorinish, approximately 20 Acres, 16 for

Auctioneer's confirmation of Dorinish being for sale.

at inflated prices. He had to say that he was a businessman looking for somewhere to escape to from time to time.

After several frustrating days, he was looking through the classified section of *The Times* when his eyes lit upon an advert in the auction column that began 'Island for sale'.

He read the advert and then read it again. It was perfect. Green grass, running water – it was all there. It was too good to be true. Alistair became convinced that John had set him up. He picked up the phone and rang the Lennons' home number. Cynthia answered and when Alistair asked to speak to John he was told he was still in bed. Alistair said, 'When he surfaces tell him I'm on to his little game.' He explained what had happened and Cynthia flatly denied any duplicity on anybody's part.

Still not believing the advertisement was for real, he then rang the number shown. To his surprise it was answered by an auctioneer by the name of Mr Browne, who assured him that it was all very genuine and, within two hours, Alistair was on a flight to Dublin armed with a camera and a notepad. He took a car from Dublin to Westport, the town that overlooked Clew Bay. He then hired a small boat with a one-man crew and sailed out to Dorinish, the island to be auctioned. In the past, sailing ships had sometimes stopped at the island to load stones from its shore to use as ballast in rough seas. It was for sale, uninhabited, because the Westport Harbour Board had decided to sell it when diesel engines replaced sails.

Alistair walked all over what were really two rocky outcrops joined by a sandbank. The beaches were perfect, as was the freshwater spring. Alistair took photograph after photograph and, as he did so, one thing struck him – there were no buildings of any kind.

Alistair had to get back to London develop the photographs, show them to John, get his approval and get back to Westport for the auction. This all happened just one day before the auction, all in a normal day's work for Mr Fixit. When John and Cynthia looked at the photographs they immediately fell in love with the place. Lennon sent Taylor off to Westport to bid for him at the public auction. 'Go and buy it, Al,' John said.

'Just one snag,' Alistair said. 'I need £2,000 to do that.' John replied, 'You'll have to sort that out yourself. I don't keep money like that in the house.' Alistair was aghast, 'You are joking aren't you?' Lennon shook his head in the negative and Alistair looked at his watch. 'It's 4pm, the banks are closed,' he said. John put his arm around him, 'You can sort it out,' he said. 'Go and sit in the study, make whatever phone calls you have to and buy me the island. Take Lesley [Alistair's wife] on the trip.'

The only transport Alistair could arrange was the Euston to Holyhead boat-train. He rang Lesley, who said she would pack and meet him at the railway station. Now there was just the little matter of the money. The Irish would not accept a personal cheque; it had to be a certified cheque or cash. Then, in a moment's inspiration, he decided to call Clive Epstein, Brian's brother in Liverpool. 'I can come up with £800. But how do I get it to you?' Clive said. The problem was solved when Clive decided to send his chauffeur to Crewe station. When the train stopped there, Alistair could jump off, pick up the cash and resume his journey. 'How will I identify him?' Alistair asked. 'I'll have him carry a newspaper and he'll hold it above his head,' Clive replied.

Alistair went straight to Euston station where Lesley was already waiting. It was going to be a long journey and as they settled into their first class compartment they dozed until the ticket collector arrived. 'What time does this train get into Crewe?' Alistair asked the ticket collector. 'We don't stop at Crewe,' he replied. Alistair retorted, 'You must be kidding, everything stops at Crewe!' 'You might think so, but our next stop is Holyhead.' Those were the collector's final words as he closed the door behind him and moved down the corridor.

Lesley gave Alistair one of her looks. They already had a cabin booked on the ferry and agreed that they might as well make the trip. Neither of them spoke until they reached Holyhead. They had a two-hour wait at Holyhead before sailing and, just ten minutes before the boat was due to leave, Alistair took a walk on deck. He looked over to the quay where a single naked light bulb illuminated a man who slowly raised a rolled newspaper above his head. The chauffeur had broken every speed limit between Crewe and Anglesey (and been stopped twice by the police) in order that Alistair had his £800.

Alistair arrived in Westport just three hours before the auction. He made himself known to Mr Browne, who immediately offered him a Jameson's whiskey. 'This man speaks my language,' Taylor thought.

Taylor was among a crowd of 30 or 40 locals at the auction, many of them farmers hoping to buy the island to use as pasture for sheep and cattle.

The two men talked for ages, accompanied by regular refills of whiskey. Browne was particularly interested in London where he had gone to college. He wanted to know how it had changed over the years and what the big West End shows were at the time.

Then suddenly, he changed the subject. 'How much do you want this island?' he asked, pouring Alistair yet another Jameson's. Alistair replied, 'I have to have it, but I can only afford to pay £2,000.' Browne nodded and suggested that his son, Michael, bid on his behalf, a suggestion that Alistair readily agreed with.

Alistair Taylor, the Beatles 'Mr Fixit', who obtained Dorinish by auction on behalf of John Lennon in 1967.

Between each bid, Browne would talk interminably about the island, its beauty and benefits. The bidding crawled along, reaching £1,500 in about two hours. Browne went into another ten-minute monologue before asking if there were any more bids. Michael appeared in the doorway and said, 'One thousand, five hundred and fifty pounds.' Browne immediately slammed down his gavel and shouted, 'Sold!'

Alistair looked around and Michael had gone. Uproar ensued, the other bidders were up in arms, but could do nothing – the deal had been done. The island had been purchased in the name of 'Alistair Taylor'. The news made the Irish national newspapers and, when he flew back to London, Alistair found himself upgraded to first class on the strength of his new fame.

John visits Dorinish, Autumn 1967

For tax reasons, John was unable to visit the island for six months, by which time Yoko Ono had replaced Cynthia. When he finally made the trip, Lennon's companion on the journey was John Dunbar, the owner of the Indica Gallery. The party were met in Dublin by a limousine whose driver stared in disbelief as John Lennon got into his car. Alistair sat alongside the driver and it was not long before he noticed the unmistakable odour of cannabis emanating from behind, where the two Johns also popped pills at frequent intervals during the journey. By the time the car had travelled the width of Ireland, even Alistair and the driver were stoned.

On Dorinish, John stood and surveyed his domain. 'It's sensational,' he said. 'Just fabulous.' They walked all over the island with Lennon leading the way. Suddenly he stopped. 'Stand still,' he cried. 'Look amongst the pebbles.' Nestling among the shingle and boulders were thousands of beautiful, speckled gulls' eggs. The beach was covered in them. 'Walk very carefully,' Lennon said, and they did, taking 30 minutes to walk 50 yards. With the day drawing to an end, Alistair sat with Lennon on a grassy bank. 'Thank you,' the Beatle said. 'It really is wonderful.' He pointed to a section that dropped down into the bay. 'You see that plot? That's yours.' John put his arm round Alistair. 'Build a house there. Bring Lesley. It's for you and Lesley.' Alistair was very grateful but, typically, never took John up on the offer.

Alistair later arranged for Lennon's Romany caravan to be shipped out to the island on a raft designed by Inishcuttle boat-builder, Paddy Quinn. John had taken delivery of the 1874 Romany caravan on 24 July 1967, as a birthday present for his 4-year-old son, Julian. The caravan had been renovated and decorated by the freelance designer, Stephen Weaver, who had charged John more than £3,500 to complete the project.

The caravan was floated out one summer's evening across the bay on to the island. It was quite a sight to see a caravan floating across the sea. It was later moved back to John's Surrey home in Weybridge and neighbours subsequently complained to the residents' association that the caravan was 'a hideous monstrosity'.

Alistair had a further trip over to the island with Alex Mardas who said he could build a 'floating' house – a house with no vibrations. It was an interesting concept that Alistair would have liked to have seen, particularly as the island was prone to gales directly off the Atlantic Ocean.

John and Yoko at Dorinish, 1968

It was not until 1968 that John and Yoko made a visit to Dorinish together (John's marriage to Cynthia had collapsed at the end of 1967). The couple made their trip in the company of the late actor, Robert Shaw, and Irishman Ronan O'Rahilly. O'Rahilly was the former head of the ship-based pirate radio station, Radio Caroline, and was about to become a member of the Apple staff. The group had flown into Dublin and were then driven to Westport, where Lennon met Michael Browne, the solicitor who had handled the purchase.

During the trip they viewed Achill Island and had dinner at the Amethyst Hotel (now disused) in Keel. Browne made arrangements for the party to sail to over to John's island, hiring Paddy Quinn, the same boat-builder who lived on Inishcuttle Island and later designed a raft to float John's caravan over to Dorinish.

Quinn had no idea who his famous passenger was. 'It was only afterwards that I discovered it was John Lennon. As far as I was concerned, he was a customer. Beatlemania and the Swinging Sixties had not quite reached the west of Ireland,' Quinn said.

The party spent an hour and a half walking around the nineteen acres of Dorinish, two small islands joined by a natural stone causeway. Afterwards they drank tea at Quinn's house where Sandy, Quinn's dog, annoyed Lennon by continually barking at his long hairy coat.

Browne (the Westport solicitor) said, 'He had a cine-camera with him and was taking shots of the scenery all around there. He was very impressed with Clew Bay. I found him very practical and businesslike. He was completely in command of himself, and interested in the logistics and the cost of building a house out there. He was worried about further erosion on the island. He was concerned that something should be done to prevent it.' Lennon went on to commission an architect to do soil borings.

John Lennon and Yoko Ono at the Mulranny Hotel, Co Mayo, on 22 June 1968 just after they had touched down by helicopter. (*The Mayo News*)

Lennon made a second visit with Yoko, Pete Shotton and 'Magic Alex' (aka Alex Mardas), the head of Apple Electronics, who said he could build a 'floating' house for John and Yoko. The group made use of a helicopter during their visit and all stayed at the Great Southern Hotel in Mulranny, a seaside village nearby. The hotel later named a suite after John, but Lennon was never to see Dorinish again.

The Mayo News of 29 June 1968 reported the visit with the headline 'Beatle was "enchanted" with Mulranny visit'. The report went on to say:

> The time was 4pm on Saturday last (June 22). The Great Southern Hotel, Mulranny, which stands majestically over the picturesque Mulranny village, and from which there is a panoramic view of island-studded Clew Bay, was experiencing its usual routine in the off-period, except for the extra arrangements being made for the expected arrival of Mr Frank Aiken, Minister for External Affairs, as a guest.
>
> Then the phone bell rang, which a busy receptionist, Margaret Nealis, duly answered. It was a personal call for the hotel manager, one of the many he must attend to each day, except this one said that, 'Mr John Lennon of the Beatles and a party of seven are to land by helicopter in two hours' time on the hotel lawn. They will be guests for the weekend for a strictly private visit.'
>
> Little wonder that an air of excitement spread through the hotel as the Dublin-born hotel manager, Bo Lalor, called the heads of staff together to brief them on arrangements for the arrival of the VIPs. And, little by little, the tension mounted as the 150 hotel guests took up vantage positions in the sun to get a centre circle view of the Beatles millionaire.

On Saturday afternoon, Mr Lennon and his party had landed by helicopter on the four-acre uninhabited Dorinish Island in Clew Bay, which was purchased by a London businessman for the Beatle twelve months ago for £1,500 after it was put up for sale by Westport Harbour Board. After touching down on the island, the helicopter immediately left again for Westport. Back at the hotel, the Minister for External Affairs had arrived and was photographed on the hotel steps and the guests were anxiously scanning the skies as tension mounted to a crescendo.

On Sunday at 9.30pm the helicopter touched down and Mr Lalor was on the spot to welcome John Lennon and his Japanese lady friend, Yoko Ono, Ronan O'Rahilly and Jeremy Banks of Radio Caroline. They made a motor trip to Achill Island, without being recognised and on return were taken on a conducted tour of the hotel grounds by the manager. On Sunday night a special Irish concert was arranged by Mr Lalor and compèred by Tony Chambers. Taking part were the Molloy Brothers, Mulranny, Dominick Grady, Shraloggy, Newport, Ms Peggie Jennings, hotel receptionist and a native of Hollymount, and Mr Larry Mc, Newport. Later, Mr Lennon played a tape recording of a new record by the Beatles entitled 'Revolution', which will be soon released. It was the first time for the recording to be heard in public. Mr Lennon and his friends were immediately whisked to a private suite in the hotel. Garda Sean Murray was on duty to see that the Beatle was not mobbed.

After lunch on Monday, John Lennon and his party left by helicopter for Shannon Airport where a plane was waiting to take them back to London. The news of John Lennon's visit brought members of the cross-channel press hurrying to Mulranny. They were anxious to interview Mr Lennon as to whether his marriage was about to break up, but he refused to meet them.

He was enchanted with the Mulranny countryside and very pleased with his island purchase. 'The fact that the area is in no way commercialised adds to its beauty,' he told me. He would make no comment on a rumour that the other members of the Beatles group were planning a visit to Mulranny. My visit to the hotel on Saturday was to cover the arrival of the Minister for External Affairs. Little did I expect that

I would be the only pressman on the spot to cover the surprise arrival of the Beatle millionaire.

Hippie Island, Ireland

The next phase in the history of Dorinish started on 13 November 1969, when Lennon offered free use of the island to any hippies wishing to establish a commune. Lennon had heard that a group of New Age travellers – called the 'Diggers' and led by Sid Rawle, who was known at the time as 'King of the Hippies' – were looking for an island to set up a commune. Lennon summoned Rawle to the Apple offices where he offered Rawle custodianship of Dorinish, soon known as 'Beatles Island', to be used for the public good.

Rawle accepted, printed fliers and distributed them among the 'Flower Power' people in London. A group of 25 adults and a baby travelled to Dorinish. 'We decided we would hold a six-week summer camp on the island. Then we would see what came out of that and decide if we wanted to extend our stay,' said Rawle. 'It was heaven and it was hell. We lived in tents because there were no stone buildings on the island at all. Most of the time was really good.'

The hippies stayed for two years, growing vegetables on the island, lighting bonfires to keep warm and storing food in specially built hollows. They bought groceries in Westport once a fortnight. The commune had no boat, so they relied on the local oyster fishermen for transport. They had an agreed system of alerting the boatmen when they needed a lift.

'During the day, if we put up three sheets on the hill that was an emergency. One sheet was "come round and pick us up whenever you've got time", two was "we'd like to see you in a bit of a hurry" and three was "get a move on".'

Post would arrive addressed to Hippie Island, Ireland. Some of the local people were hostile to the New Age travellers. 'Hippie Republic under siege' was the headline in *The Connaught Telegraph* in March 1971 over a story that reported, 'After a year of seething anger, Westport has finally declared war on the Republic of Dorinish!' In 1972, after a fire destroyed the main tent used to store supplies, most of the Diggers moved off Dorinish, and Rawle went back to Britain. He was one of the founders of the Tipi Valley commune in Wales where 150 people lived for twenty years.

The final part of John's and Yoko's connection with Dorinish came after

John's death. In 1983, Michael Kavanaugh, director of the Ireland West Tourism organisation, sent a telegram to Yoko inviting her to scatter John's ashes on Dorinish. In the telegram he stated that the people of Mayo would regard it as a tremendous honour if she agreed. She declined the offer and John's ashes were eventually scattered in New York.

Yoko eventually sold Dorinish in 1985 to the Gavin family in Murrisk, near Westport. The family had intended to use it for grazing purposes, but it was eventually made available as a wildlife reserve and remains that way today. Yoko commented at the time:

> Putting Dorinish up for sale is an expression of the love we have for Ireland and its people. John would have wished the island to be returned to the Irish. John is still there in spirit. His grandfather was born in Dublin, and John always thought of himself as Irish.
>
> John was always very concerned about the Irish cause and thought a lot about the Irish people and always associated sympathetically with their suffering. He was aware of how severe the Irish plight was. For John, buying the island was a bit like Jewish people buying a bit of Jerusalem. It was a place where we thought we could escape the pressures and spend some undisturbed time together but because of what happened our hopes never came to be. We often discussed the idea of building a cottage there. It was so beautiful, so tranquil, yet so isolated. It seemed a perfect place to get away from it all.

5

'Republican' Beatles

On his 1972 album *Some Time In New York City*, Lennon made reference to the presence of British troops in Northern Ireland by writing two songs, 'The Luck of the Irish' and 'Sunday Bloody Sunday'.

'Sunday Bloody Sunday' referred directly to the events of 30 January 1972 when a peaceful civil rights march through Derry's Bogside area turned into a riot and British paratroopers opened fire on the crowd. Thirteen unarmed civil rights protesters were killed and the episode became known as 'Bloody Sunday'.

'The Luck of the Irish' was actually written by Lennon in November 1971, but it was to take on a new life when it was used at a demonstration in the days following Bloody Sunday. Yoko contributed to the lyrics, which appear now to be a rather naïve comment on an extremely complex situation, with lines such as 'Let's walk over rainbows like leprechauns' and 'Why are the English there anyway?'

* * *

On Wednesday 11 August 1971, John and Yoko had been among 1,000 protesters taking part in an anti-internment rally and demonstration march past the Ulster Offices in London, where Lennon was photographed holding a sign that read:

'Victory for the IRA against British Imperialism'. An interviewer later asked John whether his support of the IRA conflicted with his anti-violence views. He replied:

> I don't know how I feel about them, because I understand why they're doing it and if it's a choice between the IRA and the British Army, I'm with the IRA. But if it's a choice between violence and non-violence, I'm with non-violence. So it's a very delicate line. Our backing of the Irish people is done really through the Irish Civil Rights [Northern Ireland Civil Rights Association], which is not the IRA.

And then came Bloody Sunday in January 1972. FBI files include an informer's account of a meeting in February at the Irish Institute on West 48th Street, New York, just days after Bloody Sunday. According to the FBI informer, some of the proposals included procuring weapons for the IRA, whilst another called for the boycott of British goods. But one thing that caught the FBI's attention was the willingness of Lennon to offer to perform at a 'mass demonstration' organised by the Socialist Workers Party (SWP).

The demo occurred on 5 February, organised by the Transport Workers Union in Manhattan. Lennon joined Jerry Rubin and about 5,000 others outside the New York offices of the British Airline, BOAC, where he announced that, 'The purpose of the meeting is to show solidarity with the people who are going to march tomorrow in Northern Ireland.' [There was a civil rights march planned for 6 February] Referring to his Irish ancestry, Lennon told the crowd, 'My name is Lennon and you can guess the rest.' He added that his native Liverpool was '8 per cent Irish'. Then, along with Yoko, he sang 'The Luck of the Irish'. Lennon had also dictated a press statement about the situation in Northern Ireland. It read:

> Today at Forty-fourth [Street] and Fifth Avenue, outside the BOAC building, there was a demonstration in protest against the internment and killing of Irish people in the civil rights movement. Present among the five or six thousand were senators and congressmen also. John sang 'Luck of the Irish', the proceeds of which they announced would be donated to the Irish civil rights movement.

> The police were particularly cooperative as most of them were Irish. The meeting was a great meeting and it got lots of media coverage. The weather was freezing cold. The Lennons looked like refugees – John hadn't shaved for a few days, and Yoko was wrapped up like an Eskimo. At first they went round unrecognised, but finally they were announced.
>
> The people joined in singing with the Lennons and great applause and shouting was heard, especially on such lines as 'Why are the English there anyway?' and 'The bastards commit genocide'. The whole thing was a success, there was no violence, and if you hear otherwise it's a lie.

It was during this period that Lennon began to identify himself as Irish, rather than British, and began to openly support both the Troops Out movement and the Northern Ireland Civil Rights Association. Also on the album *Sometime in New York City* John Lennon recorded a song, 'Woman is the Nigger of the World'. Lennon had become interested in the Feminist movement. He was intrigued by something Yoko said during an interview in *Nova* magazine, published in March 1969: 'Woman is the nigger of the world'.

The song made its debut on the New York-based TV show, *The Dick Cavett Show*, in May 1972. On the show Lennon was to say: 'It was actually the first women's liberation song that went out.' He added, 'The whole story is the title, the lyrics are just a fill-in, except for the line "Woman is the Slaves of the Slaves", this I had taken from the writings of James Connolly, the Irish Socialist'. Connolly had been shot by a firing squad following his involvement in the Easter Rising of 1916. This shows how intensely engaged Lennon was with Ireland and the Irish around this time.

His 1974 *Walls and Bridges* album included a booklet containing a history of the Lennon name, in the form of the entry from *Irish Families: Their Names, Arms, and Origins* by Edward MacLysaght.

An interesting development in relation to the song 'The Luck of the Irish' was its use in a political documentary of the time *The Irish Tapes*, produced and directed by John Reilly and Stefan Moore. The production was a video film with a pro-IRA slant and was supported financially by John and Yoko. John had recorded a demo disc of the song and he gave this version to Reilly and Moore to be used on the soundtrack. Around this time a secret memo addressed to the US Attorney General, John Mitchell, from Senator Strom Thurmond suggests that John Lennon

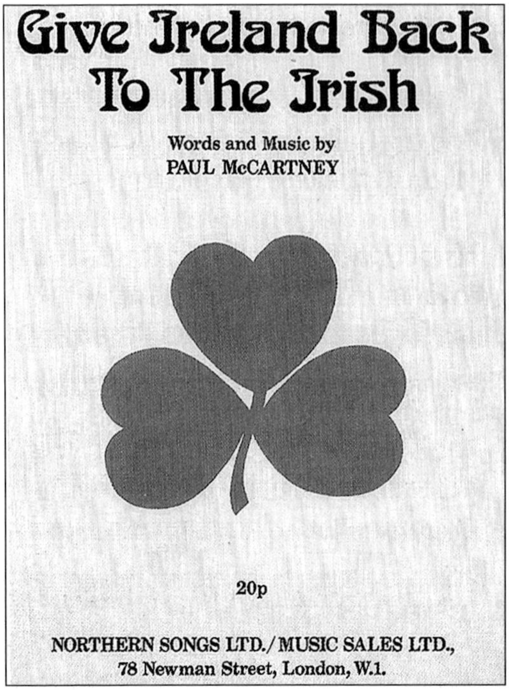

should be deported as an 'undesirable alien', due to 'his political views and activism'.

In February 2000, the FBI released files that indicated that they had investigated links between Lennon and New York-based Irish Republican activists in the 1970s. These are part of a 300-page Lennon file, which the FBI had resisted releasing since his murder in December 1980. Eighty pages from the report had already been released after a court settlement with Professor Jon Wiener, a California-based Lennon biographer and author of *Come Together: John Lennon in His Time*. Wiener states that the files include 'the first solid evidence' that the FBI had an interest in Lennon's involvement in Irish issues, as prior to that he [Wiener] had not been aware of the FBI connecting Irish Republican activists to Lennon in New York.

It goes without saying that both MI5 and MI6 would also have had an interest in Lennon and his political activities and would have shared relevant information with the FBI and the CIA. In fact, Wiener says a further ten documents still held by the FBI were 'almost definitely' compiled with the help of MI5. The FBI claims that these ten files are 'national security documents' which originated with 'a foreign government' (in other words, Britain). Wiener thinks that this probably has something to do with surveillance of Lennon's political activities in the UK as well as his arrest for possession of cannabis in 1968.

McCartney's Irish Touch

At almost the same moment that Lennon was composing his two Irish songs, Paul McCartney, always considered the least political of the pair, was in London recording his response to events in Northern Ireland and invoking his own Irish ancestry with his offering 'Give Ireland Back to the Irish'.

An unfortunate aspect of the ongoing political situation in Ireland, from a musical point of view, was to surface in the mid-1970s, when Paul McCartney and his band Wings were pencilled in to perform in Ireland. Paul himself had no qualms about bringing his band to Ireland, but it is said that his late wife, Linda, had some misgivings. Her fears were based around the fact that Paul's song 'Give Ireland Back to the Irish' and its potentially inflammatory lyrical content, had caused some concern in particular sections of the political community

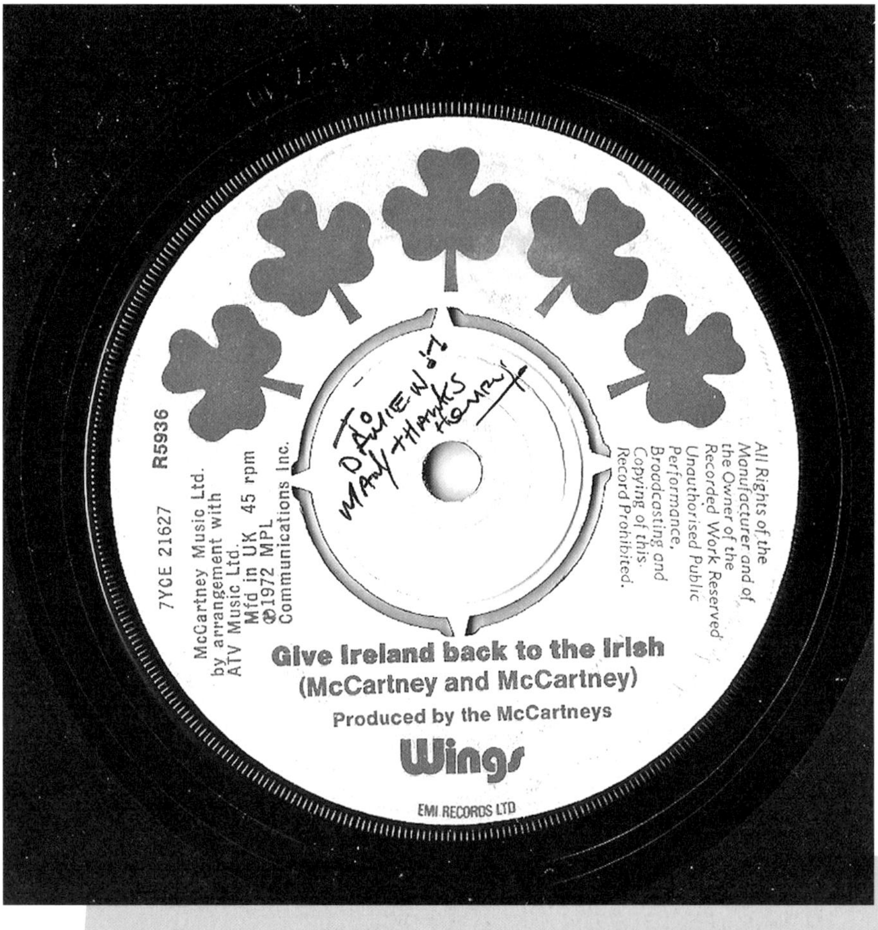

An autographed copy of the Wings 1972 single 'Give Ireland Back to the Irish'.

in the north of Ireland. It is now known that planning for an Irish tour by Wings was at an advanced stage, so much so that one Dublin prompter had produced posters and tickets for what would have been the group's Dublin concert.

Unfortunately they never did make it on to Irish soil and, by this time, the band had been drawn to the more lucrative American stadium tour circuit.

The song was issued as a single in February 1972, and it topped the charts in both Ireland and Spain. To publicise the single, Apple had prepared a 30-second radio and TV commercial in which Paul was featured, but the Independent Television Authority banned it from British television networks, as did BBC Radio One and Radio Luxembourg.

During the recording of the song at Island Studios, Paul was asked by a reporter for the US-based ABC TV Network if he was worried about making a political point. He replied:

> No. You can't stay out of it, you know, if you think at all these days. We're still humans, you know, and you wake up and read your newspaper, it affects you. So I don't mind too much, it doesn't worry me, like I say. I don't now plan to do everything I do as a political thing, you know, but just on this one occasion, I think the British Government overstepped their mark and showed themselves to be more of a sort of repressive regime than I ever believed them to be.

The release of the controversial track had given McCartney and his band mates more than a few headaches. McCartney said at the time:

> I'm a taxpayer, so that entitles me to an opinion. I'm living in the West, so we're allowed to talk over here, right? So when the English paratroopers, my army who I'm paying rates for, go into Ireland and shoot down innocent bystanders, for the first time in my life I go, 'Hey, wait a minute. We're the goodies, aren't we?' That wasn't very goody and I'm moved to make some kind of a protest, so I did: 'Give Ireland Back to the Irish', which was promptly banned in England. But it was Number One in Spain, of all places! That was rather odd, Franco was in power. Maybe they couldn't understand the words and they just liked the tune.

The fact that the song was immediately banned from British airwaves didn't help the record's sales, but added to its credibility. It went down surprisingly well with audiences when performed during Wings' British and European tours. As McCartney noted, it was a highlight of his live performances: 'It makes a great announcement. You can say, this one was banned and everyone goes "hooray!" The audience loves it. Everyone is a bit "anti" all that banning, all that censorship.' McCartney's decision to play the song in concert may have been politically motivated, but he was also forced into performing it through lack of more suitable material. Wings' repertoire was limited and the band often had to perform songs twice to pad out their live sets. No matter how politically motivated he was, McCartney had little choice other than to perform the song in concert.

For one member of the group, Henry McCullough, the song was to cause problems for his family. McCullough's brother Samuel was beaten up because of Henry's involvement with the single.

Henry McCullough, Guitarist with Wings 1972–73

Henry McCullough, a guitarist from Portstewart in Derry, was the only Irish musician to perform with Paul McCartney as a member of Wings and appeared on a number of the group's early releases, including the controversial 'Give Ireland Back to The Irish'. His career had begun with bands such as The Skyrockets, Gene and The Gents, Sweeney's Men, The People, and Irish psychedelic band, Eire Apparent. By the time he joined Wings in 1972 he had already toured the world with Jimi Hendrix, as well as Joe Cocker and the Grease Band.

In 1972 Paul McCartney recalled:

> We're trying things out in Wings at the moment, but there's nothing too set with Henry McCullough. He might come in. All we really want to do is to get a good band to go round and play with. I don't care if we're three, four or five, so long as it sounds like a good band. What we're doing is working up to going out. It's been a long time since I played live, that's why I want to get back. I've really decided that I miss just playing to people.

Speaking to Adrian Smyth in November 1999, Henry McCullough takes up his own story about his part in the early days of Wings:

> I received a phone call from Ian Horne, my roadie, who asked me to go to a rehearsal the next day. I had a couple of pints of Guinness before I went along the first time. That helped. It was a wee room. The equipment was set up and Paul asked me to play and said the rest of them would fit in. We got into some rock n' roll, things like 'Blue Moon of Kentucky', 'Lucille', some things off the *Wild Life* album and some reggae. Also there were a couple of new ones he'd written. On one song he was kind of playing away on a tune I hadn't heard before, so I asked him what to do. He said, 'We're all just trying it out', and just continued playing. We all joined in, it went on a bit further and in no time at all, a song was written. It was written on the spot and we all contributed. I'd only met Paul twice, but he seemed full of energy and enthusiasm. He comes in and throws off his coat and gets right into it.

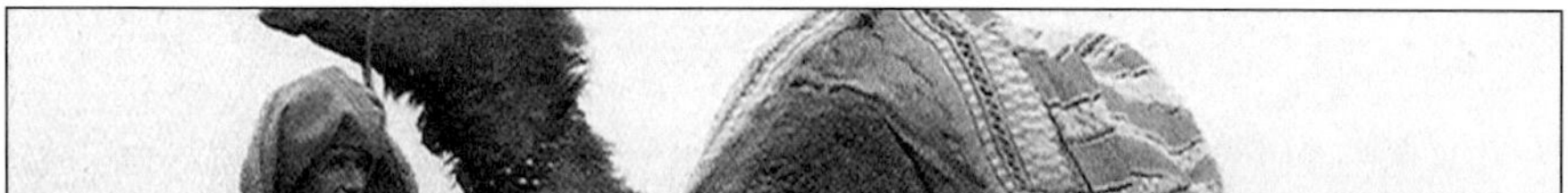

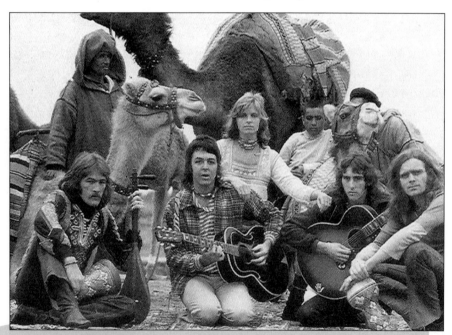

Wings take a short break in Morocco in 1972. L–r: Denny Seiwell, Paul McCartney, Linda McCartney, Denny Laine, and Henry McCullough. *(Henry McCullough)*

> I can't help having respect for Paul and all the songs he's written and what he's achieved. But, it's just another band as far as I'm concerned, and that's the way Paul wants it. Originally Denny Laine was going to be the lead guitarist and vocalist as well, but I felt Denny felt a bit restricted playing guitar and singing at the same time. He probably felt he couldn't do both.

Wings didn't make Henry's fortune: he was on £70 a week back in 1972, just enough to get him a small car. There were no session fees but he got a £500 bonus for the *Red Rose Speedway* album. There was also the odd perk, such as after he had finished the *Red Rose* album, the band jetted off to Morocco for a few weeks. According to McCullough, McCartney is a perfectionist, 'You just have to go along with that. Ninety per cent of what we played on each song was the same every night, so it was almost like being back in the showbands.'

On the recording of the 'My Love' track from the *Red Rose* album, McCullough created one of the greatest guitar solos in rock music. He recalls:

> Recording 'My Love' I had problems with the solo. I just couldn't get it right and the tension was running high when, just before yet another take, I asked if I could try something a little different. We'd worked it out and rehearsed it and we had a full orchestra and it was recorded live. We had the whole orchestra waiting and George Martin behind the glass. I went over to Paul and said, 'Just a minute, do you mind if I change the solo?' It was actually one of my best solos I ever played. And afterwards Paul came up and hugged me. I think it proved a point to Paul regarding myself.

McCullough remembers performing the song on *Top of the Pops* – it was a less than glorious experience. As he approached his solo he realised he was about to get sick. He prematurely leapt from the stage, still playing the solo, and promptly threw up behind the scenery. Paul was very tolerant and never said anything.

On the question of Paul's wife, Linda, joining the band, McCullough remembers:

> One of the odd things to us musicians was Paul's insistence on having

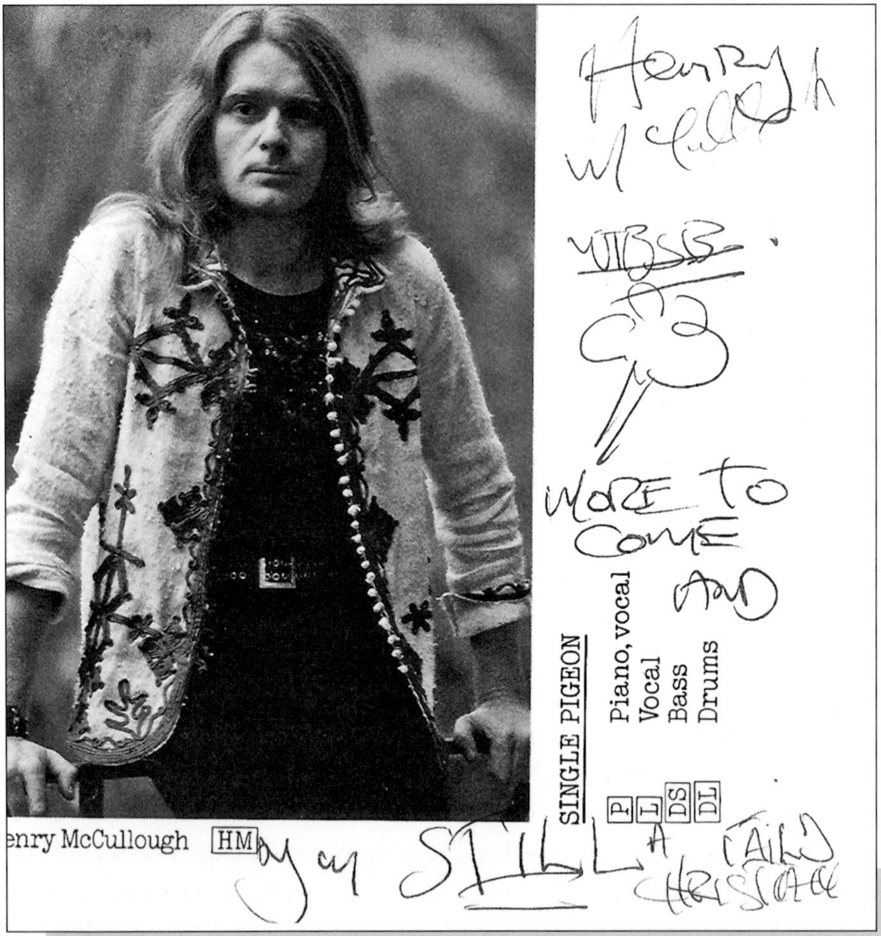

An autographed copy of the Wings album *Red Rose Speedway* from 1973.

his wife Linda, a non-musician, playing keyboards in the band. Well, of course it was a bit frustrating. We did have discussions about bringing in a piano player to do the job properly. I was very fond of Linda, we would all sing and do little harmonies and have a good time up on Paul's farm in Scotland. She wasn't a musician at all but at the end of the day she was able to play something. She was taught the parts by Paul and she never ventured too far from that. She could shuffle maracas, she could play the tambourine. I think she handled it really well.

Wings' first tour was low-key. According to Henry:

> We just got in the back of the Transit, with dogs and kids and the truck behind and just turned up at universities. Paul would stick his head in and say, 'Is it all right if we play here tonight?' and of course it was. That was the bonding period, in the back of a bloody Transit with no windows. I went on tour around England and Europe with Wings. We did most of the organising ourselves and we certainly weren't doing it for the money.
>
> The band was great live. We had a lot of great rocky numbers. I had a great time as everybody else did. The odd time we would have done 'Long Tall Sally' as an encore, and Paul was brilliant at it. We were like a bunch of kids really after the gig.

Henry McCullough had said in a interview in 1973: 'I don't suppose we'll be together for ever; I'm sure Paul's got more of a tie to the Beatles than to Wings. Wings has all the makings of a great group, but our battle is to keep it as a band and not let it fall apart as it could so easily do. It's worth going at it. I'm there 100 per cent, I know we've got a lot to offer.'

Despite these words, by May 1973 there was speculation about McCullough's position within the group. The suggestion was that Henry was unhappy and contemplating a return to the Grease Band. Shortly before Wings were due to record their third album, both Henry and drummer Denny Seiwell quit. The reasons they left are probably many and varied. As Paul said, some months after the break, 'Henry preferred to lead a more bluesy way of life and he left over musical differences. He was very good at the other stuff but more into blues.'

Henry left shortly before Wings were due to fly to Lagos, Nigeria, for the recording of *Band On The Run*. He and Paul came to a showdown over styles of playing and he was unhappy about taking directions from Paul. Henry recalls: 'I had a row with Paul over what to play and where to play it. And it was quite severe – "You'll fucking do this, like I'm the boss", Paul said. [I said] "We'll see about that, you c***", and I just packed my guitar, stuck my amp in the car and set sail. And that was my stint in Wings done.'

About two months after he left Wings, Paul wrote McCullough a cheque for £5,000 and said: 'Here Henry, thanks very much. I really appreciate it. Nice one.' Henry says, 'we drank a half-bottle of whiskey, smoked a couple of joints, shook hands and that was that. He's a lovely man. A genuine, hard-working person and a dedicated artist.'

Another Beatle connection for Henry McCullough came from George Harrison. In 1975 he recorded a solo album entitled *Mind Your Own Business* for George's new Dark Horse label. Henry recalls: 'I didn't spend that much time with him, but he seems a nice chap. But when he lost the 'My Sweet Lord' copyright lawsuit everybody on the label had to go their own way.'

In 2001 the acclaimed television documentary *Wingspan* was shown around the world. Henry recalls:

Henry McCullough with one of the authors of this book, Damian Smyth, pictured here in Dublin in 1999. *(Mick Lynch)*

> I watched the documentary with great joy, the music was great and it made me realise more than before that I'm part of rock history. I actually sent Paul a wee note to say I'd enjoyed watching it and it brought back many memories and I got a nice letter back from him to say thanks and he hoped I was well and to keep plucking them silver strings. And he drew a wee caricature of himself, with that little rounded face of his. It was nice to hear from him.

Almost 30 years after its original release, 'Give Ireland Back To The Irish' was still causing problems for McCartney. When he wanted to include it on *Wingspan – Hits and History*, EMI asked for it to be removed. He said at the time, 'I feel that, like a lot of people, but I don't support their [the IRA's] methods. I certainly don't want to be in support when a bomb goes off in London and people are killed. I would have a hard time supporting that. So when EMI rang me up and said, "Look you know, we're pretty nervous and you don't have much time on the album. We should pull that one", that was really why it got pulled.'

6

Paul Marries in Monaghan

On Thursday 26 July 2001 it was announced that Paul McCartney had become engaged to Heather Mills. Paul had met Heather at a charity function in May 1999 when she was appealing for help for her own foundation, The Heather Mills Trust, which provides limbs for victims of war. Mills was a former swimwear model whose left leg was amputated below the knee after she was knocked down by a police motorcyclist in 1993. A spokesman for McCartney said that Paul and Heather planned to marry some time in 2002.

Paul, who had lost his first wife to cancer three years earlier in April 1998, had proposed to Heather during a trip to the British Lake District. As part of Paul's research into his family tree – particularly his maternal grandfather, Owen Mohan, and grandmother, Mary Teresa Danher – the pair made a secret visit to Co Monaghan. The couple stayed in Castle Leslie, the seventeenth-century, 1,000-acre estate in the village of Glaslough, and decided that this should be the fairytale venue for their wedding.

Within a few months, on Wednesday 20 February 2002, Paul and Heather were back in Dublin making a second fleeting visit to Ireland. Heather was in town for a disability conference at Dublin Castle. The couple arrived on Tuesday and stayed at Brown's Hotel on St Stephen's Green for their 24-hour visit. Their

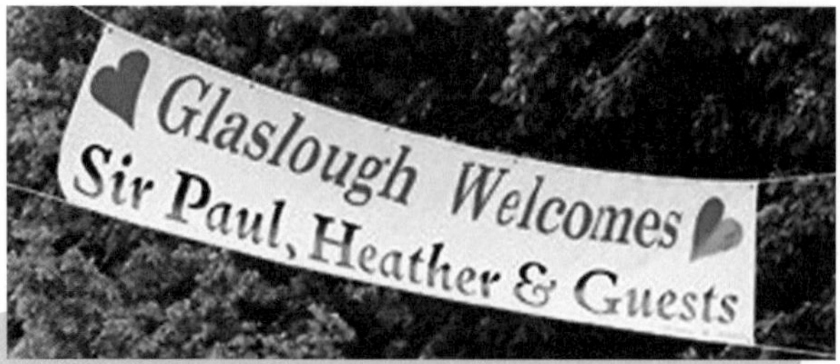

Local residents offer the happy couple a warm welcome. *(Damian Smyth)*

day-trip caught fellow hotel guests by surprise and diners in the restaurant were stunned when the pair turned up for dinner. Even staff members were not aware that the celebrity couple had booked into the small hotel. The pair stayed in the top suite which houses a double bed once slept in by Marilyn Monroe. As he signed autographs for fans at the hotel, Paul said, 'We're having a very pleasant time here. Dublin is a great city, really nice.' He went on to say, 'Heather has gone up to Dublin Castle and I'm going to collect her there later. We fly out this afternoon. I'd love to stay longer but we can't.'

On 10 June 2002, the day before their wedding in St Salvator's Church in the grounds of Castle Leslie, Paul and Heather came to the gates of the estate to formally announce that the wedding would take place the following day.

Just after 4pm a Land Rover driven by Paul pulled up inside the gates of the castle and the couple emerged from the vehicle to rapturous applause. A spot was marked on the ground so the couple would be an adequate distance from the press. A huge cheer greeted them as they emerged from inside the gates and walked the short distance to the waiting media. Paul presented his bride-to-be with a red rose and kissed her twice for the cameras. Paul and Heather spoke briefly:

Paul: Okay! We'd just like to say a couple of words if you don't mind. We'd just like to thank ... [interrupted by somebody throwing Heather a small flower].

Heather: It smells nice, thank you.

Paul: Em, we'd just like to say a couple of words, thanking, thanking all of the people who've wished us good wishes, the people who've written in to us, and the people we've met on the street who've said congratulations and wished us all the best. We'd like to take this opportunity of thanking those people. Right! And what would you like to say? [Turning to Heather]

Heather: Just the same. Thanks for all your support and well wishes, and really nice letters, really appreciate it, thank you.

Paul: So we're gonna go …

Reporter: Are you nervous?

Paul: We're just a bit, yeah!

Heather: Excited.

Paul: Excited yeah! So we're gonna go back into the castle and, eh, and as you know through Uncle Jack, it is tomorrow.

[*This draws a cheer from the assembled crowd.*]

Heather: But it's a secret!

Paul: But it's a secret, alright!

Female Reporter: Will you be spending the night together? Will you be spending the night in separate rooms?

[*This was either ignored or not heard by the couple.*]

Paul and Heather come to the gates of Castle Leslie to meet the press and formally announce their wedding. (*Damian Smyth*)

Paul: I'm not supposed to tell anybody anything. So what we're gonna do is basically a family wedding. So we're gonna have family and friends and we're just gonna have a bit of fun. So there you are. Thank you very much.

At the media's insistence, Paul gave Heather another kiss, and then they walked towards the crowd. Amongst the gifts offered was a framed coat of arms (displaying the origins of both the McCartney and Mills names) from the Beatles Ireland fan club.

Paul: We'll collect the autographs and we'll do them in there, otherwise we'll be here for hours.

Heather: We'll get them collected for signing.

Fan in crowd: Will you be watching the match tomorrow, Paul?

[*In reference to Ireland's World Cup game against Saudi Arabia*]

Paul: Yeah! Oh yeah! We've got nothin' else to do.

Paul and Heather waved to the crowd and returned to the castle with the souvenirs. Twenty minutes later Geoff Baker, Paul's publicist at the time, returned with all the autographs.

News reports on the day claimed that the couple were refusing to sell their wedding pictures to a glossy magazine and that they were turning down an offer of £1.5 million sterling. Instead they were to issue one picture that the media had to purchase, with the money going to a landmine charity.

Geoff Baker said, 'Any occasion like this is for everybody, not just for the person with the largest cheque-book.' He added, 'Paul and Heather are due to stay at the castle until the ceremony, although they will not be spending Monday night together. That would be bad luck.'

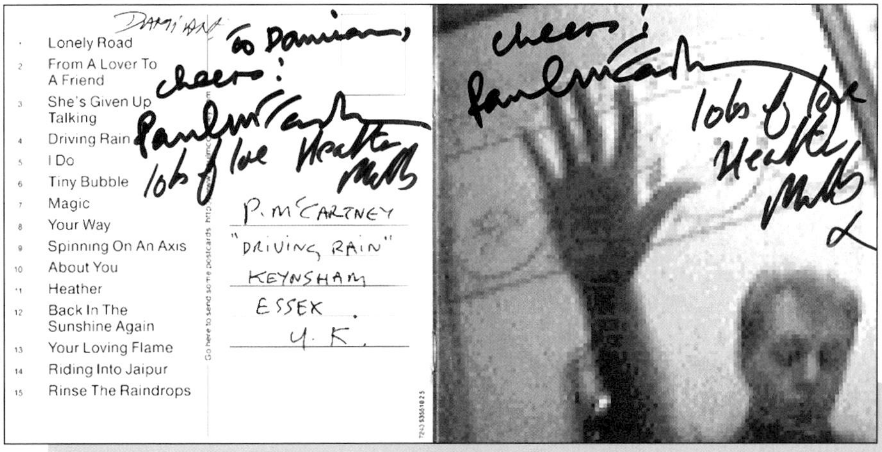

Two autographed albums signed by Paul and Heather in Glaslough on 10 June 2002.

The Wedding Video

Paddy Barron, a freelance cameraman from Greystones, Co Wicklow, was brought in by a New York-based film and video company to assist with the production of the official wedding video. According to Barron, the brief McCartney gave the production company was that every aspect of the event was to be recorded. It was, in fact, to be a kind of fly-on-the wall documentary covering the days before and after the wedding. This meant that as well as the actual wedding ceremony itself, the crew was given exclusive access to all areas of the preparations and permission to follow Paul and Heather's every move. It also meant that Barron got closer to the centre of the story than any other member of the media. Surprisingly, he says he wasn't asked to sign any confidentiality contracts for his part in the production of the wedding video.

The crew was in attendance from three days before the actual wedding, making arrangements for the video-shoot with the wedding planners. Paddy met up with the rest of the team at the Armagh Arms Hotel, which was a short distance from the wedding venue. Normally a cameraman, on this occasion he had been asked to take on the job of soundman.

The day before the big day, the couple arrived by helicopter from Belfast Airport. The crew filmed their arrival at the castle, after which the couple retired to their rooms. They later appeared outside for the impromptu press reception at the castle gates. That night, a party was held at the castle for close friends, family and guests. It lasted until after 3am and at one stage during the night's entertainment Paul played drums.

According to Barron, on the day before the wedding Paul's daughter, Stella, came up to the wedding video production team and said to them, 'Look! I don't want to be in the film at this wedding, I don't want anything to do with this, please don't put me in the video.' So they had a production team meeting about her request, and decided that if she didn't want to be in the video she wouldn't be in it. In fact, the only time she was filmed was a few days before at Castle Leslie, when there was a McCartney family dinner in the main dining room of the castle. On this occasion, Paul discovered it was the film producer's birthday and he sang 'Happy Birthday'.

On the morning of the wedding, Ireland played Saudi Arabia in the World Cup. Two hours before the wedding, in a room in Castle Leslie, Paddy Barron, Paul and Mike McCartney, the cameraman and video producer were all gathered together to watch the match, accompanied by a barman and butler to serve food and drink. There was beer on tap and a big-screen TV. All Barron could think about was his press colleagues outside the castle trying to get the big scoop and there he was, in the 'eye of the storm'.

Paul and Heather married at St Salvator's Church in the grounds of the castle, in a ceremony conducted by the Venerable Cecil Pringle, Archdeacon of Clogher. Paddy Barron recalls that for the shoot they used two cameras, one high up to capture the overall view of the proceedings and the second at the side of the altar. He says it was very much like any other wedding video set-up, only with better cameras.

The guest list for the ceremony included Paul's children, Stella, Mary and James from his marriage to Linda, and Linda's daughter, Heather, from her first marriage. The Beatles' former producer Sir George Martin, long-time friend Chrissie Hynde, Jools Holland, Pink Floyd guitarist Dave Gilmour and US actor Steve Buscemi, who starred in *Reservoir Dogs*, were also invited to the ceremony. Barron remembers having 'a good laugh with Dave Gilmour', who was there with all his family and his new baby.

As Paul and Heather walked down the aisle after exchanging their vows, the organist played Paul's own composition, 'The Wedding March', from the film

St Salvator's Church in the grounds of Castle Leslie where Paul and Heather were married. *(Mick Lynch)*

The Family Way, for which he wrote the soundtrack in 1966. Just after 5.30pm the church bell sounded, signalling that the couple had taken their vows. 'After the church,' says Paddy Barron, 'we moved with the guests to the reception and by now there were up to about 300 guests in attendance. I was amazed with the food. All vegetarian and very Indian. The reception was very much like most weddings I have ever been to, just a bit bigger. As for the food, it was served buffet-style. You just got the stuff and went back to your table, no big fuss.'

During his wedding speech, Paul recalled his Liverpool childhood. He got emotional when he said he felt that John and George were probably looking down on him and wishing him well. Heather sang Paul's favourite Beach Boys' song, 'God Only Knows', and the newly-weds then showed a 20-minute video that featured the couple kissing in twenty different locations throughout the world.

It seems that Paddy Barron wasn't the only person who was less than impressed with the video. He commented:

> What she had put together was footage of Paul and herself on holidays, just Paul and herself holding hands, walking around, kissing, on elephants in India, walking on the Great Wall of China, all that kind of stuff. And it was the most boring thing. You could feel the tension in the room, it just got so, so boring. Five or ten minutes would have been enough. You could feel people getting bored and this went on for twenty minutes! I think she was trying to put out a message to the world that she loves Paul so much. I just thought it was so false. In fact I said to my colleague at the time, 'I bet you this is another celebrity wedding that will end up in shambles like most of them.' The noise level had become very embarrassing and very awkward: people just got bored at what they had to sit through.

Castle Leslie, the seventeenth-century castle set on the 1,000-acre estate, which was the fairytale venue for their wedding. (*Mick Lynch*)

The first dance was Tony Bennett's 'The Very Thought of You', the couple's favourite song. Later, Chrissie Hynde, lead singer with The Pretenders, sang backing vocals on a medley of 1970s disco hits. Barron remembers that Ringo, who had made a speech in the church, left halfway though the reception or just after it, which he thought was a bit odd.

The gifts ranged from a breadmaker, courtesy of Paul's cousin, Kate Robbins, to donations to Heather's landmine charity. One unique gift was a framed sketch of the couple from Paul's artist cousin, Ian Harris. 'What do you give a multi-millionaire?' said Harris. 'At least this is different.' Mike McCartney gave the happy couple a Frisbee with the initials 'P' and 'H'. Paul tried it out, tossing it around the castle grounds.

The guests were given silver Waterman ballpoint pens engraved with the words 'Love Paul and Heather' before leaving. The British musician and television personality, Jools Holland, spoke for many when he said, 'It was marvellous, a beautiful traditional family wedding', adding, 'I may have had one too many pints of Guinness.' Paddy Barron added:

> When it was time for Paul and Heather to go, they had arranged a fireworks display over the lake at the castle. So, just before the display began, Paul and Heather made their way to a jetty on the lakeside and boarded a small boat to take them to the middle of the lake to view the fireworks. There were flowers all over the boat. It was very romantic.

On Wednesday 12 June, Paul and Heather left by helicopter and headed for Belfast International Airport where a private jet was waiting to take them to the Seychelles Island of Cousine in the Indian Ocean where they would spend their honeymoon.

As for the footage shot by the video crew, it was handed over to the producer of the New York-based production company for editing in New York and was presented to Paul and Heather at a later date. The unedited footage was to be held in a London archive. About a week after the event, Barron received a call from New York. It was the production company enquiring whether he had any footage he had not submitted. As it happened, he did have some footage remaining on tapes in his possession. He promptly packaged the tapes and took them to Greystones Post Office where he posted them to New York.

The only security scare during Paul and Heather's time at Castle Leslie was the arrest of a man at the gates of the castle who had tried to drive into the grounds before the ceremony. Security said he tried to enter the grounds with a guitar on the passenger seat of his car. A Garda sergeant on the scene said, 'I think it was a case of a man having too much drink and deciding to give the couple a song.'

McCartney Returns to Glaslough

According to the *Ireland On Sunday* newspaper:

> One year on from the wedding, locals in Wright's Pub in the village of Glaslough found themselves with some unexpected company. To celebrate their first wedding anniversary and his birthday on 18 June, not to mention the impending arrival of their first child, Paul and Heather made a surprise return to Co Monaghan. They were put up for the night at Castle Leslie and enjoyed a private dinner there before slipping down to the village pub for a quiet drink accompanied by Samantha Leslie.
>
> At about 10.30pm they dropped into Wright's, the quaint little pub where, incidentally, the movie version of Spike Milligan's *Puckoon* was filmed. Paul enjoyed two pints of Heineken while Heather settled for a glass of Ballygowan. According to one of the regulars, 'Nobody asked for an autograph, but he did shake all the locals' hands, and, no, he didn't buy any of us a drink.' During their time there they walked up and down the village and shook hands and spoke with locals.

During December 2004, Paul and Heather made their second visit of the year to the area, taking the opportunity to visit Castle Leslie for the fourth time since their wedding in 2002. They stayed in the Red Room at the Castle, where they spent their wedding night. Their daughter, Beatrice Milly, who was one year old in October, was blessed in the church on the castle grounds.

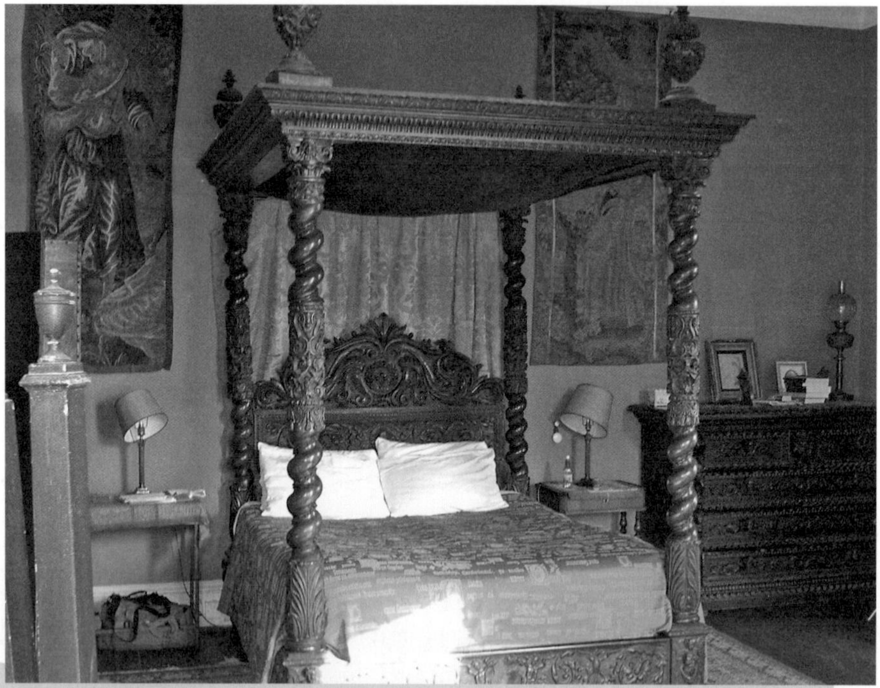

'The Red Room' where Paul and Heather spent their wedding night, on the second floor of Castle Leslie. (*Mick Lynch*)

7

The Beatles Return to the Irish Stage

Since the break-up of the Beatles in 1970 there have been only two appearances on stage in Ireland by former members of the group. As part of a world tour, which coincided with the release of his *Vertical Man* album, Ringo appeared at the Point Theatre in Dublin in 1998 with his All-Starr Band. In May 2003, Paul played the Royal Dublin Showgrounds (RDS) on the Irish leg of his 'Back in The World' tour.

Ringo at the Point, 1998

Set List:

[*Ringo on lead vocals except where stated*]

It Don't Come Easy
Act Naturally
Show Me the Way (Peter Frampton)
Sunshine of Your Love (Jack Bruce)
Shooting Star (Simon Kirke)

Boys
Yellow Submarine
No No Song
La De Da
I Feel Free (Jack Bruce)
Molly Malone (Jack Bruce)
All Right Now (Simon Kirke)
Baby I Love Your Ways (Peter Frampton)
A Whiter Shade of Pale (Gary Brooker)
I Wanna Be Your Man
Love Me Do
Photograph
I'm the Greatest
With a Little Help from my Friends

As the lights went down the screams went up for the arrival of the All-Starr Band on stage. The cheers got louder when Ringo arrived and kicked straight into 'It Don't Come Easy' and 'Act Naturally'.

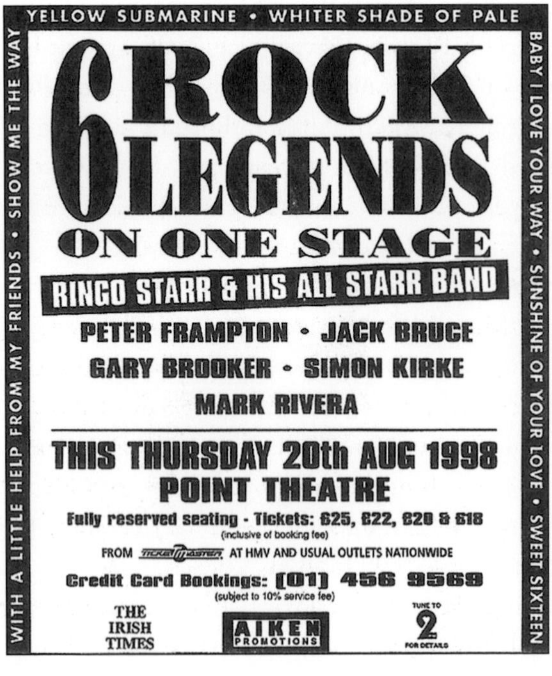

Dressed in dark trousers, a glittery silver top, and two-tone jacket, Ringo introduced the legendary Peter Frampton. Renowned for his trademark sound, the 'voice-box' guitar technique of forming words by channelling the sound through a mouthpiece, Frampton belted out the classic, 'Show Me the Way'. Jack Bruce then performed the legendary Cream number, 'Sunshine of Your Love', and Simon Kirke sang 'Shooting Star'. But it was Ringo the

A front-row ticket for the Ringo Starr concert in Dublin.

crowd had come to see and he obliged with 'Boys'. A banner in the crowd read 'Ringo no tomatoes', which brought a cheeky grin from the Liverpudlian.

Next came a moment to cherish for a female fan in the front row. She made her way up to the stage and handed Ringo a portrait of himself that she had drawn. During his performance of 'Yellow Submarine' he held the portrait up to the crowd and, in his distinct Scouse accent, he said, 'My face is a little bit thinner than that.' He continued with the 'No No Song' and, in an effort to please all the front row fans, he performed his current single at the time 'La De Da'. 'This song is Number One in Poland,' he informed the crowd.

While Ringo took a well-earned rest, Jack Bruce performed 'I Feel Free' and then proceeded to do a solo version of 'Molly Malone'. Kirke sang the much loved Free classic 'All Right Now'; then Frampton did 'Baby I Love Your Way' and Brooker, together with Mark Rivera on keyboards, performed 'Whiter Shade of Pale'.

Ringo returned to sing 'I Wanna Be Your Man' and 'Love Me Do'. 'Photograph' and John Lennon's 'I'm the Greatest' brought the show to a close, with the crowd roaring for an encore. Ringo obliged minutes later, finally finishing the show with the appropriate 'With a Little Help from my Friends'.

The show was billed as 'Six Rock Legends' and may have been nothing more than a glorified karaoke show but the capacity audience didn't care. This was the first time a Beatle had performed in the Republic of Ireland since 1963.

Prior to the concert, Ringo allowed some of his Irish fans to meet him backstage. Some members of the Beatles Ireland fan club were ushered down a long corridor and met him in his dressing room. They presented him with a bodhran. 'I bet this is a drum', he joked, 'but where is the stick?'

He signed a letter to become an Honorary Member of the fan club and he was impressed with the other Honorary Members, reading them out loud, pausing briefly on Julian's name. 'Ah Jules,' he said, and swiftly passed over Pete Best's name, before mentioning that the original Quarrymen were before his time. He signed a letter for the club and even included his trademark Star logo.

Almost a decade on from that meeting, Ringo continued to remember his Irish fans. In the summer of 2007, Dublin teenager Laura Meehan wrote to him in Los Angeles looking for an autograph – and in October that same year she received a signed photograph.

Clockwise from left: Ringo sent this autographed photo to Irish fan Laura Meehan in October 2007; Ringo pictured backstage with a bodhrán, a gift from the Beatles Ireland fan club (*Beatles Ireland fan club*); Ringo backstage before his Point Depot concert.

Paul at the RDS, 2003

After the success of his American and Japanese Tours of 2002, Paul and his band hit the road again. The line-up was Rusty Anderson on guitar with Abe Laboriel on drums (both musicians who backed Paul on the *Driving Rain* album), Paul 'Wix' Wickens on keyboards, and Brian Ray on guitar and bass. The new tour, entitled 'Back in the World, 2003', was to lead the band back to Europe through more than 30 live dates, including, for the first time in 40 years, a highly anticipated return to Dublin on 27 May 2003.

There was some controversy prior to the gig, primarily regarding the high ticket prices, and a ban on fans taking photographs, which resulted in cameras being confiscated on entry to the RDS. As well as this, the free programme, which had been given out with previous tours, was not available in Ireland. Instead, a collector's tour programme was available for sale, featuring more than 70 pages of exclusive photos, interviews and information relating to Paul's recent activities.

Commenting on the high prices, Paul said, 'I just let the promoters do that. I say "what do things cost" and they tell me and I'm always shocked. Is the suggestion that I do it for free? I suppose I do already have a lot of money. But these promoters have a living to make.'

Paul flew into Dublin on 26 May, the day before the concert, and checked into the Four Seasons Hotel. That evening Paul, Heather and several of his entourage went to O'Donoghue's Bar in Baggot Street.

The following day two guards on motorcycles, with sirens blaring, escorted Paul's black limousine, carrying himself and Heather, on the short journey from their hotel to the concert venue where they arrived shortly after 4pm. During this short journey he gave his only Irish interview to Tom Dunne of Today FM (see Appendix 5, p 179, for the full interview).

The Concert

Set List:

Hello Goodbye
Jet
All My Loving
Getting Better

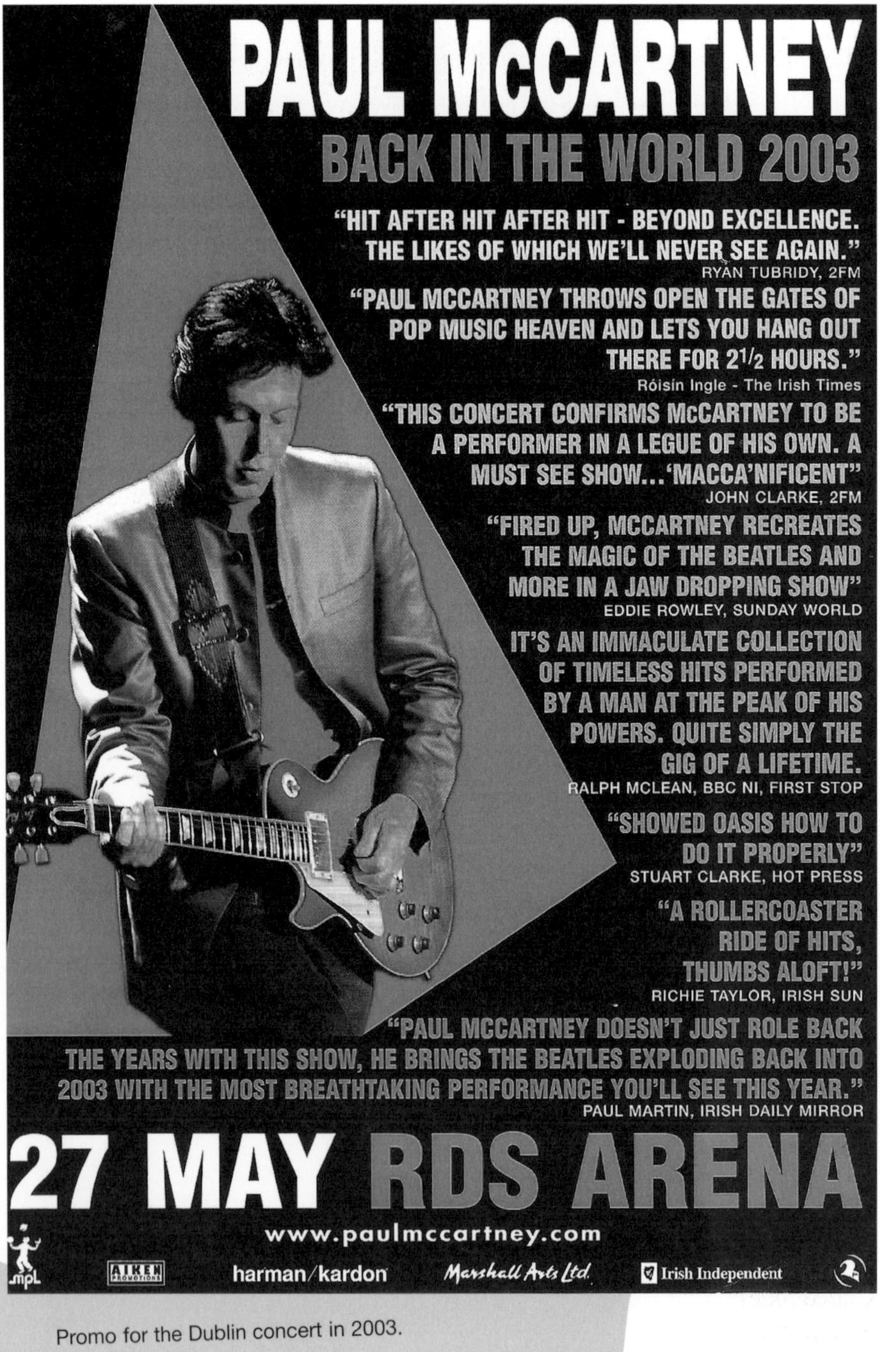

Promo for the Dublin concert in 2003.

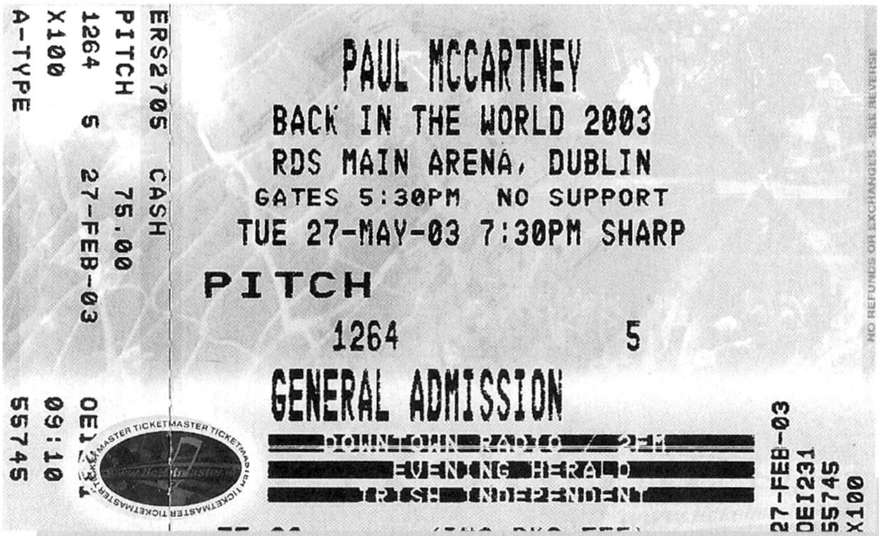

Ticket for Paul's first solo Irish concert in May 2003.

Let Me Roll It/Foxy Lady
Lonely Road
Your Loving Flame
Blackbird
Every Night
We Can Work It Out
You Never Give Me Your Money
Carry That Weight
The Fool On the Hill
Here Today
Something
Yellow Submarine
Eleanor Rigby
Here There and Everywhere
I've Just Seen a Face
Calico Skies
Two of Us
Michelle

The pre-show to Paul's Dublin concert, 2003. *(Damian Smyth)*

Band on the Run
Back in the USSR
Maybe I'm Amazed
Let 'em In
My Love
She's Leaving Home
Can't Buy Me Love
Birthday
Live and Let Die
Let It Be
Hey Jude
The Long and Winding Road
Lady Madonna
I Saw Her Standing There
Yesterday
Sgt Pepper's Reprise

'Hello Dublin! We have come to rock you tonight,' were Paul's opening words as he appeared solo on a Dublin stage for the first time. He opened with 'Hello Goodbye', 'Jet' and 'All My Loving'. 'Getting Better', should have been re-titled 'Getting Wetter' as the rain, which marred the opening sequence of the show, continued to fall during the early part of the gig.

After 'Let Me Roll It' (with a bit of the Jimi Hendrix track, 'Foxy Lady', thrown in for good measure) he discarded his black jacket, to good-natured wolf-whistles, revealing a red 'Adopt-A-Landmine' T-shirt, in support of Heather's charity. Following a rendition of 'Lonely Road', he moved to the piano and introduced Abe Laboriel on drums. Before playing 'Your Loving Flame', he dedicated it to Heather. The other band members then exited the stage leaving the audience in the company of Paul.

Alone on stage, he introduced the Beatles classic 'Blackbird' by telling the story of how he was inspired to write the song. He told the audience that the song was written at a time in the 1960s when the question of civil rights in the United States was prominent. He explained, 'Sometimes we call girls birds, so I was imagining the struggles of a young black woman and came up with this song.'

During a sequence of songs from the *Abbey Road* album, he surprisingly forgot the lyrics to 'You Never Give Me Your Money', despite singing the song correctly at the sound check earlier, but 'Carry That Weight' was sung without a glitch.

Paul rocks at the RDS on 27 May 2003. *(Beatles Ireland)*

The concert was particularly memorable for Paul's easy and good-humoured rapport with the audience. He proved himself a gifted storyteller, as well as a powerful performer of rock 'n' roll. He told the crowd the gig felt like he was returning home, especially given that Liverpudlians consider Liverpool to be the 'capital of Ireland'. He then paid tribute to the two missing members of the Fab Four:

> You know, sometimes in life I don't think we always say what you mean to say to people. Sometimes maybe you're going to give someone a compliment but the moment isn't right, or you just think I'll leave it till another time, and it's particularly sad after someone passes away because you think I wish I'd said that, I wish I'd told him that. By then it's too late and I wrote this song after my dear friend John passed away. Let's hear it for John! So I wrote this song for him, like I say after he died and it's in the form of an imaginary conversation with me and him.

He then launched into 'Here Today'. At the end of the song, still alone on stage, he continued reminiscing, this time about George:

> While we're in this mood, I don't know if many of you knew it, but George was a very good ukulele player. He was fantastic, he really loved it and he was a big fan of George Formby ... For those of you that don't know, George Formby was a film star of the forties, who played the ukulele, and a British film star, and George was such a big fan of his that George was in his fan club. It's true, and he used to go up to Blackpool for the convention and there would be, like, about 50 of

Paul performs 'Back in the USSR' at Dublin's RDS, just three days after performing in Red Square, Moscow. (*Damian Smyth*)

these guys in a room all singing, 'When I'm Cleaning Windows!' So what would happen, if you'd go around to George's house, sometimes after you'd have something to eat, the ukuleles would come out, and he'd say, would you like one? And in fact he gave me this one. [Audience applauds] That's the first time a ukulele's got a round of applause! So I was around his house one of these nights, and we were playing the ukuleles and I said I'd do a song on the ukulele and I played it for him. And now I'd like to play it for you tonight as a tribute to Georgie.

Paul and his band treat the Irish fans to 'Calico Skies' during his RDS concert. *(Damian Smyth)*

After he performed 'Something' he went on to say, 'When George listens to me doing this he says "Nah, nah, it doesn't go like that. It goes like this".' Then Paul performs a speeded up version. Someone at the front shouted, 'What about Ringo?', which drew huge applause from the sell-out crowd and prompted Paul and the crowd to sing the chorus of, 'We All Live in a Yellow Submarine'.

Less chat and more music followed with a trio of Beatles classics, 'Eleanor Rigby', 'Here There and Everywhere' and 'I've Just Seen a Face', followed by 'Calico Skies' and 'Two of Us'. After a storming version of 'Back in the USSR' he added, 'Just the other night we were in Red Square in Moscow and you can imagine how that went down.'

Band member Paul Wickens then explained how he had been getting stick from the other band members for not learning any local language from the countries they had visited. He placed a black Guinness hat on his head, as he raised the pint that he had perched on his keyboard, addressing the crowd with 'Sláinte' and sampling the famous Irish beverage.

The music continued with 'She's Leaving Home' and 'Can't Buy Me Love'.

Following 'Live and Let Die' and 'Let It Be', Paul decided the time was right for a bit of crowd participation. 'Okay, there's a bit at the end of this next song that I've got a feeling you just might want to join in. Okay, sing along with us,' as he plays the opening chords to 'Hey Jude'. During the song the band left the stage, one by one. The crowd got vocal with chants of, 'We want more! We want more', and then the traditional Irish chant of 'Olé! Olé! Olé!' until Paul returned with 'The Long and Winding Road'.

'Oh, Dublin! Oh, Ireland! We love ya. Dublin's bubblin'. I tell you what I've got a feeling you, you wanna keep on rockin' alright,' he declared, before launching into 'Lady Madonna'. As he kicked into 'I Saw Her Standing There' and 'Yesterday' he declared his amazement that the crowd had any energy left and thanked them for their welcome.

After the gig there was a party for all the crew at Luttrelstown Castle on the north side of Dublin. The following morning Paul and Heather had a free day in Dublin and they used the time to announce to the world's media that Heather was pregnant and expecting their first child before the end of the year.

As research for this book, Michael Lynch spent the day behind the scenes at Paul's RDS gig:

> The band began their sound-check with 'Coming Up' around 4.45pm and for the next 50 minutes went through a selection of cover versions, including a Dublin remix of the Eurovision Song 'Volare', 'Yakety Yak' and 'C Moon'. McCartney performed fourteen numbers in total, most of which wouldn't make the main set-list later.
>
> There were only ten to fifteen people visible during the sound-check, most of them roadies, but he responded regularly to the small applause with, 'Thank you, uncontrollable people, you wild bunch.'
>
> The soundcheck ran over the allocated time, so the opening time for the gates was now put back from 5.30pm until 6pm, and Paul finished the soundcheck ten minutes prior to that.
>
> As the crowd rushed in to get the best positions at the front of the stage, we walked around backstage and, while there was no sign of Paul, all of his band were casually walking around and we got to speak to each of them individually.

There was a sense of sadness and disappointment in their voices that the tour was coming to an end. 'I'm having a ball on this tour,' said Abe. Wix spoke of fulfilling a dream three days earlier when he got to meet Gorbachov in Moscow, 'I've always wanted to meet him,' he added.

We asked them if they'd get to see any of Dublin, while they were here. 'We've got a day tomorrow to look around, but tonight we're going out to party in a castle [Luttrelstown Castle, as it was later revealed] near Dublin,' said Abe. Before we got a chance to invite ourselves, we were quickly told that it was a private party.

The pre-show was building momentum around us but the sudden downpour had upset their plans. 'We're now doing a rain-show, so it's umbrellas all round,' shouted Abigail, the pre-show tour manager. 'I'm scrapping the stilts,' shouted another clown, as the stage got wet. It was great to witness a show of this magnitude being prepared from behind the scenes. 'Be very careful on stage. They're drying it as I speak, but it

Irish fan Pat Moore and one of the authors of this book, Michael Lynch, meet Paul McCartney backstage before his Dublin Concert. *(Bill Bernstein)*

could be slippy,' Abigail added. 'It's a 7.45pm show time,' she concluded.

We were escorted in to meet Paul in his dressing room as the pre-show began. 'Oh! It's the people in the Beatles Ireland T-shirts, come in,' he said as we entered his dressing room. We shook hands and introduced ourselves. 'What song was it you were looking for?' he enquired. We told him it was 'Another Day', to which he replied 'Oh! We've never actually rehearsed that one, so we can't do it!'

I informed him that it was a Number One single here in Ireland, which he seemed pleased about. We asked for a photograph and were told that his official photographer would take one for us and e-mail it to us. We also got autographs as Paul signed a copy of his *Blackbird* book for Pat Moore and I handed him a photograph of us shaking hands in Monaghan the day before his wedding, which he gladly signed.

Handshakes all round and, with that, it was time to leave. The clowns were already on stage, and the countdown to Macca's first Irish concert for almost 40 years had begun.

Now five years on from that RDS performance, Paul is embarking on what could be his last big world tour. He has already performed in his home town, Liverpool, and Kiev recently, and Irish fans have their fingers crossed in anticipation of a rumoured return visit in the not-too-distant future.

8

Calling All Beatles Fans: Beatlemania, Dublin-style

Over the weekend of the 7 November 1993, a little bit of Beatlemania returned to Dublin at the Adelphi Cinema, Middle Abbey Street, the scene of the Beatles' one and only live appearance in the Republic of Ireland, exactly 30 years previously. The short season of Beatles' films showing in the Adelphi at the time seemed to be an ideal opportunity to promote and advertise the idea of a new Irish Fan Club.

'Beatles Ireland', the brainchild of Beatles fan Pete Brennan, came into existence after he had placed an advertisement headed, 'Calling all Beatles fans', in Dublin's *Evening Press* newspaper in July 1993. With the rejuvenation of guitar bands, thanks to the Britpop explosion – and, in particular, Oasis with their self-confessed adoration of the Beatles – it was hip to be a Beatles fan again in the 1990s. Coincidentally, the Beatles were just about to release the definitive version of their own story in the form of *The Beatles Anthology* TV Series and the *Anthology* series of CDs.

The management of the cinema had obtained permission to show the first two Beatles films, *A Hard Day's Night* and *Help!* from Walter Shenson, the film's producer, who at the time held the worldwide rights to both films. Neither film had been seen in a public cinema anywhere in the world since they were originally released in the 1960s. Irish Beatles fans were given an opportunity to see *A Hard Day's Night* four times on Friday and *Help!* on Saturday over the anniversary weekend.

The Beatles Fan Club in the UK

The first official Beatles Fan Club was formed in Liverpool in May 1962 and was run by Bobbie Brown. When Bobbie became engaged in 1963, Freda Kelly took over the running of the club.

Freda Kelly was born in Ireland in July 1945 and arrived in Liverpool when she was thirteen. She found work in an office in the city centre and attended the Cavern Club regularly where she met Brown and began to help with some of the fan club work. As she took control of the club, she started to work as a shorthand typist in Brian Epstein's North End Music Store (NEMS) office. On her first day in the job, there were just two fan letters waiting to be answered, however as the group's popularity increased, she was receiving up to 400 letters a day.

When NEMS Enterprises moved to London, Freda's father refused to let her go, so she remained in Liverpool and moved into new offices that she shared with Bill Harry, the editor of the *Mersey Beat* magazine. The fan club soon boasted more than 16,000 members. Freda was the only full-time employee and, helped by part-time workers, she would send each of those 16,000 members a membership card, a photograph, a quarterly newsletter and, eventually, a Christmas record.

As the club continued to grow, it was divided up and its national headquarters was moved to London. Freda continued to handle the northern area of the club and, in October 1966, became Joint National Secretary.

The Adelphi Cinema, Dublin, on the weekend of the 30th Anniversary of the Beatles' concerts there. Things look a little more subdued in 1993. (*Damian Smyth*)

Newspaper advertisement marking 30th anniversary of Adelphi concert.

Late in 1967, whilst also working for both NEMS and Apple, she took over the full running of the club once more. By March 1972, she was expecting her second child and decided she no longer wanted to run the club, particularly as the Beatles had by that time disbanded. She suggested to Apple that the club should close when all the current memberships had expired and the company agreed.

For most of the 1970s, the memory of the Beatles had been consigned to musical history. Even in the group's hometown of Liverpool, a vote in October 1977 by the city council rejected a plan to build a lasting monument in honour of the group, a decision they would later come to regret.

The Beatles Ireland fan club

This original Irish Beatles fan club had the advantage of being in existence at the same time as the band itself. As part of the club's activities, regular weekend pilgrimages would be made to Liverpool to attend Mersey Beat shrine, the Cavern Club. Irish visitors could pay about *2s 6d* for membership of the junior club and sessions took place between 1pm and 4pm each Saturday.

One regular Irish visitor was B.P. Fallon who, just a few years later, would graduate from teenage Beatles fan to Beatles employee, working for the band's Apple venture in Savile Row. Fallon was partly educated in England and would make a point of getting to the Cavern whilst transiting to and from school. While in the club, he would spend his time ingratiating himself with Brian Epstein or anyone that would listen, telling them how much he wanted to get

Poster for Ireland's first Beatles convention.

into the music business, a tactic that paid off in the end, when he proved his worth by becoming involved with a string of major music acts in the late 1960s and 1970s as a public relations guru.

One of the quirkier aspects of Beatlemania in 1963 came from the breakfast cereal manufacturer Kellogg's. The company launched a campaign in Ireland where images of the Beatles appeared on boxes of corn flakes. Irish consumers were given the chance to win a Beatles fan club badge by returning the top of the cereal box to the company.

Beatles Ireland attracted well over 200 members at its height through its monthly meetings, magazine and, latterly, its website. It forged links with people connected with the Beatles, not only from Ireland, but also from all over the world. Paul McCartney and Ringo Starr are Executive Honorary Members. Cynthia Lennon, Pete Best, Yoko Ono, Gay Byrne, Geoff Rhind, Gerry Marsden, Allan Williams, Richard Lester, Harry Prytherch (of the Remo Four), and the original Quarrymen, Rod Davis, Colin Hanton, Eric Griffiths, Len Garry and Pete Shotton are all Honorary Members. Sir George Martin and Julian Lennon are Executive Patrons and the Patron is Astrid Kirchherr.

As time went on, Beatles Ireland started to form very close links with the music scene on Merseyside and, in particular, the children's charity Merseycats, an organisation well known for its charity work in Liverpool and made up of original Mersey Beat groups of the sixties. Taking a leaf out of their book, Beatles Ireland took on a charity role in aid of Our Lady's Children's Hospital, Crumlin, south Dublin, through musical fund-raising events.

In November 1998, the club held its first ever Beatles Ireland Convention on the 35th anniversary of the group's appearance in Ireland. Held in the Olympia Theatre, Dublin, the line-up was headlined by the original Quarrymen and included Ireland's only Beatles tribute band, also known as the Quarrymen. A crowd of over 500 attended the celebrations.

As part of the weekend, an exhibition of Beatles photography, a sixties memorabilia market, a video show and a number of interviewees were lined-up. Among the special guests were the original 1950s Quarrymen and Alistair Taylor, Brian Epstein's personal assistant and general manager at Apple. They kept the assembled throngs amused with a plethora of knowledge and endless anecdotes in the nearby Castle Inn.

The (Irish) Quarrymen and The Classic Beatles

Ireland's only Beatles tribute band is the Classic Beatles (formerly known as the Quarrymen), a Dublin-based quartet that has worked with Sir George Martin as well as ex-Beatles' solo band members.

The band started life as the Quarrymen in 1990, and the Irish public saw them first on the RTÉ TV show, *Secrets*, with Gerry Ryan in March 1991. This was followed up by an appearance on the late night programme, *Nighthawks*, in mid-1992. After this trip into the big time it was back to busking on Grafton Street, but not for long. By mid-1992, the Quarrymen had taken up residence in Madigan's pub in Rathmines, Dublin. The band cut its teeth during this phase, performing a show reminiscent of the Beatles' Hamburg days – full of fun and engaging humour, they stuffed the venue every Saturday night for three years.

The band's then manager, John Casey, was very much the driving force for the group. Indeed, it was Casey who organised the band's first trip to Liverpool in April 1992, so that the group could play in the Cavern reconstruction on the Albert Dock complex. Rob McKinney (the band's 'George') said, 'It was our first

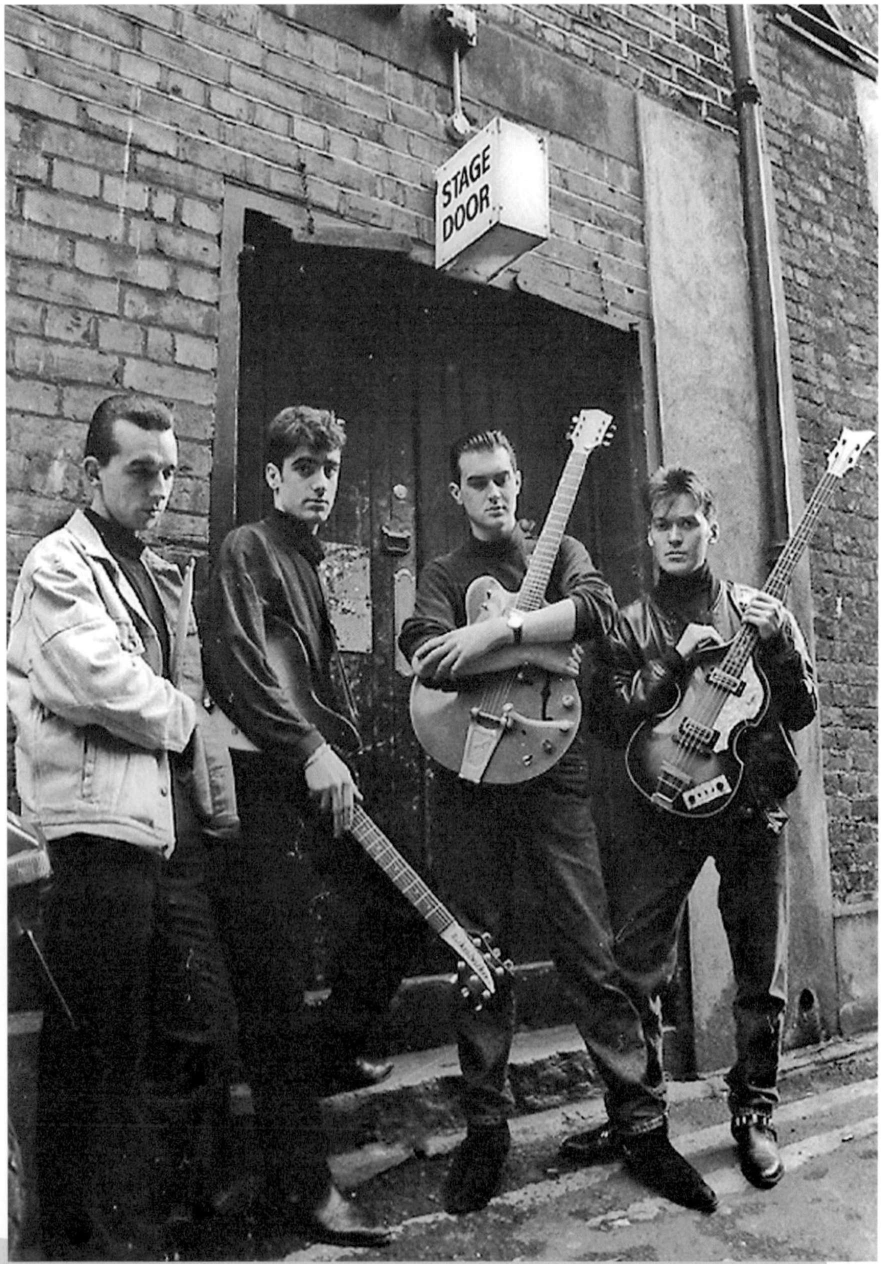

The Irish Beatles' tribute band, the Quarrymen, as they were known for most of the 1990s, pictured here looking very 'Beatles in Hamburg'. *(Damian Smyth)*

group trip out of Ireland: we took 50 regulars from Madigan's. It was a great buzz seeing all the places we had heard and talked so much about.' 1993 saw the Quarrymen still in residence at Madigan's doing the Hamburg apprenticeship week in, week out.

It was around this time that one of John Casey's more unusual transport arrangements was brought to an end. For some time the band had had the use of an old London black taxi. It functioned in three ways – as equipment-transporter, away-from-base changing room, and mobile advertiser. Actually, it was quite an effective travelling advertisement for the group, but it fell well short of the demands the band made on it – eventually going on its last fare to the big taxi rank in the sky.

Following their debut on English soil, they were asked by Cavern City Tours to play at the International Beatles Convention in Liverpool, August 1993. Over the weekend of the convention they played a lunchtime session at the Cavern, Mathew Street, and included in their number some guys from John Lennon's original 1957 Quarrymen line-up. They were amazed at the reception they received from Beatles fanatics there and went on to play a further five conventions.

In December 1993, on the occasion of the 13th anniversary of John Lennon's death, the Quarrymen were interviewed and performed on *Heading Home*, presented by John McDonald, a radio programme from Dublin-based Anna Livia FM. 1994 saw a return to the annual Beatles Convention in Liverpool and an interview with BBC Radio Merseyside's Spencer Leigh. On his show, they met up with Cynthia Lennon, guest of honour at that year's festival. On Saturday 15 October 1994, the Quarrymen made an appearance on one of RTÉ's most popular television shows, *Kenny Live*. The band performed 'I Saw Her Standing There' to open the show.

In 1994, to commemorate the 25th anniversary of the Beatles' Apple Rooftop gig, the Quarrymen performed on the roof of the Anna Livia FM radio station high above Grafton Street in Dublin. The performance went out live on the *City Limits* radio show at 11.30am on Saturday 29 January 1994, a day before the anniversary of the original Apple gig. *Evening Herald* reporter, Eamonn Carr, gave the band the banner headline 'Rocking on top of the World' in the Wednesday 26 January edition of the paper, as well as a feature in his section 'The Rap'.

In Carr's feature, Fran King explains, 'We link up with the *City Limits* radio

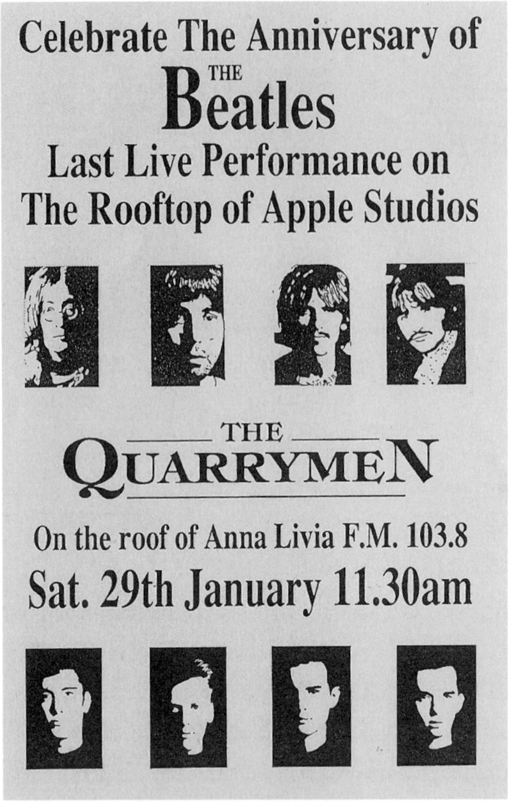
Celebrate The Anniversary of
THE
Beatles
Last Live Performance on
The Rooftop of Apple Studios
THE
QUARRYMEN
On the roof of Anna Livia F.M. 103.8
Sat. 29th January 11.30am

show, but before that we'll be doing an early Beatles set. When we go on air, we will play the same songs as the Beatles did on that fateful day in 1969.'

These are just a few of the highlights of the Quarrymen's thirteen years together, before they became known as the Classic Beatles in January 2000. The band was, and is, a pioneer in the Irish tribute band scene and paved the way for a plethora of tribute acts in the mid-1990s. There isn't a venue in Ireland that the Classic Beatles has not played.

So popular was the band's appeal that by 1994 that they were invited to play live in front of over 60,000 people in Dublin's Phoenix Park as part of a welcome home for Ireland's returning World Cup soccer heroes. They also had the pleasure of performing with the legendary Beatles producer, George Martin, and his 70-piece orchestra for three sell-out and critically acclaimed performances in Dublin's National Concert Hall in October 1999. In 2001, they were invited to London, again by Sir George, to perform for an MTV Lennon Tribute Special. Band members for this event included ex-Paul McCartney guitarist, Robbie McIntosh, and keyboard player Paul 'Wix' Wickens, together with David Bowie band members, Gail Ann Dorsey and Zachary Alford.

9

Meeting John Lennon

From the moment he saw them on *Thank Your Lucky Stars*, Richard Hall was besotted by the Beatles. He could tell they were no flash-in-the-pan, that they had something different. They had a certain kind of magic all of their own. So it was not surprising that Richard and his wife Maureen should want to try to meet their heroes. They did so, twice: once in Germany, when they gatecrashed a press conference in the early Beatles years, and again in 1968. The story of their second (1968) meeting was told in a short film entitled *It's Only Gathering Dust*, run by the Irish Film Institute in Dublin on 1 October 2006. Richard recalls:

> In 1968 my brother got married in Andover, Hampshire. Myself, Maureen and Renate – a young German girlfriend of ours – decided to travel by car from Germany to Ostend, and then from Ostend to Dover for the wedding.
>
> I considered travelling through Kent, Sussex and then into Hampshire. As I pondered this decision I realised that doing so would mean that I would not be in a position to drop in on our old friend John Lennon at his home. I decided that we would go via Surrey and make a stop in Weybridge. Maureen suggested that we go to the wedding first and then try and go to see John Lennon later but, as I was doing the driving, I overruled

her and insisted that we go to see John first and then go to the wedding.

We drove through Kent and then into Surrey and were soon in Weybridge. It's not difficult to find the vast estate of St George's, as the entrance is marked by the arch of a large brick gate. Amazingly, there was no security at the gate and I was able to drive through the gate and directly onto the estate.

We didn't have any idea where John's house was and as we drove along the drive we stopped a lady out walking her two small Scotch terrier dogs to ask for directions. With an accent of pure British aristocracy she pointed along the road: 'It is a large house situated on a small hill.' I thanked her, got back in the car and carried on up the road. About 500m from where we left the lady and her dogs, graffiti-daubed gates appeared before us. It was quite obvious that this was indeed the Beatle's home.

I parked the car outside the gate and the three of us began to walk up the slight slope towards the house. As we drew nearer to the house we could see a figure busily having a shave in an upstairs room. This figure was easily recognisable as John Lennon even at that distance. We knew then that he was home. Nonetheless it was proper that we follow procedure and so I approached the door and knocked.

After a short while the door was opened and John's housekeeper greeted us. I asked, 'Could we please speak to Mr Lennon?' The housekeeper replied, 'I will go and see if he is in', and, with that, she turned and went back in to the house, closing the door behind her. I thought, 'Sh**, she is going to come back and tell us that he is in Australia or Canada or the States and we know he is in there.' The housekeeper never returned.

Instead, fifteen seconds later, the door was reopened by the man of the house, a certain Mr John Lennon, accompanied by his young son, Julian. At this time Julian would have been only five years old, and it was very noticeable by John's actions for the first few minutes of our encounter that, like any first-time father, he was anxious for the safety of his son, by maintaining a human barrier between Julian and us.

When he was satisfied that we offered no threat of any kind, to either himself or, more importantly, to Julian, he relaxed and walked all three of us around the outside of his home. He showed us the old gypsy caravan that had been psychedelically decorated for Julian, in the same fashion as John's Rolls Royce and George Harrison's Austin Mini. I admired, and passed comment on, his garden to which he very quickly told me that the garden was the responsibility of the gardener. He admitted having no interest at all in the garden and what was planted there. He then turned interviewer and asked us if we thought the Beatles were really as good as the press said they were. I recall telling him that the Beatles were, in fact, far better than the press said they were.

Maureen reminded him about the gatecrashing incident at the press conference in Essen. I had a photo with me that I had taken at that press conference and I asked if he would sign it for me. As he was about to sign I said to him, 'Please just sign it "Lennon". Not "To A.N. Other', not "Love from", not "John", just "Lennon".' I had written to him on many occasions, I had never received a reply, but in my letters I had always referred to him as just plain 'Lennon', never calling him 'John' at all.

He paused before signing, looked at me and said, 'So you are the little sh*** that calls me Lennon', to which I replied, 'So you do get the mail then?' 'Yes,' he said, 'I do get the mail, but there is so much, it is impossible to answer it all. It is even difficult to read it all.' Well at least I had confirmation that he had read some of my letters, even if I was never going to get a reply. I still have that photograph framed.

As he was attempting to sign, the biro wouldn't penetrate the glossy finish of the photo at first so he leant hard and his signature is actually etched into the print. It will never fade, unlike the ink from the biro that has faded with time, so that it is now necessary to hold the photo, in its frame, at an angle in order to see the signature.

During the course of our audience, Renate discovered, much to her embarrassment, that not only could she speak fluent German and English, but she had also instantly mastered fluent gibberish. Every time she opened her mouth to speak to John her tongue ran away and never came back. She was in total awe of him and when he held her hand as I photographed them together she stared at him in disbelief.

We remained with John and Julian for more than three-quarters of an hour, and it was I in fact, who brought our visit to a close, by thanking him for his time and his autograph. As we were about to turn to leave, Maureen asked him if he had anything she could take as a souvenir. He then disappeared back inside the house. I was embarrassed by Maureen's request and wasted no time telling her so. I said, 'I do not believe it. You are amazing! This man, John Lennon, has given us so much of his time and now you want more? You really are amazing!'

Maureen just looked at me and said, 'Well, you never know – he might give me a cup or an ashtray or something small – just to remember today by.' I wondered out loud what would you need to remind you that you been given a tour of John Lennon's garden and met his precious son. Why on earth are you ever going to need something to remind you of that?

Before Maureen could answer, John reappeared with a statuette in his hands, which he handed to Maureen. Maureen reached out and took it from him, saying, 'Thank you, thank you so much.' As it passed from John to Maureen I could see the statue had a little plinth and I clearly read the words:

'She's Leaving Home'. 1967. John Lennon. An Ivor Novello Award

Bronze and beautiful it was and I could not believe what was happening. I immediately turned to John and said, 'You can't give that to her, you must take it back, you won this for your music, you should not give this away.' I was also looking at Maureen, pleading with my eyes for her to give it back. Maureen was holding on tight to the statue and though she allowed me to turn it round in her hands she would not let it go.

John looked at me and then at Maureen and his words – words I will never forget –were, 'Look, it's only gathering dust in there and if she wants it then let her have it and let her keep it, it's only gathering dust in my house.' It's only gathering dust. Fair enough, you don't argue with a Beatle. More photographs were taken with all three of us individually holding the gift with John. Maureen took my photograph.

John Lennon hands over his Ivor Novello Award for 'She's Leaving Home' to Irishwoman Maureen Hall outside his Weybridge home on 7 June 1968. (*Richard Hall*)

I am still amazed she didn't drop the camera. As it turned out she was so excited by the recent events that she was unable to hold it steady and so my photo never came out. Although I was disappointed at the time, it doesn't matter now. I don't need a photo to remind me of the day I met and shared time with John Lennon.

10

Drive My Car: The Beatles, an Irishman and an Austin J4

Hamburg is a seaport, like Liverpool, and it is also on the same line of latitude as Liverpool, 56° north. However, unlike Liverpool, Hamburg had no thriving music scene in 1960s when the Beatles first appeared there. How did the Beatles arrive in Hamburg?

Allan Williams, the Beatles' original manager, met Bruno Koschmider (owner of two clubs in Hamburg) for the first time when Koschmider was in England looking for British bands to appear on his premises. The meeting took place in the 2 Is Coffee Bar in Soho, London, a venue where Tommy Steele and others had been discovered. When Williams heard Bruno was looking for live bands, he arranged for Derry and the Seniors to be the first Merseyside band to go to Hamburg. Bruno was very impressed with this band, and asked whether he could arrange others.

William's first two choices were unwilling to take up the offer: Rory Storm had commitments to play a summer season at Butlins in Pwllheli, North Wales, while Gerry and the Pacemakers were not keen on the idea at all and simply refused, although they were eventually to play Hamburg a few months later. Williams was by now at his wits end and so, out of desperation, he booked the Beatles for Hamburg, even though they had no drummer at the time.

After a hastily arranged audition at the Wyvern Social Club on 12 August 1960, Pete Best became the band's first regular drummer. All Williams had to do was arrange transport. Enter Irishman Sean Newman.

Like so many Irish people of that time, Sean arrived in Liverpool to escape starvation and unemployment in a 1950s Ireland where the economic situation was dire. He arrived in Liverpool straight off the mail-boat from Dublin early one morning in the mid-1950s, carrying a battered, brown, leather suitcase holding all his worldly possessions and held together with his own leather belt. He dragged it, and himself, up the hill from the boat terminal at Liverpool's Pier Head.

He almost immediately found work in a local garage, despite 'the no blacks, no Irish' signs that were commonplace all over England at the time, and recalls that he first met Allan's wife, Beryl, not then aware of the turmoil about to be unleashed on his life by her husband. They have remained lifelong pals despite Williams embroiling the lugubrious Irishman in a string of adventure-strewn frolics.

Williams was a regular customer at the garage around that time. One of his vehicles was a battered Austin J4 van painted in a nondescript two-tone cream and brown, which could actually seat twelve people at a pinch. It was a late 1950s model and in such terrible condition that it probably should have been scrapped long ago. But the van was Williams' way of transporting some of his groups, including Gerry and the Pacemakers and the Beatles, around the Liverpool area. Newman remembers servicing the van a few times when, in early August 1960, Williams made the announcement that he was about to take one of his bands to Germany and would need the van in tip-top condition. 'I can remember meeting the Rolling Stones in the Blue Angel and saw the Beatles regularly in the Jacaranda and I was only around twenty years of age then myself, so I was quite caught up in what was going on,' recalls Sean.

Having hastily arranged passports and visas, Williams, his wife Beryl, her brother Barry Chang (known to one and all as 'Lord Woodbine'), and the five ex-Silver Beatles (now re-named simply the Beatles), along with their equipment, crammed into the cream-and-brown Austin van and set off for Hamburg.

The Beatles' van, which Irishman Sean Newman had serviced, being loaded for Hamburg. John Lennon (lower left) looks on.

Unsurprisingly, Williams had not applied for work permits, which later led to George's deportation from Germany.

They took the ferry from Harwich to the Hook of Holland. Having got there in one piece, Williams forgot that they had to drive on the right-hand side of the road and, as a result, the group nearly had an accident at the first roundabout they encountered.

A few days later, the Beatles were left to fend for themselves in the red-light area of the city as Williams made his way back to Liverpool. He continued to use the van for the next couple of years after which it was put into storage.

Newman often wondered about the fate of the battered Austin J4, pictured in all the Beatles books as it was lifted aboard the cross-channel ferry bound for Germany. For years, he has been scouring scrapyards, auctions and second-hand car sales all over Ireland and the UK for a replica of that Austin van with a view to re-registering it with the original licence plate number and to perhaps clambering aboard the Beatles nostalgia circus himself. Newman later said in an interview:

> We didn't really appreciate its future importance and one day Allan decided he wanted to sell it. So I advertised it. This West Indian came to have a look and gave my assistant Ruddy a £100 deposit. He wanted it delivered to Moss Side in Manchester, where he lived. I explained that we didn't deliver that far, but to get the balance of the cash I decided I would drive over with it. This guy had a grocer's shop and so I parked outside. Then, when I was inside talking to him, someone parked in front and at the rear of the bloody van, blocking it in. After driving over the thirty odd miles I'm having a bit of a row with this guy who is blithely telling me that he didn't have the rest of the money. As we were exchanging verbals he was casually chopping up a yam with a huge machete. I was a little apprehensive at that point and thought it best to withdraw in the best fashion of gallantry. But I couldn't drive the bloody van away, as it was hemmed in. Allan never did get the balance of the money and that legendary old van vanished somewhere in Manchester, presumably ending its days delivering vegetables and fruit.

By the 1980s Sean Newman was back in Dublin and still friendly with Allan Williams. On Easter Monday 1984, the now defunct Dublin-based radio station, Radio Nova, broadcast an interview with Allan Williams and Bob Wooler, the former Cavern DJ, as part of a day-long Beatles special. Sean Newman was invited to take part in the final segment of the show to reveal his old connection with the Beatles – a connection that had, up to that time, remained one of the best-kept secrets in the story of the Beatles' formative years (see Appendix 5).

Appendix 1

An Irish Beatles' Who's Who

Andrews, Eamonn

Like fellow Irishman and broadcaster Gay Byrne, Eamonn Andrews carved out a broadcasting career in Britain in the 1960s, first as a boxing commentator, and then as a chat show host on television.

Voted 'Television Personality of the Year' four times in the UK, Dublin-born Andrews was a highly respected and much-loved broadcaster, chiefly associated with two popular television programmes, the panel show *What's My Line?* (BBC, 1951–63; ITV, 1984–87) and the biographical tribute programme *This Is Your Life* (ITV, 1955–87).

In the 1960s, the launch of television in Ireland brought him his most exciting and rewarding challenge as the Chairman of the RTÉ Authority. After his contract with the BBC finished in 1964, he moved to commercial television, presenting *World of Sport* (ITV, 1965–68) and his own late-night chat show, *The Eamonn Andrews Show* (ITV, 1964–69), with an array of guests, including his first Beatles interview on 11 April 1965.

The Beatles arrived to take part straight from an all-star winners' concert to mark the New Musical Express Annual Poll. They participated in Andrews' main discussion forum as part of the show and lip-synched to 'Ticket to Ride' and 'Yes it is'.

It was not until 1969 that Eamonn Andrews would have any contact with the group again, this time in the persons of John and Yoko. Just a few hours after John and Yoko had journeyed back from their Amsterdam 'bed-in', they met Andrews for his TV programme *Today*. The couple's 'Bagism' concept was the main subject of Andrews' fun-poking interview, in the course of which John and Yoko appeared from inside a white bag and then, remarkably, tempted Andrews himself to join them there. Just two days later both John and Yoko took part in another live ABC TV programme, again with Eamonn Andrews.

Andrews went on to further his entertainment career, mostly in Britain. A self-confessed workaholic, he returned to *This Is Your Life* in 1969 and hosted the programme for another two decades. Although his last few years were stricken by illness, he continued to work, even signing a new three-year deal for ITV just before he died on 5 November 1987. His life and career are commemorated with a bronze statue at the RTÉ Headquarters in Donnybrook, Dublin.

Bachelors, The

The Bachelors were the first of the Irish 'boy bands' to invade Britain's shores in 1962. They took on the might of British groups and had some major success in Britain in that year. Formed in 1957 in Dublin by brothers Con and Dec Cluskey, they have appeared with almost every showbiz legend in the world, including Judy Garland, Tom Jones, Engelbert Humperdinck, Sammy Davis Jnr, Bob Hope, Morecombe and Wise, Tommy Cooper, Tony Bennett and Cliff Richard – right through to Ant and Dec.

They appeared with the Beatles, as guests of the band on the BBC radio series *Pop Go The Beatles*, recorded at Maida Vale Studios, not far from EMI's studio in Abbey Road, North London, on Monday 17 June 1963 – the programme was aired the following Tuesday. In 1993, the Bachelors played with George Harrison a second time at the Water Rats' dinner at the Grosvenor House Hotel, London, alongside Lonnie Donegan, Bert Weedon and Chas McDevitt.

Barron, Paddy

Paddy is a freelance professional lighting, cameraman and director from Greystones, Co Wicklow and has worked in areas of documentaries, factual, music, and film-making for over fifteen years.

Paddy was asked by a New York-based film and video company to assist with the production of the official wedding video for Paul and Heather's Castle Leslie ceremony. Paddy was in fact the only Irish person involved in the video production of the wedding over the three days of filming. Normally a cameraman, on this occasion he had been asked to take on the job of soundman. (See Chapter 6)

Bowyer, Brendan

Brendan first captured the public's imagination in the early 1960s when he was the lead singer with the Royal Showband who helped put Waterford on the map as a dancehall heaven. Brendan's recordings with 'The Royal', as they were fondly known, yielded an unprecedented five Number One hits in Ireland with their first five singles. In 1962 the Waterford band were supported on one of their British tour dates by an up-and-coming Liverpool band called the Beatles.

Royal Showband with support from the Beatles in April 1962.

Perhaps best remembered for 'The Hucklebuck', which charted in 1965, The Royal Showband were also the first Irish pop act to make it in the entertainment Mecca that is Las Vegas and it is in that US city that Brendan still spends much of his time.

Boyd, Pattie

Pattie Boyd's Irish roots are well documented. She is a descendant of the Irish Boyds of Ballymacool, Co Donegal. The Boyds of Ballymacool are descended from the Scottish Earls of Kilmarnock. The first Boyd of Ballymacool Estate was John, born 1739, who purchased the estate from the Span family in 1798. He was High Sheriff of Donegal and was a major in the 36th Regiment of the Donegal Militia. He was married to Martha, daughter of Colonel Stewart, Governor of the Bahamas.

He was succeeded by his nephew, William Henry Porter, under the condition that he assumed the surname Boyd, which he did by Royal Licence in 1891. He was father to Mary Rosalie Boyd, the famous South African poetess.

The founder member of the Apprentice Boys of Derry was John Boyd (1767–1836). He was the Accountant General of the Court of Chancery, a Captain in the Letterkenny Corps of the Donegal Militia, and a Freeman of the City of Derry. In 1830 he presented to the Apprentice Boys the saddle on which Governor Walker rode at the Siege of Derry in 1689.

George Harrison's first wife was born Patricia Anne Boyd in Hampstead, London, on 17 March 1945, the eldest of three sisters, the others being Paula and Helen. Due to their father's work, the entire family moved to Kenya in the 1950s and returned to London when Pattie was in her late teens. In 1962 Pattie began her modelling career. She met George Harrison on the set of *A Hard Day's Night*, the Beatles' first film. George proposed to her on Christmas Day 1964 and the couple were married on 21 January 1966, only to divorce eleven years later, on 9 June 1977. She later married Eric Clapton and in 2007 published *Wonderful Tonight: George Harrison, Eric Clapton and Me.*

Brambell, Wilfrid

Irish-born character stage actor and star of *Steptoe and Son*, the mercurial Brambell played Paul McCartney's troublesome grandfather in *A Hard Day's Night*, although only 52 years old at the time. Something of a theatrical snob, he professed 'positive amazement' at the group's professional attitude while filming.

Byrne, Gay

Who wants to be a multi-millionaire? Gay Byrne could have been if he had accepted the Beatles' offer to be their manager in the early days of their career. The most famous face in Irish broadcasting, Byrne first met the band while working with Granada Television in the early 1960s. After hearing how thousands of screaming girls were trying to jam into the Cavern to see the unsigned local band, programme producers sent down a film crew to capture raw footage of the Beatles before they became famous. Gay Byrne recalls:

> I was doing a show called *People and Places* with Granada television when we heard about this phenomenon happening at the Cavern. So we sent down a camera and showed them playing on the programme. The reaction was so good we invited them to the studio (their first ever television interview) and people went wild. It was a very prestigious show to be on at the time and we invited them back three or four more times.
>
> They came into the studio one of those times – it was well before Brian Epstein came on the scene – and they asked if I would like to be their agent. But I just looked at Lennon who had asked me and laughed it off and said, 'I'm not agent material.'

'Charlie'

Paul McCartney had to hire guards to protect his property in Cavendish Avenue as fans were continually breaking into his house when he was away. One of the guards was an Irishman, known only as 'Charlie', who started working for Paul around 1969. Not the best of security guards, Charlie would end up talking to the girls he was told to keep out of the property as he sat in the garage at the side of Paul's house, which had become a larger-than-life sentry box.

Delaney, Patrick

A former member of An Garda Síochána, Patrick, more familiarly known as 'Paddy', joined the Liverpool Parks Police and later became a doorman at the Locarno and Grafton Ballrooms on West Derby Road, Liverpool. One night in 1959 he was asked if he would work the door of the Cavern Club. He turned up in a dinner-suit with matching tie and cummerbund. At the time Paddy started working there, there were fights almost every night as a group of hooligans had virtually taken control of the club.

Paddy agreed to take on the job permanently for £1 per night if he could have some other men to help him. He soon cleaned up the place and became the regular doorman at the Cavern until the venue closed, spending a total of seven years working for the club.

Following a number of incidents in which he initially tried to stop them from entering because of their appearance, Paddy became a friend of the Beatles and often chatted with them at the door. For a time he also worked for *Mersey Beat* magazine, helping to deliver copies locally. His memories of the years he served at the Cavern are contained in an unpublished manuscript, *The Best of Cellars*.

Dennis, Ted

Ted Dennis was the head cleaner at the Adelphi Cinema in Dublin. On the day the Beatles played there, he was given the task of helping RTÉ reporter Frank Hall. Dennis says, 'Frank Hall had requested a step ladder for his cameraman, Jacky Merryman, but because of the hysterical fans the use of the ladder would have been too dangerous.' He also helped keep the Beatles supplied with refreshments.

Fallon, B.P.

Dublin-born B.P. Fallon has been a DJ since 1964. He is also an author and has published three books of his words and photographs, one of which, *U2 – Faraway So Close*, details the period of time when he joined U2 as 'Guru', 'Viber' and DJ on their global *Zoo TV* tour. He has also been DJ on solo tours by both Keith Richards (USA, 1993) and Ronnie Wood (Ireland and England, 2002). He was the manager of New York Doll, Johnny Thunders, and was the publicist to Led Zeppelin, Ian Dury, Bob Geldof and Marc Bolan. He is described as 'Purple browed beep' by Bolan in the T-Rex hit 'Telegram Sam'. Phil Lynott famously told *Melody Maker* in 1976, 'B.P.'s brilliant, though I'm not sure what he does.'

Among his other jobs, Fallon was at the Beatles' Apple Records – where one of his tasks (allegedly) was to test Paul McCartney's grass (and we're not talking about the horticultural kind). Fallon first saw the Beatles on three consecutive nights in August 1963, firstly at the Cavern, then at the Grafton Ballroom in Liverpool the next night when they did two half-hour sets, and finally, on the third night, as they were being screamed at in the Blackpool Opera House.

Working at Apple Records led him to appear on *Top Of the Pops* with John Lennon and the Plastic Ono Band for John's third solo single 'Instant Karma'. Fallon says:

> I remember waiting with them in the dressing room and they were getting ready to go on and Lennon said, 'Are yew gettin' up?' as if he was asking some drunk biddy at a teddy boy dance. He said the Plastic Ono Band was everybody and so I borrowed a tambourine from the BBC Orchestra and banged it away. Lennon's vocal was live and I probably put him off his timing. When I went back, there was this seven-foot geezer asking, 'Where is the tambourine? Had you permission to borrow it? Are you a member of the Musicians' Union?' Then John came in with Yoko and he could have passed by, but he saw what was going on and made mincemeat out of him and the guy crawled away. I mimed on bass the next time.

Flanagan, Jack

Jack was the garage foreman for Independent Newspapers and he was the man who drove the Beatles away from the Adelphi after the second of their two concerts on the evening of 7 November 1963. He used an *Evening Herald* newspaper delivery van to whisk the group back to the safety of the Gresham Hotel in O'Connell Street.

Flavelle, Jackie

Jackie Flavelle was a bass player from Northern Ireland, whose professional career had begun in 1959 on the Irish showband scene. In 1966 he was headhunted by top English jazzman, Chris Barber, who had become a star in the trad boom of the late fifties and early sixties. Paul McCartney wrote and produced a single called 'Catcall' and gave it to the Chris Barber band in 1967. The Quarrymen and the Beatles at the Cavern had occasionally played it since its composition by Paul in the late 1950s. In the Chris Barber Band version, Flavelle took part in the recording of this single, playing bass.

Back in Ireland, Flavelle became a presenter with Downtown Radio and a successful freelance musician.

French, Tony

A cousin of George Harrison who lives in Dublin, Tony French traced George's family tree back to the thirteenth century when the Harrison ancestors, who were Norman knights, came over from France and settled in Ireland.

Foran, Tony

Apprentice projectionist at the Adelphi in 1963 at the time of the Beatles' Dublin performances.

Geldof, Bob

His older sister took a teenage Geldof to the Beatles'Adelphi concert in November 1963. As the leader of the Boomtown Rats, an Irish New Wave band of the seventies and eighties, Geldof remembers his second encounter with George Harrison: 'I remember when the Boomtown Rats started, we played a gig in Oxford and I was shocked and stunned when George Harrison walked into the room: There was a living Beatle.' Geldof and the Boomtown Rats went on to have a string of hits in the UK and broke through to international popularity with the 1979 single, 'I Don't Like Mondays'.

Geldof is now better known for his humanitarian work, particularly the spectacularly successful series of Live Aid concerts in 1985. Memorably, Paul McCartney closed the London show. In 2005, Geldof helped organise another day of mega concerts called Live 8. The London concert, from Hyde Park, was opened and closed by Paul McCartney.

Hall, Frank

Frank Hall was an Irish journalist, satirist and broadcaster, born in Newry, Co Down, in 1921. He left school at the age of twelve to work in a local shop. He moved to London and worked there as a waiter before returning to Dublin where he began a journalistic career with the *Irish Independent* and the *Evening Herald*. He then moved to RTÉ where he worked in the newsroom. It was while working at RTÉ that he interviewed the Beatles at Dublin Airport in 1963.

From 1964 to 1971 he presented *Newsbeat*, a regional television news programme. He also presented *The Late Late Show* for the 1968–1969 season, but public demand led to the return of the previous presenter, Gay Byrne, the following year. When *Newsbeat* ended, Hall started writing and presenting *Hall's Pictorial Weekly*, a political satire show that ran for over 250 episodes until 1982. In 1978, Hall was appointed Irelands' national film censor. He died in Dublin in 1995.

Hall, Richard and Maureen

No relation to Frank, Richard and Maureen Hall met John Lennon outside his home on 7 June 1968. Richard and Maureen were making their way from Germany to a wedding in the south of England when they decided to make a short detour to John Lennon's home in Weybridge, Surrey. Lennon presented Maureen with the Ivor Novello award that he had won for 'She's Leaving Home'. The statue was recently sold for the second time, for a sum in excess of $24,000.

Healy, John

Irish Independent journalist who travelled the short journey with the Beatles in the *Evening Herald* van, following their Dublin Adelphi gigs.

Kane, Trevor

Kane was a major entertainment promoter in Northern Ireland in the 1960s. He promoted the Beatles' second visit to Northern Ireland at the King's Hall, Balmoral on 2 November 1964. One of his arrangements with the group was to provide a limousine from Belfast Airport for the duration of the group's trip.

Kelly, Freda

Irish-born Freda arrived in Liverpool with her family at the age of thirteen. On leaving school, she began to work at Princes' food factory and became a Cavern regular. At the club she met Bobbie Brown, who was then running the Beatles Fan Club, and began to help her with the club work. She got a job as a shorthand typist at NEMS Enterprises and when Bobbie became engaged in 1963 Freda took over the running of the fan club.

When NEMS Enterprises relocated to London, Freda's father would not allow her to move south, so she continued to run the club from her northern base with the help of part-time workers, becoming joint National Secretary of the fan club in 1966. She married a local musician, Brian Norris, a former member of the Realms and the Cryin' Shames, on 4 April 1968 and soon after left her fan club activities to concentrate on raising her first child.

Lush, Harry

William Henry (Harry) Lush was a schoolteacher for most of his working life. On retiring from teaching, he took a position at the Adelphi Cinema in Dublin, becoming the manager. A fluent Irish speaker and friend of both Éamon de Valera and Patrick Kavanagh, he welcomed the Beatles to the Adelphi Cinema on 7 November 1963, the only occasion they were to play Dublin. He immediately warmed to them and remembered them as 'very gentlemanly lads', who had respect for their elders and 'called you sir'. 'They were only in their teens and they could have been in my class and I would have got on really well with them. Bands like the Rolling Stones couldn't hold a candle to them.'

Born on 17 October 1916, in Kilglass, Co Sligo, he was the eldest of five sons of T.J. and Mamie Lush. His father was a flax mill owner and farmer, his mother a teacher. Partition caused the flax mill to go out of business, and the family moved to Tinahely, Co Wicklow.

As manager of the Adelphi Cinema, he promoted Irish by screening Irish-language versions of public information films, which were also available in English. He also encouraged the use of Irish in the day-to-day business of the Adelphi, which was part of the Associated British Cinemas chain. The cinema, with seating for 2,300 patrons, was one of the top entertainment venues in Ireland. Hollywood stars often made personal appearances to promote their films at the cinema. Among those he met were Gary Cooper, Marlene Dietrich, John Wayne and Ronald Reagan, the future president of the United States. Speaking of Reagan, Harry said, 'He came here when he was a cowboy actor, with a lovely actress called Patricia Neal. They did an act that was very popular.'

Éamon de Valera was struck by the boundless enthusiasm of this Irish-speaking Protestant. Harry introduced Cary Grant to Mr de Valera, who in turn introduced Harry to President John F. Kennedy.

Mahon, Gene

Gene Mahon, a Dublin-born graphic designer who had moved to London in the 1960s to work for an advertising agency, returned from lunch one afternoon in February 1968, to find a note from the Beatles' ex-road manager, Neil Aspinall.

Gene Mahon. (*Richard DiLello*)

The message asked Mahon to come over to 95 Wigmore Street as soon as possible. In 1967 Mahon had first encountered Aspinall and the Beatles when he was involved in the design of the sleeve for *Sgt Pepper's Lonely Hearts Club Band*. He was art director of the back sleeve, which featured the photograph of the

Beatles with Paul turning his back to the camera, over which were printed the lyrics to the songs. It was Mahon who pulled the line from the lyrics and inserted it as the final credit on the back sleeve: 'A splendid time is guaranteed for all.'

This time Aspinall requested that Mahon get a photograph of an apple for a record label, a simple enough request. Inspiration struck. Mahon suggested that the A-side of the record should be a whole apple, with no writing on it whatsoever. On the B-side the apple should be sliced in half and show all the label copy.

The next day Mahon went to a photographer named Paul Castell and asked him to take photographs of two apples: one red and one green; each photographed whole to begin with, then sliced; and both against a variety of coloured backgrounds. Two days later Castell returned with transparencies of an assortment of apples on black, red, blue, green and yellow backgrounds.

Paul McCartney was the Beatle lavishing his days and energies on the project with Mahon. A shiny green Granny Smith apple on a black background was finally chosen as the iconic Apple apple. From the initial commission to the final approval of the design, the project had taken six months to complete. Mahon was later commissioned to work on other Apple design projects.

McCullough, Henry

Henry McCullough was a member of Wings for almost two years. He began his musical career in Northern Ireland with the Skyrocket Showband, later joining Jean and the Gents before becoming a member of Eire Apparent in 1967. The group began to play in England and were spotted at London's UFO Club by Chas Chandler, then manager of Jimi Hendrix. The group's road manager was Dave Robinson (later to launch the successful Stiff Records label) who also doubled up as their PR man. They played a number of gigs with Jimi Hendrix, but the group never achieved the success they deserved. When the band broke up Henry moved on to Sweeney's Men and then Joe Cocker's Grease Band.

He was already friendly with Denny Laine, but it was Paul's road manager that informed him that Paul was holding auditions for a new lead guitarist. Henry auditioned on a Tuesday and was asked to return to audition again the following Thursday. Later Paul rang the Irishman to ask him to join the band, just in time to contribute to Wings' first single, appropriately called 'Give Ireland Back To The Irish'. In the early 1980s he had an accident with a knife that severed the tendons in his playing hand. He eventually recovered and is still performing to this day, mostly around Ireland. (See Chapter 5 for a more detailed account.)

McCann, Donal

Many have hailed Donal McCann as the best actor Ireland ever produced. He will be best remembered for his RTÉ role in the television drama *Strumpet City* in the 1970s.

He had attended Terenure College, Dublin, in the 1950s. It was there that he began thinking of a career in the theatre. The college had a strong Shakespearean tradition and it became clear to some of his teachers that he was 'actor material'. In spite of this he left school for a short spell, studying architecture at Bolton Street, Dublin, before going on to work at *The Irish Press* newspaper. He eventually went to the Abbey School of Music and Drama in the early 1960s, from where he joined the Abbey Theatre Company.

During his time with *The Irish Press*, he interviewed the Beatles in Dublin at the Adelphi concert in 1963. His father had been the Lord Mayor of Dublin and was also a playwright – Donal appeared in one of his plays. Donal McCann died in July 1999 at the age of 56 after a battle with cancer.

Moloney, Paddy

Best known as part of the legendary traditional Irish music group, the Chieftains. Paddy Moloney formed the group in Dublin in 1962 with Kevin Conneff, Sean Keane and the late Derek Bell. The band broke new ground for Irish traditional music around the world and over the years they have collaborated with the Rolling Stones, Chet Atkins, Willie Nelson and Sting. The Beatles gave up part of their 1969 Abbey Road session so that the Chieftains could mix a new album at EMI. The Chieftains had just recorded their second album in Edinburgh in 1969. Paddy takes up the story:

> I wasn't happy with the acetate, because I thought the album had lost a lot of presence. I rang up a guy called Harry Christmas at the EMI offices in Dublin to see if I could get a studio for a few hours. Harry

> suggested Abbey Road but at the time the Beatles had it booked solid for six months, recording the *Abbey Road* album. The Beatles heard we had wanted to use the studio and they gave us the OK to use it, so I got my half-day in Abbey Road.
>
> Paul McCartney came in at one stage and said 'hello' and we had a chat about music for a while. Later John Lennon came in and casually said 'hello' but he didn't make any conversation. They all kind of came in one by one to see what was happening. It was a great half-day for everyone!

Although John Lennon didn't appear particularly friendly that day, it seems the music of the Chieftains definitely made an impression on him. Paddy continues:

> I was honoured many years later when I heard John Lennon and Yoko Ono had attended the first Chieftains concert in New York in 1972. I actually saw them leave just before the end of the show. Of course that's not to say that the show was bad or anything but it was just they wanted to get away before they got mobbed!

Moloney later got a call from Paul McCartney during 1980. McCartney had a new composition called 'Rainclouds', a track that Paul was working on at the time of Lennon's death and originally rehearsed with Wings in October–November 1980.

Paddy Moloney joined McCartney, Denny Laine and George Martin on the afternoon of Tuesday 9 December at Air Studios, London, where they spent the rest of the day recording. Moloney was the first of several asked to contribute to the project, overdubbing a Celtic-flavoured uilleann pipes solo to complete the song released as a single in Britain on 29 March 1982.

Murphy, Gerry

A Drogheda promoter who, in February 1963, sent a letter to the Beatles' manager, Brian Epstein, inquiring about the possibility of having the group appear at a venue in Drogheda town, Co Louth.

Murphy, Jack

Photographer with the Independent News and Media group of newspapers, who accompanied the Beatles in the *Evening Herald* van, along with reporter Liam Kelly. He remembers the occasion, 'At the time we got in the van with the group, we sat as they did, on old newspapers, until we got to the Gresham.'

Murphy, Kieron 'Spud'

Kieron 'Spud' Murphy began as a photographer in his native Dublin, before moving to London in 1970. He worked for the weekly rock paper, *Sounds*, on the recommendation of his friend and fellow Irishman B.P. Fallon.

In April 1971 Murphy was sent by *Sounds*, with journalist Steve Peacock, to cover John Lennon recording what would become the *Imagine* album. Phil Spector was the producer:

> The studio was attached to John and Yoko's home, Tittenhurst Park, outside London. Meeting him was the high point of my life. I'd never met anyone so famous and I suppose I still haven't. They'd been recording all night and sleeping through the day. When I got there it was 5pm and he was having breakfast. I remember being amazed at seeing him tuck into bacon and eggs; I thought people who are this famous eat more rarefied foods. But there he was putting salt and pepper on it like an ordinary mortal. More people began to arrive, like Klaus Voorman [bass player] and Alan White [drummer] and Nicky Hopkins who was playing piano; they were all having a cup of tea.
>
> Then Phil Spector arrived. It was almost as if he'd come up out of the floor in a puff of smoke. He had a very heavy presence: he just seemed to arrive without coming into the room. And the interesting thing was that John looked almost as in awe of Spector as I was of John. He leapt up to give him his chair, fussed around him and got him tea or coffee. Everybody else is being a bunch of boisterous lads, swapping football stories and whatever, but Spector just sat there, and Lennon was getting very fussy. Then Spector says to him, very quietly, 'John, I think we should make a start', whereupon John leapt to his feet and literally took the cups of tea out of peoples' hands, frogmarching

> them into the studio. 'Phil wants us now,' said Lennon. I was amazed to see that John Lennon had to obey anyone.
>
> He'd just written a new song – he was literally making the album up as he went along and he was teaching it, playing it for them. It turned out it was 'How Do You Sleep?', the big anti-McCartney diatribe. I thought at first it was a slag-off of the fans, because the first line is, 'So Sgt Pepper took you by surprise', but it began to click when he sang, 'The only good thing you did was "Yesterday",' and so on.
>
> I don't remember any discussion about the subject, but Yoko was sitting on the floor writing out the lyrics. Phil Spector was in the control room, just muttering the odd word. John was very deferential towards him, very nervous.

Two months later, Lennon invited Murphy back to Tittenhurst Park to hear the finished album:

> It was the height of summer now. Yoko made iced tea and we walked around the grounds and it dawned on me that he was quite nervous. He kept saying, 'We'll go in and have a listen in a minute.' He'd been labouring over this for months and suddenly he's got to play it to a member of the public who might hate it. So we'd have more tea and then another walk.
>
> Hours later we went in. He put the album on and said, 'Look, I can't bear to listen any more. You have a listen and tell me what you think.' A few hours later I staggered out to see him, and he really quizzed me. I'm going, 'it's brilliant!' He's saying, 'Do you think people will like it, it's such a departure from the last album?' He seemed taken aback I was so enthusiastic. He was really proud that King Curtis had played the sax part on one track: 'We managed to get King Curtis! He didn't seem to get that people would kill their own mothers to play on one of his albums.'

Murtagh, Joe

The head boiler man at the Adelphi Cinema. On the day of the Beatles' visit he had been given the secondary task of selling programmes. Joe Murtagh was the first individual in Ireland to get a full set of Beatles autographs when they arrived at the Adelphi. He told the Beatles, 'You're not leaving until you sign.'

Nerney, Michael

Assistant manager to Adelphi manager Harry Lush during the Beatles' visit to Dublin in 1963. One of Nerney's jobs after the concert was to give Jack Flanagan the signal to start the getaway van's engine. He also assisted Frank Hall in rounding up female fans for interview.

Newman, Sean

In his book, *Allan Williams is The Fool on the Hill,* Williams devotes a few pages to his relationship with Irishman Newman. A Co Meath native, Newman was William's Liverpool garage mechanic pal, responsible for servicing the battered van pictured in all Beatles books being lifted aboard the cross-channel ferry for its first fateful journey to Hamburg. As a matter of interest, it was Sean who dreamed up the slogan, 'The Mug Who Gave The Beatles Away'.

Owen, Janet

Teenager who left school at sixteen and, thanks to George Harrison, got work with NEMS Enterprises as a general dogsbody, delivering wages and letters to the Beatles' homes. She continued working for Apple and attended the premiere of *Yellow Submarine* with the Beatles.

She painted a psychedelic door for the Apple Boutique and it included contributions from all four Beatles: John painted a Chinese pagoda; Ringo wrote the word 'Love'; Paul drew a honey bee; and George drew the Tibetan symbol for nirvana. She later worked for Dick James Music and, to this day, still possesses that door which has travelled from London to Wexford, Mayo, Swords, Drogheda and finally to her home in Co Meath.

Speaking to Pete Brennan about her time with the Beatles she said, '"All You Need Is Love" was the beginning of the magic and "Give Peace A Chance" was the end of the magic. It went black and white with John and Yoko and the colour of the sixties disappeared.'

O'Rahilly, Ronan

The son of a wealthy Irish industrialist, Ronan O'Rahilly was an entrepreneur who started putting his own moneymaking plans into action at an early age. He was responsible for beginning the pirate radio boom in Britain when he launched Radio Caroline in 1958. After the Marine Offences Bill had banned the pirates from the airwaves, the Beatles hired O'Rahilly as a business adviser to Apple. O'Rahilly, who is originally from the Clondalkin area of west Dublin, is still in the broadcasting business to this day in the UK.

Young Ronan had been packed off to London to seek his fortune and settled into London's Soho clubland. Ray Charles was his hero and soon Ronan was operating his own rhythm and blues club. He bought the Rolling Stones their first set of stage equipment and briefly managed them together with his friend, Georgiou Gomalski, before entrepreneur Andrew Oldham snapped them up, but he still had the blues singer Alexis Korner and northerner Georgie Fame as his protégés.

He was influential in the early days of Eric Burdon and the Animals, even suggesting the name for the band. Live gigs at small venues were a slow way to achieve popularity, but nobody would record his artists, so O'Rahilly created his own record label and paid for his own acetates. When presenting these to the BBC, he learned that the Corporation only played music by established artists, which begged the obvious question, 'How do you get established?' At Radio Luxembourg he fared worse. Station bosses laughed heartily, showing him the programme schedules block-booked by the major labels. Independents had no chance of airplay at all. The answer: give up his artists and hope a major label would sign them.

O'Rahilly told Radio Luxembourg directors, 'If, while managing my own artists, I have to create my own record label because nobody will record them, and if I then find that no radio station will play their music, it seems that the only thing now is to have my own radio station.' Radio Luxembourg thought this was hugely funny and showed him the door. As a result he set up Radio Caroline.

O'Rahilly's last known connection with the Beatles was in June of 1976. During a press conference at the World Trade Center in New York, he introduced a new four-piece band, comprised of Mickey Gallagher, Charlie Charles, John Turnbull and Norman Wattroy, 'who call themselves Loving Awareness. The band announces that they intend to change their name to the Beatles! They say they had written to John, Paul, George and Ringo suggesting that, since they no longer use the name, they relinquish it to Loving Awareness, who will be happy to carry on in their tradition.' The Beatles' reply was, 'Don't even think about it!'

In 2007 Ronan was inducted as a fellow of the Radio Academy, a registered charity dedicated to the encouragement, recognition and promotion of excellence in UK broadcasting and audio production.

Reid, Eileen

Eileen Reid was born in the Iveagh Buildings in the Liberties, Dublin, in 1943 and has spent her whole life in show business, having first joined a band at the age of fifteen. She went on to audition successfully for the well-known Irish showband, the Cadets. The band had a distinctive look, wearing naval-style uniforms.

The Cadets toured with Johnny and June Cash when they came to Ireland in October 1963. The highlight of the tour was a concert in the National Stadium in Dublin. Eileen and the Cadets were introduced to the Beatles as a major force in the Irish music scene and Eileen was photographed with both John Lennon and Paul McCartney when they came to Dublin in November 1963.

Rhind, Geoff

Geoff Rhind was the Liverpudlian youth who took the famous photograph of the Quarrymen performing at the Woolton Village Fête on the day John Lennon met Paul McCartney, 6 July 1957. Geoff moved to Dublin in the 1960s, where he still lives today, working as an artist and musician. He retains the original negative of his famous picture, taken with his black plastic Kodak Comer camera.

Geoff Rhind and Yoko Ono, pictured in Dublin on 7 May 2004. *(Pete Brennan)*

Ronan, Ken

On the day the Beatles came to Dublin, 14-year-old Ken and his mate skipped school in the hope of meeting the band – they were successful, meeting them in the Gresham Hotel. Ken now runs a B&B outside Killaloe, Co Clare.

Walsh, Tommy

The only person to photograph John and Yoko during their visit to Dorinish Island in 1968. At the time, Tommy Walsh was working for *The Mayo News* and had been sent to photograph the then Irish Minister for External Affairs, Mr Frank Aiken, at the Great Southern Hotel, where he happened to meet John and Yoko.

Whyte, Mal

Mal Whyte is a native of London but spent most of his working life in Ireland as an actor. He plays the uilleann pipes, tin whistle and bodhran. As a lad in London in the early 1960s, he had a newspaper round in the Brompton area of Knightsbridge, which included Emperors Gate. From November 1963 until July 1964, under the family pseudonym 'Hadley', John Lennon, Cynthia and their baby son Julian lived at 13 Emperors Gate, in Flat 3 on the fourth floor.

Just before Christmas 1963, Mal was on his daily paper round, when he arrived at the door of Number 13. As he approached the door, it opened slowly and there was John Lennon in his slippers, dressing gown and black-rimmed spectacles. Whyte proceeded to pull Lennon's paper out of his bag and, at the same time, Lennon stuffed a ten shilling note into the young boy's hand, saying in his very Liverpudlian accent, 'There you go, that's the smallest I have. Happy Christmas.' This was to be the one and only time that the young Whyte would see Lennon at this address. Later on in life, Mal Whyte went on to pursue an acting career in Ireland taking on roles in productions such as *The Last Of The High Kings, Michael Collins, Father Ted* and *Fair City*, to name but a few.

Appendix 2

Day Trippers

Paul and Heather visit Barretstown, 2004

The year 2004 saw Paul back in Ireland not once, but twice. Paul and Heather joined Hollywood legend, Paul Newman, to turn on the showbiz magic at the 10th anniversary Gala Ball of Barretstown Castle in Co Kildare, on 4–5 September. The Barretstown recreation camp for children with cancer and other serious illnesses has given over 10,000 sick children therapeutic recreation programmes since it was set up by Newman with his own money in 1994. Paul McCartney and U2's The Edge helped strum up a fortune for sick children over this weekend. The famous rockers took turns to sign and play a glittering green guitar – designed specially for the auction by Irishman Mark Nicholls – that raised a whopping €55,000 at the charity bash, with Paul belting out rock classic 'Peggy Sue'. Paul told the huge crowd, 'I'm delighted to be back in Barretstown to celebrate ten years with the kids and their families. It's amazing to see how it's grown and developed over the years.' Later on in the evening the Barretstown project got another huge boost when Dubliner David Mellon forked out €175,000 for a limited edition Porsche car.

The Edge, Mark Nicholls, Paul McCartney and Paul Newman, with a specially designed guitar which helped raise funds for Barretstown's 10th Birthday Gala. *(Maxwell Picture Agency/Barretstown)*

John Lennon's half-sister, Julia Baird

Julia was the first daughter of Julia Lennon and John Dykins, born on 5 March 1947. Her parents did not marry when they began to live together because Julia was not divorced from Freddie Lennon (see Chapter 1). In 1965, when she was just eighteen, she met Allen Baird. Allen was living in Belfast, studying psychology. At the same time as John's fame was on the increase, Julia married Allen and went to live in Belfast. They have three children.

'For me, Ireland was an escape hatch. I was grateful to be away from the furore surrounding John. No one in Ireland knew he was my brother, apart from Allen's family, who very discreetly never mentioned his public antics,' she said. The last time Julia spoke to John was when she was in Ireland: she had just given birth to her first child and John phoned to congratulate her. Julia now lives in Chester with her partner Roger and in 2007 she published a book called *Imagine This – Growing up with my brother John Lennon.*

Ted Carroll and the Liverpudlians

During the mid-sixties a consortium of businessmen from Liverpool, including the playwright Alun Owen (who had accompanied the Beatles on their 1963 visit to Dublin), were planning to open a basement club on the bottom of Dublin's Harcourt Street, modelled on the famous Cavern Club.

Since he was the pre-eminent Dublin club owner of the day, the consortium approached Ted Carroll with a view to buying his club. Unfortunately the Liverpudlians' business plan never got off the ground and Dublin never did get its own Cavern.

Donovan

He was born Donovan Phillip Leitch, in Glasgow, Scotland, on 10 May 1946. Bob Dylan first introduced him to the Beatles at the Savoy Hotel, London, in May 1965. He became a friend of the group and wrote a song in tribute to them called 'For John And Paul'. The name of the song was changed to 'Sunshine Superman' when it was released and it reached Number Two in the British charts in December 1966.

Donovan was also at Rishikesh with the Beatles during a six-week period in 1967 and he composed 'Hurdy Gurdy Man' in company with the four Beatles, Beach Boy Mike Love, and actress Mia Farrow. George Harrison immediately added a new verse to the song. Unfortunately, Donovan's record company, Pye, talked him out of including George's verse on the finished track as they wanted releases of singles to be kept to a length of under three minutes. The record reached Number Four in the British charts. Mickie Most produced the number and Jimmy Page, John Bonham and John Paul Jones backed Donovan on it. The

George Harrison verse, the third in the song, was reinstated in 1990 on a CD called *The Classics Live*. Donovan also included George's verse in his live performances in 1991.

While in India, Donovan taught John some guitar styles and John was to comment, 'Donovan is as important and influential as Bob Dylan and we are listening: the man's a poet.' Paul and George attended Donovan's Royal Albert Hall appearance on Sunday 15 January 1967, and all four Beatles went to see him on the opening night of his week-long engagement at the Saville Theatre on Monday 24 April 1967. George Harrison was to give him his first lesson in playing the sitar in January 1967. During 1968 it was alleged that Paul McCartney made a guest appearance on Donovan's 'Atlantis' single, playing tambourine and providing some backing vocals, an event Donovan denies. He does confirm, however, that Paul dropped into the studio during the recording of 'Mellow Yellow' and at one point sang the title of the song.

A fifteen-minute session between the two artists, also from 1968, has been captured on an American bootleg album, *No 3 Abbey Road, NW8*. The interlude was taken from a studio warm-up between Donovan and Paul. In their book, *The End of the Beatles*, authors Harry Castleman and Walter J. Podrazik mention that the two stars sat down together with acoustic guitars and exchanged songs-in-the-works, with Paul offering 'Blackbird' and 'Heather' and Donovan selecting numbers from what eventually became the album *HMS Donovan*.

Donovan married Linda Lawrence in 1970 and the couple had two children, Oriole and Astrella. He lived in Fermoy, Co Cork, for twenty-odd years, but then decided to move to Spain, to be closer to his children and grandchildren, but he returns to Ireland frequently, the most recent visit being June 2008.

George and Donovan

In the middle of 1971, folk singer Donovan sent an invitation to his old friend, George Harrison, to join him for a short holiday in Ireland following the break-up of the Beatles. George and his wife, Pattie, flew to Dublin and joined Donovan and a large gathering of musician friends for what could only be described as a three-day party at the home of Lord Gowan, Castle Martin, which is a run-down eighteenth-century stately home just outside Kilcullen in Co Kildare, 30 miles west of Dublin.

In an interview with the authors of this book, Donovan recalled it was both a 'wonderful' and 'strange' time. Like many of his contemporaries, he says he had come out of the sixties having been 'ripped off by the music business and the taxman'. He admitted it was ironic that it was McCartney's nemesis, lawyer Alan Klein, who was to play a major part in his career and his decision at the time to become a tax exile in Ireland.

> It was towards the end of my time as a tax exile that I found myself in Ireland as the guest of Lord Gowan. The day I arrived at Castlemartin, I made my way from the village of Kilcullen. On entering the house it was evident, and very obvious, that this once great house had seen better days. My next move was to locate the owner. After a short tour of the house and several failed attempts to make contact with anyone, I suddenly came across a man at the top of a ladder who was attempting to paint one of the rooms blue. I asked if could I speak to Lord Gowan. The man on the ladder said, 'You have found him.' As the day went on, the house began to fill with all types of avant-garde artists. After three days of non-stop partying around the castle, during which George and I had time to talk about the future and our dreams for the 1970s, it was time for us all to make our way back into reality.

George and Ronnie Wood

Called 'The Quiet Beatle' for his reclusive ways, Harrison was stabbed several times in the chest by a knife-wielding intruder during a pre-dawn attack at his home, Friar Park, near Henley-on-Thames, in the early hours of Thursday 30 December 1999. This was to rekindle memories of the tragic news of John Lennon's death just over nineteen years earlier: on yet another morning Beatles fans were to wake and discover that a member of the group had been seriously hurt in a violent attack.

As the day progressed, it became known that at around 3.30am George had heard the sound of breaking glass – neither the burglar alarm nor any other security equipment had alerted the household as it slept. George went downstairs to investigate, while his wife, Olivia, called the staff on the internal phone.

He found an intruder in a downstairs room, tackled him, and was stabbed

George and his wife Olivia, pictured in Ireland in 2001.

four times in the chest with a 6-inch knife. George screamed for help and Olivia ran downstairs, where she saw him locked in a struggle and proceeded to hit the intruder over the head with a table lamp, which apparently stunned him into submission.

By now a member of the Harrisons' staff had reported the attack to the police who arrived shortly after. The attacker, identified as Michael Abram from the Beatles' home town of Liverpool, was arrested on suspicion of attempted murder. His mother was quoted in a Liverpool newspaper at the time as saying, 'He has been running in pubs shouting about the Beatles ... he hates them and even believes they are witches.'

Following George's recuperation, he expressed a desire to get away from Britain for a short break. George and Olivia travelled to Ireland in January 2000 at the invitation of Rolling Stones guitarist and Co Kildare resident, Ronnie Wood, who had, like so many others, taken advantage of the Irish government's tax exemption for artists. During their week-long stay at Wood's Straffan home, George made one statement to the press in which he said both he and Olivia were overwhelmed by the concern expressed by so many people. He said they thanked everyone for their prayers and kindness. George had a long association with Ireland and had often visited his cousins in Dublin as a child. This short trip in January 2000 was to be his last visit before his death in 2001 from lung cancer.

Cynthia Lennon

Cynthia Lennon pictured in Dublin in the 1990s with Pete Brennan. *(Pete Brennan)*

In the early 1980s, Cynthia Lennon lived in a cottage in Ruthin, North Wales, but sold up and bought a bungalow in Ireland at Kilmacanogue, Co Wicklow, for £36,000. Cynthia commented at the time, 'The move was for tax reasons. I have only about a tenth of the original settlement I had got from John [£75,000].'

At the time of her move to

Wicklow, Cynthia was married to John Twist. He had persuaded her to move so that she could write a book about her life. A publisher was interested and she went ahead with the project. The book, entitled *A Twist of Lennon*, was published in 1978. Cynthia later said, 'I think John Twist believed it would make our fortune, but all it did was provoke fury in John and Yoko.' After a short stay in Ireland Cynthia moved back to the UK and in 2002 married night club owner Noel Charles. She recently published a new biography called *John* and currently lives in Majorca in Spain.

Paul and Linda

During the period between the recording session in New York for the *Ram* album and the start of the Wings project in 1971, Paul and Linda made a trip to Ireland. The holiday and Ireland itself became the setting for another idea that was simmering. McCartney has said that he had wanted 'someone' to do a big band version of *Ram*, but there were no takers. So that 'someone' was to become McCartney himself.

This lesser known album would be called *Thrillington* and was based on a fictitious individual called Percy Thrillington (played by McCartney). Paul's company, MPL Communications, went to considerable lengths to convince the public that Percy 'Thrills' Thrillington existed. Not only were business cards produced but the company even went as far as to create a biography and promotional photographs.

Paul and Linda used their trip around Ireland to take photographs for possible use as part of the album's artwork. During their tour they found a young farmer whom they asked to model for photographs. According to McCartney, the idea was that they wanted to find someone that no one could possibly trace. They paid him the 'going rate' and photographed the unknown farmer in a field, first wearing a sweater and then an evening suit. The photographs were never used since, as McCartney said, 'He never quite looked Percy Thrillington enough.'

Lennon's Legacy

Since John Lennon's death in 1980, Yoko Ono and Lennon's two sons, Sean and Julian, have all made working visits to Ireland. Yoko Ono has never enjoyed a

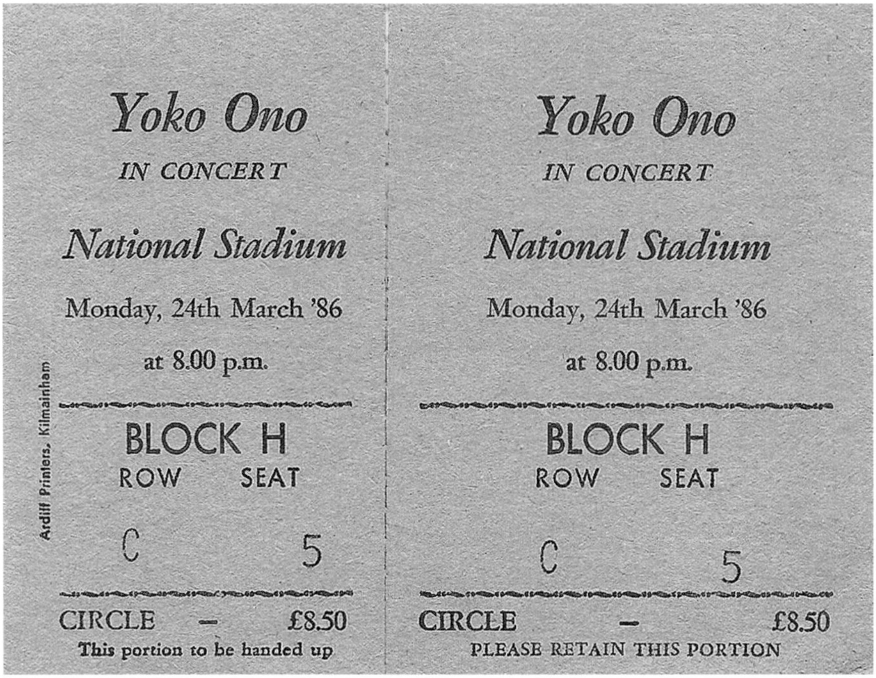

comfortable relationship with Beatles fans, especially since her now famous meeting with Lennon at a preview of her work at the Indica Gallery in November 1966. The British press took an immediate dislike to her and the Irish media have not been far behind their British colleagues in their questioning of Yoko's role in Lennon's life. This became very evident when it was announced that she was about to embark on a solo world tour in February 1986.

As part of her tour she was to give a performance at Dublin's National Stadium. When the news was announced, a Dublin daily newspaper speculated what might happen at the event: 'It's not clear what Yoko Ono will be going to do at her gig in Dublin. Perhaps she is going to make ice cubes or bake a cake.'

At around the same time another member of the Lennon family, John's first son, Julian, was about to set off on a series of European concerts to promote his new album. As part of this tour, he was due to play the same venue as Yoko, this time on Friday 16 May.

In late February 1986, Yoko began her world tour in Brussels. Due to poor ticket sales, the US leg of her tour was cancelled. Yoko's tour rolled on with performances in the Netherlands, West Berlin and Warsaw, where only a third of

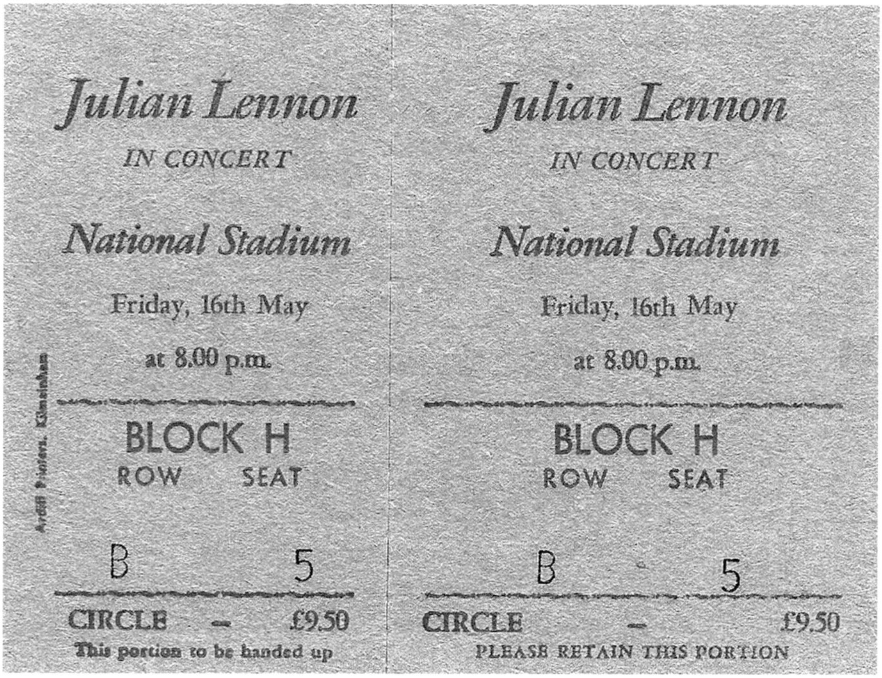

the 6,000-seater stadium was filled. By mid-March, Yoko and son Sean arrived in London to take up residence at the Dorchester Hotel in Park Lane. During her stay in London, Yoko and Sean met up with Julian. This was to be one of only a few such meetings, since relations were strained, as they remain to this day.

Yoko was due to fly into Dublin from London on the afternoon of Monday 24 March, the same day that Julian's second solo album, *The Secret Value of Daydreaming*, was released, but was forced to stay in London. As a result, Yoko's Dublin concert never took place. Unfortunately, due to poor ticket sales, Julian's gig in Dublin was also cancelled.

Fortunately both artists have returned to Ireland to pursue individual projects since the 1980s. Julian was to take up a short residence in Dublin for most of 1998, to complete his album *Photograph Smile* at Windmill Lane Studios.

Sean Lennon performed his first solo concert in Britain – and indeed one of his first solo concerts anywhere in the world – at the cramped Camden Falcon rock 'n' roll pub in North London on Thursday 7 May 1998. In November of that year Sean made his musical debut in Ireland as support to the French duo, Air, at Dublin's Olympia Theatre on 5 November 1998. Two nights later, his father's

Left to right: Sean Lennon pictured in Tower Records, Dublin, in November 1998 *(Mick Lynch)*; Yoko Ono at the Irish Museum of Modern Art, Dublin, for an Amnesty International Human Rights charity event in May 2004. *(Damian Smyth)*

original group, the Quarrymen, took to the same stage as special guests at a Beatles tribute night organised by the Irish Beatles fan club, Beatles Ireland.

Sean Lennon was touring in promotion of his debut album, *Into The Sun,* which he had finished in January of that year. Prior to his appearance at the Olympia Theatre on 5 November, Sean played an acoustic gig at the Dublin branch of Tower Records that also included a signing session afterwards for a small number of fans who had turned up. He was later interviewed by Tom Dunne as part of his TV series, *Planet Rock Profiles*, broadcast some weeks later on RTÉ and Ulster television.

Yoko made her way back to Ireland in May 2004 when she was asked by Amnesty International to launch a major collection of art in aid of the human rights charity.

Professor Ciaran Benson of University College, Dublin (UCD), asked Irish artists to donate one of their paintings to the collection, which was to be known as *In Time of Shaking*. As part of her involvement in this event, Yoko was to meet the press at the Irish Museum of Modern Art. Yoko's PA had promised the assembled press that she would be available for a photo-shoot lasting about 40 minutes, but went on to say, 'You can look, but don't touch.' At the press conference Yoko said, 'We did the "bed-in". The rest is history. We tried our best and today I feel as though John is here with us because this is the kind of thing that he would have loved to see happen. John believed that he was Irish.'

Following the press launch, Yoko and U2 guitarist Dave 'The Edge' Evans declared the exhibition officially open. The following night Yoko made an appearance on RTÉ's *The Late Late Show*.

In March 2003, an exhibition opened at The Apollo Gallery in Dawson Street, Dublin. *The Art of John Lennon* was a display of original work by Lennon, which he had created whilst living in New York at the Dakota Building from 1973 up until his death in 1980. The exhibition was opened on Thursday 27 March and ran until 4 April. A year before, the exhibition had had a short run in Belfast, but Yoko did not attend either showing, simply passing on her best wishes.

Paul McCartney's 'Liverpool Oratorio', Dublin Performance

Carl Davis was commissioned to compose the *Liverpool Oratorio* by Brian Pidgeon, the general manager of the Royal Liverpool Philharmonic Orchestra. Carl approached Paul to suggest that they collaborate on the venture and base it around a character similar to Paul himself.

Paul and Davis worked on and off for eighteen months on the piece that began with the words, *non nobis solum sed toti mundo nati*, the Liverpool Institute High School for Boys motto, which means, 'Not for ourselves alone, but for the whole world we were born'.

The first movement, called 'War', told the story of how the hero, Shanty (modelled on Paul), was born in Liverpool during the Second World War in the middle of an air raid. In the movement called 'School', Shanty plays truant at the age of eleven to sunbathe in the graveyard of Liverpool Cathedral. In the third movement 'Crypt', Shanty goes to a church dance in the crypt where he meets Mary Dee, who is to become his wife. He tells her his father has died. In the movement called 'Father', Shanty comes to terms with the loss of his father. A few years later Shanty marries Mary in the movement called 'Wedding'.

In 'Work' Mary runs an office staffed entirely by women and has a heavy schedule and then discovers she is pregnant. Shanty rows with his wife and says he doubts her love for him. She runs out on him, telling him she is pregnant, and is knocked down by a car and taken to hospital. Shanty prays that she will be saved, saying that he will change his ways if she is.

The oratorio has a happy ending with Shanty, Mary and their child happily reunited in a movement called 'Peace'. The work was given its world première at Liverpool's Anglican Cathedral on Friday 28 June 1991 before an audience of 2,500 as part of the orchestra's 150th anniversary celebrations (which had actually occurred the previous year). A second performance took place at the Cathedral on Saturday 29 June.

The American première took place at Carnegie Hall, New York, on Monday 18 November 1991. Paul and his family were in the audience. The performers were basically the same as those from the Liverpool Anglican Cathedral debut, with the exception of Kiri Te Kanawa who was replaced by Barbara Bonney.

During the five years after its debut, the oratorio was performed 99 times in twenty different countries. The oratorio was performed for the fifth time as part of the Belfast Festival at the Ulster Hall on Thursday 21 November 1991, followed by a performance at St Patrick's Cathedral in Dublin on Sunday 24 November. Paul and Linda were not present in either Belfast or Dublin, however Paul sent a message of thanks before the Belfast performance:

> Having written the *Liverpool Oratorio* to celebrate the 150th anniversary of the Royal Liverpool Philharmonic Orchestra, I was very happy to hear that the Northern Ireland Symphony would be giving the work its Irish Première.
>
> Being myself the product of a Catholic mother and a Protestant father it was important to me that the religious aspect of the piece be written in such a way that people of differing views could come together in harmony and perhaps understand that, whatever the religion, 'God is good'.
>
> I cannot be there tonight unfortunately, as I am starting work on my next project but I hope in some small way this performance will promote a feeling of cooperation amongst those who hear it. Have a marvellous evening. Spread the message and, who knows, one day (as the choir sings) we may all, 'Live in peace together'.

A further performance of the oratorio took place at St Anne's Cathedral in Belfast. This was performed by the Northern Ireland Symphony Orchestra and Youth Chorus with Alan Tonque conducting. This was the same line-up as the Dublin performance.

Maurice E. Stewart, Dean of St Patrick's Cathedral, Dublin, said at the time; 'St Patrick's Cathedral welcomes Paul McCartney's *Liverpool Oratorio*. This year, 1991, is of double significance for us here. Our city has been honoured to be the European City of Culture, while in St Patrick's we are celebrating the 800th anniversary of our foundation as a cathedral.'

Some of the proceeds of the performance were devoted to the fund to restore the great Willis organ at St Patrick's Cathedral, which was scheduled for rebuild at the time.

Richard Lester

The Irish Times film correspondent, Michael Dwyer, conducted an interview with Richard Lester on 25 September 2001 at the Irish Film Centre, Temple Bar, in front of an invited audience.

To film historians, Lester is the most stylistically ground-breaking director of his generation, but among Beatles fans, Lester is known as the man responsible for bringing the band to the big screen, directing *A Hard Day's Night* in 1964.

The Allan Williams Story

On Tuesday 8 October 2002, Irish actor Ronan Wilmot staged the world première of his musical based on the life of the Beatles' promoter, Allan Williams, at the New Theatre on East Essex Street, in Dublin's Temple Bar. The première played to a full house, with Allan Williams and his wife, Beryl, in attendance as personal guests of Mr Wilmot. They had just arrived from Liverpool the day before.

They had all first met on one of Wilmot's early trips to Liverpool: Allan and Beryl had been running the digs where Wilmot stayed. Wilmot, a former Royal Shakespeare Company actor, said, 'We have remained friends since that first visit. I thought Allan's early days with the Beatles would make a good musical.' After contacting Williams and getting his approval, he began writing the show under the title *The Man Who Gave the Beatles Away – The Allan Williams Story*.

It is a play with music and the first act deals with the early Liverpool days and characters like the late Lord Woodbine. The second act was set in Hamburg. The play did a five-week run but closed after that.

Sgt Pepper in Dublin

On 30 March 1967, photographer Frank Herrmann was sent to Abbey Road Studios on a routine assignment for *The Sunday Times* to spend one hour with the Beatles who were busy recording their latest album, *Sgt Pepper's Lonely Hearts Club Band.* During the session, Frank Herrmann shot two rolls of film capturing the Beatles lounging around the famous studios, eating their lunch, chatting with producer, George Martin, smoking lots of cigarettes, drinking endless cups of tea, rehearsing, listening to playbacks in the upstairs sound studio and, frankly, looking very bored.

The Leinster Gallery in South Frederick Street, Dublin, had arranged for Frank Herrmann's photographs, which were on a tour of Europe, to be displayed there. This came about because one of the gallery's employees had been working with Herrmann in the UK during 2002 at the time when he was asked to illustrate George Martin's book, *Summer of Love.*

While on a three-day visit to Dublin to open the exhibition on Thursday 15 November 2007, Herrmann said, 'The photographs I took became a rarity because of the lack of access to the band in the recording studio'.

Herrmann went on to say, 'The two rolls of film sat in *The Sunday Times* library until 1988 and by that time I had left the paper. In 2002, when I was asked for photographs to illustrate George Martin's book, I went to collect the remaining negatives, only to find that they had disappeared. It's is only now, thanks to digital technology, that the proofs made at the time have been painstakingly scanned using high resolution equipment to produce the images that were lost for over 40 years.' After the Dublin exhibition, the photographs went on to be displayed in Paris.

Heather Mills

Paul McCartney's estranged wife and controversial former glamour model, Heather Mills, arrived in Ireland on Wednesday 21 November 2007. It was her fifth visit in as many years and she visited to attend a ceremony that would make her an honorary patron of Dublin's Trinity College Philosophical Society.

Heather was late for the ceremony, held in the university's Edmund Burke Theatre, which was little more than half full for the occasion. Ruth Vallar chaired the ceremony and introduced Heather who launched into a rambling speech, never mentioning the high-profile breakup of her marriage to Paul McCartney. This, in spite of the fact that she was embroiled in tabloid controversy over the terms of her divorce with the former Beatle.

Paul McCartney's Irish Premiere of 'Ecce Cor Meum'

Irish premiere of Paul McCartney's *Ecce Cor Meum* on 25 May 2008 in Dublin's National Concert Hall. Originally commissioned by Magdalen College Oxford in 1998, to commemorate the 550th anniversary of the foundation of the college, *Ecce Cor Meum* [Behold My Heart] is an oratorio written for Magdalen College Choir by Sir Paul McCartney.

The Museum of Style Icons
Newbridge Silverware Visitor Centre,
Newbridge, Co Kildare

Since its official opening to the public the Newbridge Silverware Museum of Style Icons has welcomed thousands of visitors countrywide to its spectacular showcase. Located onsite at the Newbridge Silverware Visitor Centre, the Museum of Style Icons is a permanent exhibition dedicated to design and style excellence. More recently, suits worn for the promotion of the Beatles film, *A Hard Day's Night*, have been part of the museum's exhibition.

These suits were provided for the Beatles by Dougie Millings and his son Gordon. Dougie charged £31 per suit. In fact, the Beatles give Dougie Millings a cameo role in *A Hard Day's Night* – the part of the tailor. Dougie also made the suits for the original Madame Tussaud's waxwork figures of the Beatles. This is the first time any Beatles suits have been displayed in Ireland.

Appendix 3

Prime Beatles Sites in Ireland

Adelphi Cinema, Dublin

This Dublin cinema in Middle Abbey Street was a 2,300-seat movie palace in an Art Moderne style, designed by the English cinema architect W.R. Glen for the ABC group and opened in 1939. The façade was symmetrical, with art deco detailing. The tall windows once lit a fashionable balcony café. A streamlined canopy underneath the second-storey windows originally covered the entrance, with its six pairs of elegant doors.

While primarily a cinema, the Adelphi featured live acts as well, most notably the only appearance in Dublin by the Beatles in 1963. Other performers to appear at the Adelphi include Marlene Dietrich, Louis Armstrong, Diana Ross and Roy Orbison. In 1976, the cinema was triplexed, and later became a quad.

Open until 1995, the Adelphi was demolished shortly after and part of its façade retained to provide car parking for the expanded Arnott's Department Store. Not only was the fine entrance removed to provide a massive holding area for cars, but the façade was clumsily extended upwards to mask the taller building. This is obvious to all, as the stonework has failed to weather to the same colour.

Border Crossing, Newry, Co Down

This point is just north of the border from the Republic and into the North on the Dundalk-to-Newry Road. The Beatles were interviewed by Ulster Television at this pre-arranged spot en route for Belfast on 8 November 1963, after their Dublin concert the previous evening.

Castle Leslie, Glaslough, Co Monaghan

Castle Leslie stands on the site of an earlier castle and was designed by Charles Lanyon and W.H. Lynn in 1870 for John Leslie, MP. Designed in the Scottish baronial style, the house presents a rather dour and austere façade and is sited in such a way as to mask the gardens from the visitor. The garden front is relieved by an Italianate Renaissance cloister, which links the main house to a single-storey wing containing the library and billiard room. In contrast to the exterior by Lynn, the interior shows the hands of Lanyon and Leslie himself through its strong Italian Renaissance feel. Castle Leslie was the venue for Paul's wedding to Heather Mills in June 2002.

Castlemartin House, Kilcullen, Co Kildare

Castlemartin House is situated just 1km outside Kilcullen and is an eighteenth-century house now owned by Sir Anthony O'Reilly. Kilcullen was also the scene of one of the most fiercely fought battles of the 1798 rebellion. A monument to the memory of 1798 is now erected on Kilcullen Bridge. General Dundas was the Chief British Officer in Co Kildare and he used Castlemartin as his headquarters. In 1971 folk-singer Donovan and George Harrison were invited to stay at the house for a few days. (see Appendix 2, for the full story.)

Dorinish Island, Clew Bay, Co Mayo

The island which John Lennon purchased in 1967 for £1,500. It was purchased in the name of J. Alistair Taylor and, for tax reasons, John was unable to visit at first, but did so after six months. (See Chapter 4 for the full story.)

Dromoland Castle, Co Clare

Amongst Ireland's finest castle hotels, Dromoland is one of the few that can trace its ownership back through history to Irish Gaelic families of royal heritage. The castle offers its guests deluxe accommodation and the experience of living like landed gentry, surrounded by breathtaking scenery, absolute luxury and exceptional service. The castle is just eight miles from Shannon Airport, making it an ideal base from which to explore the rugged magnificence of the Burren. George, John, Pattie and Cynthia took an Easter break at Dromoland in 1964.

Gresham Hotel, Dublin

Rebuilt in the 1920s after the ravages of the Civil War, the Gresham Hotel in

O'Connell Street is a Dublin landmark. Robert Atkinson, an English architect who was Director of the London Bartlett School of Architecture, designed it. In line with many of the later buildings on this stretch of O'Connell Street, it has quite a restrained, rather austere, façade. The ornament has been almost completely removed, leaving a stripped, classical style. The Beatles stayed here for one night after the Dublin concert in November 1963.

King's Hall, Belfast, Northern Ireland

The King's Hall was opened on 29 May 1934 by His Royal Highness, the Duke of Gloucester, and quickly became a landmark of international renown. In April 1991 the British Department of the Environment recognised its presence and features by placing it on the list of buildings of special architectural and historical interest. The Beatles appeared here on 2 November 1964 and, with an audience of 17,400, it was the largest audience the Beatles had ever appeared before in the UK.

Mulranny Great Western Hotel, Co Mayo

Now re-named the Park Inn and part of the Radisson SAS Group, north of Westport. Originally constructed by the Midland Great Western Railway, the hotel first opened for business in March 1897 and became a famous destination during the lifetime of the railway between Westport and Achill. The hotel had passed though a few private interests since 1897 but closed in 1987 and fell into disuse. After a €17-million development which took little more than a year to complete, the hotel re-opened in 2005 as the Park Inn, under the umbrella of the Radisson SAS Group.

This magnificent Victorian country hotel was the chosen venue for John Lennon and Yoko Ono's short stay in 1968 when Lennon came to inspect Dorinish Island, which he had bought in 1967. In tribute to Lennon, and as part of the new development, the hotel now has a suite called the 'John Lennon Suite', decorated in a retro style.

Old Terminal Building, Dublin Airport

The original Dublin airport terminal was the most important pre-war Irish building in the International Style. Designed by a team of architects within the Office of Public Works led by Desmond Fitzgerald, the design was more or less complete by 1937 and the building completed by 1940. Because of wartime reporting restrictions in Ireland, the building details were not published until 1945. This meant the building never got the recognition it deserves. On the ground floor arrivals area in the terminal, the Beatles were interviewed by the Irish media in November 1963.

Ritz Cinema, Fisherwick Place, Belfast, Northern Ireland

The Beatles first appeared in Northern Ireland here on Friday 8 November 1963. The Ritz Cinema opened in 1936 and was early on given the nickname of 'Ireland's Wonder Cinema'. The building was massive, designed by architect Leslie Kemp in elegant art deco style, and seated over 2,200 people In addition to showing films, the building boasted a Compton organ and a café on the first floor. After the ABC circuit bought out Union Cinemas, which originally operated the Ritz, it became known as the ABC. Later, Cannon Cinemas acquired the theatre and divided it into a four-screener. It was demolished in 1994 and replaced by a hotel.

Appendix 4

The Beatles and the Irish Charts: 1962–2008

The Irish Singles Charts began in October 1962 (the same month that the Beatles' debut single peaked in the UK charts). Listed below are the peak positions of all their singles that have made the Irish Charts. 'Weeks on chart' totals may include several separate chart runs.

The Beatles (Singles) Chart Status

Chart Entry	Song Title	Peak Position	Weeks on Chart	Record Label
29/03/1963	Please Please Me	10	2	Parlophone
10/05/1963	From Me To You	1	12	Parlophone
13/09/1963	She Loves You	2	19	Parlophone
20/12/1963	I Want To Hold Your Hand	2	9	Parlophone
30/03/1964	Can't Buy Me Love	1	8	Parlophone
20/07/1964	A Hard Day's Night	1	9	Parlophone
07/12/1964	I Feel Fine	1	8	Parlophone
06/04/1965	Ticket To Ride*	1	6	Parlophone
02/08/1965	Help!*	1	8	Parlophone
13/12/1965	Day Tripper / We Can Work it Out	1	5	Parlophone
20/06/1965	Paperback Writer*	1	6	Parlophone
15/08/1966	Yellow Submarine / Eleanor Rigby	1	8	Parlophone
01/03/1967	Penny Lane / Strawberry Fields Forever	2	8	Parlophone
20/07/1967	All You Need Is Love	1	9	Parlophone
16/12/1967	Hello Goodbye	2	8	Parlophone
25/01/1968	Magical Mystery Tour (EP)	17	1	Parlophone
30/03/1968	Lady Madonna	3	7	Parlophone
14/09/1968	Hey Jude*	1	14	Apple
03/05/1969	Get Back (with Billy Preston)	1	10	Apple
14/11/1969	Come Together / Something	3	9	Apple

06/03/1970	Let It Be*	3	7	Apple
21/06/1970	The Ballad of John and Yoko*	1	10	Apple
01/04/1976	Yesterday	4	7	Apple
29/04/1976	Help!	10	2	Parlophone
29/04/1976	Get Back (with Billy Preston)	8	2	Apple
22/07/1976	Back in the USSR	11	5	Parlophone
13/06/1982	Beatles Movie Medley	12	6	Parlophone
10/10/1982	Love Me Do	4	6	Parlophone
23/01/1983	Please Please Me	15	3	Parlophone
16/07/1987	All You Need Is Love	19	2	Parlophone
23/04/1995	Baby It's You	12	4	Apple
07/12/1995	Free As A Bird	5	6	Apple
07/02/1996	Real Love	8	5	Apple

* *entered chart at No 1*

Paul McCartney (Singles)

Chart Entry	Song Title	Peak Position	Weeks on Chart	Record Label
06/03/1971	Another Day	1	9	Apple
26/02/1972	Give Ireland Back To The Irish	1	4	Apple*
21/12/1972	Hi Hi Hi / C Moon	18	4	Apple*
25/01/1973	Hi Hi Hi / C Moon (re-entry)	14	1	Apple*
18/07/1974	Band On The Run	7	5	Apple**
19/06/1975	Listen To What the Man Said	4	6	Apple*
27/05/1976	Silly Love Songs	1	12	Parlophone*
27/08/1976	Let 'em In	2	10	Parlophone*
01/12/1977	Mull of Kintyre / Girls' School	1	14	Parlophone*
13/04/1978	With A Little Luck	3	8	Parlophone*
13/07/1978	I've Had Enough	11	1	Parlophone*
16/11/1978	Mull of Kintyre / Girls' School (re-entry)	10	3	Parlophone*
05/04/1979	Goodnight Tonight	9	7	Parlophone*
08/07/1979	Old Siam Sir	29	3	Parlophone*
16/09/1979	Getting Closer	24	2	Parlophone*
16/09/1979	Baby's Request	24	2	Parlophone*

02/12/1979	Wonderful Christmastime	8	7	Parlophone
11/05/1980	Coming Up	3	8	Parlophone
05/07/1980	Waterfalls	4	8	Parlophone
11/04/1982	Ebony & Ivory (with Stevie Wonder)	1	8	Parlophone
11/07/1982	Take It Away	26	3	Parlophone
07/11/1982	The Girl is Mine (with Michael Jackson)	4	3	Epic
09/10/1983	Say Say Say (with Michael Jackson)	3	13	Parlophone
18/12/1983	Pipes of Peace	1	8	Parlophone
30/09/1984	No More Lonely Nights	2	8	Parlophone
18/11/1984	We All Stand Together	3	10	Parlophone
28/11/1985	Spies Like Us	8	6	Parlophone
24/07/1986	Press	15	2	Parlophone
21/12/1986	Only Love Remains	20	2	Parlophone
19/11/1987	Once Upon A Long Ago	4	6	Parlophone
11/05/1989	My Brave Face	6	3	Parlophone
11/05/1989	Ferry 'Cross the Mersey	1	8	K-Tel***
27/07/1989	This One	27	1	EMI
30/11/1989	Figure of Eight	25	1	Parlophone
15/02/1990	Put It There	17	2	Parlophone
18/10/1990	Birthday	22	2	Parlophone
28/01/1993	Hope of Deliverance	28	1	Parlophone
23/09/2004	Tropic Island Hum / We All Stand Together	30	1	Parlophone
08/09/2005	Fine Line	53	1	Parlophone
24/11/2005	Jenny Wren	66	1	Parlophone

** Wings; **Paul McCartney & Wings; ***The Christians, Holly Johnson, Paul McCartney, Gerry Marsden and Stock Aitken Waterman*

John Lennon (Singles)

Chart Entry	Song Title	Peak Position	Weeks on Chart	Record Label
03/04/1971	Power to the People	7	5	Apple*
14/12/1972	Happy Xmas (War is Over)	2	6	Apple**
27/11/1975	Imagine	1	12	Apple

09/11/1980	(Just Like) Starting Over	1	13	Geffen
14/12/1980	Happy Xmas (War is Over)	3	7	Parlophone**
21/12/1980	Imagine (re-issue)	1	13	Parlophone
18/01/1981	Woman	1	11	Geffen
29/03/1981	I Saw Her Standing There	13	3	DJM***
19/04/1981	Watching the Wheels	20	2	Geffen
20/12/1981	Happy Xmas (War is Over)	27	4	Parlophone**
14/11/1982	Love	21	3	Parlophone
22/01/1984	Nobody Told Me	5	3	CBS Epic
25/03/1984	Borrowed Time	28	2	Polydor
16/12/1984	Happy Xmas (War is Over)	21	3	Parlophone**
28/11/1985	Jealous Guy	28	1	Parlophone
08/12/1988	Imagine	29	1	Parlophone
16/12/1999	Imagine	3	9	Parlophone

** John Lennon & The Plastic Ono Band; **John Lennon, Yoko Ono & The Plastic Ono Band with The Harlem Community Choir; ***The Elton John Band featured John Lennon & The Muscle Shoals Horns*

George Harrison (Singles)

Chart Entry	Song Title	Peak Position	Weeks on Chart	Record Label
23/01/1971	My Sweet Lord	1	14	Apple
26/08/1971	Bangla Desh	18	3	Apple
21/06/1973	Give Me Love (Give Me Peace on Earth)	10	4	Apple
24/05/1981	All Those Years Ago	4	5	Dark Horse
29/10/1987	Got My Mind Set On You	1	10	Dark Horse / WEA
11/02/1988	When We Was Fab	24	2	WEA
03/11/1988	Handle With Care	12	8	WEA*
02/03/1989	End of the Line	14	5	WEA*
02/07/1990	Nobody's Child	19	2	Warner Brothers*
17/01/2002	My Sweet Lord	5	5	Parlophone

* *Traveling Wilburys*

Ringo Starr (Singles)

Chart Entry	Song Title	Peak Position	Weeks on Chart	Record Label
24/04/1971	It Don't Come Easy	4	7	Apple
29/04/1972	Back Off Boogaloo	12	1	Apple
29/11/1973	Photograph	15	3	Apple
22/02/1974	You're Sixteen	2	7	Apple

It was not until the 1990s that album sales in Ireland were tracked by retail sales. Below is a list of those albums to have made the Irish Album Charts to the present day.

The Beatles (Albums)

Peak Week	Album Title	Peak Position	Weeks in Top 40	Record Label
30/11/1994	Live At the BBC	9	9	Apple
21/11/1995	Anthology 1	6	8	Apple
18/05/1996	Anthology 2	6	6	Apple
28/10/1996	Anthology 3	6	8	Apple
07/03/1997	Sgt Pepper's Lonely Hearts Club Band	18	6	Apple
13/09/1999	Yellow Submarine Songtrack	22	2	Apple
16/11/2000	1'	1	31	Apple
20/11/2003	Let It Be (Naked)	7	6	Parlophone
23/11/2006	Love	3	13	Parlophone

Paul McCartney (Albums)

Chart Entry	Album Title	Peak Position	Weeks in Top 40	Record Label
09/05/1997	Flaming Pie	21	4	Parlophone
10/05/2001	Wingspan: Hits And History	10	5	Parlophone
20/03/2003	Back In the World	18	10	Parlophone

15/09/2005	Chaos And Creation In the Backyard	32	1	Parlophone
07/06/2007	Memory Almost Full	30	2	Hear Music

John Lennon (Albums)

Chart Entry	Album Title	Peak Position	Weeks in Top 40	Record Label
31/10/1997	Lennon Legend – The Very Best of	5	29	Parlophone
06/10/2005	Working Class Hero – Definitive Lennon	21	3	Parlophone

George Harrison (Albums)

Chart Entry	Album Title	Peak Position	Weeks in Top 40	Record Label
15/06/2007	The Traveling Wilburys' Collection	1	13	Rhino*

* *Traveling Wilburys*

(Charts Copyright, IRMA)

Appendix 5

Beatle Interviews

Granada Television, 'Scene At 6.30', 20 December, 1963

The November appearance by the group was a hilarious meeting between the Beatles, Liverpool comedian Ken Dodd and host Gay Byrne (left).

The legendary Irish broadcaster Gay Byrne presented this Granada TV programme from 1962 to 1963. Due to the large correspondence that Granada received from viewers after the Beatles' first appearance on the programme in mid-1962, Granada executives sent representatives to observe the band on 28 July at the Cambridge Hall, Southport, and on 1 August at the Cavern Club. As a result they sent a film crew – led by Dick Fontaine – to the Cavern and filmed the group performing 'Some Other Guy' and 'Kansas City/ Hey! Hey! Hey!' on 22 August.

This particular film wasn't shown until after the Beatles had become stars. However Granada officials were sufficiently interested in the group to provide them with their *People And Places* television debut on 17 October and 17 December 1962. By now the programme's name had changed to *Scene At 6.30* and the Beatles were booked to appear four times during 1963. This slot was a hilarious encounter between the Beatles, Liverpool comedian Ken Dodd, and host Gay Byrne.

Byrne: We have always thought that it might be a good question to put to Mr Kenneth Dodd and members of the Beatles, er, to what extent do they attribute their success to their hairstyles? And we'll start by asking the question now of Mr Dodd.

Dodd: We call it 'hur' ['hair' in a Liverpudlian accent] in Liverpool ... you see we always have the Judy with the 'fur [fair] hur'. A fellow once went into a shop in Liverpool where they sell these minks and things and he said to the girl, 'Give us one of those hairy coats.' She said, 'I beg your pardon, sir, what fur?' He said, 'For the Judy, who do you think?'

Byrne: [To the Beatles] Do you think he owes a lot of his success to his hair-style, fellas?

John: No. I don't think it helped at all.

George: It might have been better if he was bald.

Dodd: Bald! With the teeth and the hair, all the gimmicks, you know, I think you definitely have to have a gimmick. You've all got gimmicks, haven't you boys?

Byrne: What about the nose?

Dodd: The nose ... [He looks at Ringo and points. Everybody laughs.] He's a Martian! We were writing this film script for the boys ... you know the boys are making this new film and we've been writing the script and we've cast Ringo in the role of King Charles on account of the thing, you know, and he goes along to Nell Gwynn and pinches her jaffas.

Byrne: Tell us more about this picture, we didn't know about this.

Dodd: Oh, yes, we've written the thing. I'm writing the script, yes, with Knotty Ash University ... he's King Charles. John is a courtier and in this film he wears a long golden wig with all beautiful curls ...

John: [Camping it up]: Oh, very nice.

Dodd: ... and a blue velvet jacket and like, sort of, knickerbockers, with lace round the bottom and buckled shoes with diamante clips on and he sort of walks round on the film set and there's a policeman standing at the side, says he'll pinch him when he comes off.

Byrne: And what's he supposed to be doing, though?

Dodd: Well, John, he's a peasant. He's an evil sort. [He points at George.]

Paul and John: [Commenting on the fact that Ken appears to have mistaken George for John] He's Tom, Harry.

Dodd: Well, thingy. He's an evil smelly peasant.

Byrne: Why is he an evil smelly peasant?

Dodd: Come and stand where I am … and Paul is a jester, you see, and he's always making the King laugh. Every time he stands on his head, the King laughs like anything. He wears a kilt!

Byrne: Getting back to this group, then. Have you no ambitions to form a group yourself?

Dodd: Love to. With the boys? Kenny and the Cockroaches or Doddy and the Diddymen?

Byrne: What about yourself, would you …?

Dodd: Or Ringo and the Layabouts?

Byrne: Would you not form one yourself, Ken?

Dodd: Yes, I'd like to. Yes, because, the only thing is, I'd have to change me name, you see. I'd have to have a name like Cliff or Rock, something earthy.

Paul: Or Cliff Dodd ... Rock Dodd.

Dodd: Let's invite suggestions for an earthy name for me.

Radio Nova, Dublin, Easter Monday 1984

For Irish Beatle fans, this was a very rare opportunity to hear the one-time Cavern DJ Bob Wooler and Beatles occasional booking agent Allan Williams speak on Irish radio.

Radio Nova the Dublin-based radio station had managed to persuade Bob Wooler to take part in this broadcast. Wooler, whose encyclopaedic knowledge of the local Liverpool music scene in the 1960s made him a sought-after figure by promoters and his advice was regularly heeded. Allan Williams offered him a job at the Top Ten Club, but it burned down shortly after opening. Always of smart attire, Wooler then started full-time employment in his most notable role as compère at the Cavern Club.

Bob Wooler: Well the last time I saw any of them (the Beatles) was McCartney in late '79, I was astonished how little McCartney had changed.

Allan Williams: I can back that up.

Bob Wooler: The last Beatle I saw face to face (as close to you as I am) right now was McCartney, when he played a few shows in Liverpool on the Wings tour in 1979. Now the last time I saw them in the flesh collectively was at [the] Brian Epstein funeral service in Golders Green in 1967.

DJ Mike Edger: What was McCartney like when you saw him in '79?

Bob Wooler: Like I said, I was astonished how little he had changed, so very little. I met his wife too; of course they are both keen vegetarians whether that has anything to do with it I don't know?

Allan Williams: I will go along with that. Because Bob and I have the charisma, the Beatles are not gods to us. When I met Paul around the same period, Paul stuck his two fingers up at me and I did it back to him! That was the atmosphere, then Paul said: 'Well Allan, what are you doing now?' It was as if nothing had changed, just as if time had stood still. He was just Paul to us, mind you he never gave me a hand out.

Bob Wooler: I think you owe Paul some money for the bookings at the Blue Angel club [a nightclub opened by Williams in Liverpool in 1961] – you never paid them, remember?

Allan Williams: Hey listen; I have an IOU for fifteen pounds from Paul.

Bob Wooler: If it comes to that, the Beatles owe me as the booking agent into the Cavern Club, three bookings that Brian Epstein pulled them out of. Epstein said: 'Bob, I know you have the boys, but they have this TV show coming up, I know you know how important this is to them, please release them, okay? I promise you I will give you a replacement booking at the same fee.' I'm still waiting!

Allan Williams: Collect now, Bob, before it's too late, look you have lost one already.

[*At this point of the show, Allan Williams continued to answers questions about the Beatles' formative years and the group's time spent in Hamburg, which for the listeners turned out to be a very informative few hours. After Williams' question-and-answer session, it was back to the guests. Bob Wooler remained in the studio but contributed very little to the rest of the show.*]

Mike Edger: Allan Williams and Bob Wooler are with us for the rest of the show.

Allan Williams: Wow! Sean Newman has just walked into the studio. [Williams went on to inform the listeners that this was the man who sold the van that the Beatles had used for their first trip to Hamburg in 1960.] This Irish man, Sean Newman, sold my van, but never gave me the money.

Mike Edger: Well, are you going to pay?

Sean Newman: Straight away!

Mike Edger: Sean, what was your involvement with Allan and the Beatles in the early days?

Sean Newman: I knew Allan long before the Beatles went to Germany, in fact if I had the money I would have gone with them at the time, because I had serviced the van to take them to Hamburg and everyone was saying I should go with them, but the finance was not there so I could not make it. When Allan brought the van back to Liverpool from Germany, I passed it on to a friend who was to sell it to someone he knew in Manchester.

Allan Williams: Hey Sean! This is the first time I have seen you in years. You have put on a bit of weight.

Sean Newman: The last time I saw you, Allan, was in the Toxteth riots in Liverpool, burning my car!

Allan Williams: Hey Sean! You're completely snow white, what's the story?

Mike Edger: A question to you Allan. Why did you and the Beatles spilt?

Allan Williams: In a word 'Lennon'. You see, John had a king-size chip on his shoulder.

Mike Edger: Was it when you came back from Hamburg?

Allan Williams: Well, it was the second time. Things had moved on, it was around 1961.

Ringo Starr Interview with Dave Fanning for RTÉ, 20 August 1998

Following the Beatles' break-up, Ringo Starr had an initially successful solo recording career. He also appeared in various TV shows, including his own special, *Ringo*, and a TV mini-series, *Princess Daisy*, with his wife Barbara. He later gained a new fan-base as the voice of *Thomas the Tank Engine* in the children's TV series.

After a few years away from the limelight, he reappeared in 1989 to tour America and Japan with his All-Starr Band. This was a collaboration of 'super-group' musicians, including Joe Walsh (The Eagles), Nils Lofgren, Clarence Clemons (saxophone player with the E-Street Band), Levon Helm and Rick Danko, (The Band), Dr John, Billy Preston and Jim Keltner. The project proved to be so successful that he formed another All-Starr Band in 1992, which began an American and European tour in June of that year. By 1998, Ringo had compiled his fourth All-Starr Band line-up and his arrival in Dublin on 20 August was the mid-point of the tour.

Ringo checked into the Conrad Hotel in Dublin the day before the gig with his All-Starr Band in tow, this time consisting of Peter Frampton, Jack Bruce (Cream), Gary Brooker (Procol Harum), Simon Kirke (Free) and Mark Rivera.

At around 5pm on 20 August, the day of the concert, the All-Starr Band left the hotel for their sound-check. Ringo travelled to the venue separately, to allow him to give his only Irish interview to Dave Fanning, then a DJ with RTÉ's 2FM. The following is a transcript of the broadcast interview:

Dave: Ringo, how you doin'?

Ringo: Good thank you.

Dave: Okay! Tell me first about *Vertical Man*. Is it the first album in eight years?

Ringo: No! In six … ha, ha, ha!

Dave: Okay in six then. Why did it take so long?

Ringo: I don't think it's like waiting, it's just like a long time between albums. I did the *Time Takes Time* and then I was touring and I've been touring ever since actually, in America and Japan. And I thought, do I want to spend the time making an album … and actually *Vertical Man* came around by accident, because I just called Mark Hudson and he wrote the songs with me on the album, and I thought let's write and see if we can get on as writers. We knew each other as human beings, but not working together, and we wrote and we had a lot of fun … so then we went to Mark's studio then just to demo them, and about two hours in, I said, why are we making demos, let's make an album.

Dave: Yeah right!

Ringo: So it was a lot of fun because of that – we weren't planning to do it and then I did two weeks, two and a half weeks, on the album then I went on tour with the All-Starrs.

Dave: When you had toured before with the All-Starrs and it went so successful, was that one of the reasons why you said, hey, this is just one way of doing things, another way is in the studio making an album, let's do the album bit; I'm doing this 'live' thing, it's working fine?

Ringo: Sure, well my chops are up because I've been touring a lot and I really didn't want to go into the so-called 'real' studio and it's just a foreign environment really, when it gets right down to it, especially with the drummer being separated, they always put him beyond the glass and you're over there … so we did it in a very small room above a Chinese restaurant and there was no red light, no glass, nobody further away from me than you, and the kits, the bass player, the guitarist and it just felt to be so good that close, and so we thought, let's do the album. And with technology now, they were all directing, and I was live. You can do that now. You don't have to go to those special places.

Dave: By the same token you're very much in control of this one here. You're the front person, you're co-writing the songs, you're singing the stuff as well, so was there a little bit of, 'snap out of it lads, we got an album to make here' in the studio and you had to do that?

Ringo: No, there was a bit of 'la-de-da'. And things went wrong you know. I'm not going to die now over making an album, but if something went wrong and everyone started to say, 'Hey! La-de-da. Let's call the engineer he'll fix it, and we'll carry on later.' I'm not really into panic anymore.

Dave: Fine, so what about the writing then, I mean the co-writing?

Ringo: The writing is great, because though we were all writing it, I'm directing it 'cos I'm going to be the one singing it, so in the end we're saying what I want to say.

Dave: How do the collaborations with the co-writers happen? Is it you do the lyrics?

Ringo: No, we all kick off together. It can come from anywhere. There was a few piano licks I had. 'I Was Walkin'', I had the first three verses of that. I was on the treadmill for 'Without Understanding'. Just add a line and then we go on and work on it, and just see what happens, and it was coming pretty fast so that was the joy, so it was not like I did the lyrics and somebody did the melody – it was a real mish-mash, but if it was going somewhere I didn't want to go, I'd say let's change that and move this way.

Dave: And what about the musicians you're playing with now? I get the impression that if you had a Ringo Starr All-Starr Band number five and six, you'd like it to be [the same as] number four, because I get the impression that Number Four would be the best?

Ringo: Well, number four was the first one I put together twice. Usually I put the All-Starrs together and then we do as much as we can in a year, then I end it, then I put a new batch together. I mean, I've had Joe Walsh in a couple of the bands like the first one with Dr John and Billy Preston, and Rick … There really is no situation unless I put it together where I'm gonna play with Jack Bruce, Gary Brooker and Peter Frampton, so I have to, like, say, let's put the All-Starrs together. It's not like we're just going to pop in on each other.

Dave: Okay! So you've got Gary and Peter and Jack, and the names you've mentioned. What about anyone you ring up [saying] … I might have liked to have this guy or this person?

Ringo: Well, the thing that happens, you know, usually I phone up early in the year and say do you wanna have fun for the summer? It's never longer than two months and sometimes people are busy and so you have to move your situation around a bit, but anyone that is free so far has not said no.

Dave: You have on the album – you did 'Love Me Do', which famously you didn't play on the original Beatles single, but this time round you have this on the album, and Steve Tyler is there on harmonica. There was some track on the album, was it that one where somebody pulls Steve Tyler off?

Ringo: 'Drift Away'.

Dave: 'Drift Away', and why was he pulled off?

Ringo: His management pulled him off because he had the song on the *Armageddon Soundtrack* album from the movie, which went right to Number One, and they felt that it would detract from that, being on my album. I don't get it either, and, in a way, neither does he. I've spoke to him since and it was just one of those silly moves he made ...We only took a verse out, him singing the verse that Tom Petty, another pal, came and did for me. So you'd have to talk to the management, but it was a great case of la-de-da. We'd mixed it, mastered it, we were printing it, it was all ready to roll and suddenly we got this call and the label people going, what'll we do? I say, 'Eh la-dee-dah.' I didn't care if we took the track off completely really, but anyway we didn't, and I called Tom and Tom was great. I said, 'Tom ...' He said, 'I'll do it'. I said, 'I haven't told you what it is yet.' He said, 'I'll do it.' I said, 'Well I need you to go in and sing this verse for me.' And he said, 'Sure.'

Dave: And where does Alanis come into this? Alanis Morissette. Do you ask her in or was she just next door in the studio?

Ringo: No, she knows Mark Hudson and they came to visit 'cos she wanted to say 'hello', and I said, sure I'd like to meet Alanis, and the day she came we were doing 'Drift Away' and Steven Tyler was on it that day, and I was doing the final verse – he was doing the second verse – and I thought, hey, maybe it would be nice if Alanis did the third verse and I just asked her, would you like to do the third verse and she said sure. That's how it all fell into place like that. If she hadn't have knocked on the door, who knows what would have happened.

Dave: Okay! The album did take an awful lot less time than, say, a lot of other peoples' albums, but at the same time I get the impression that it was still too long for you, three months?

Ringo: Well no. I didn't spend that time consecutively. I did a couple of weeks, I went on tour. I did a couple of weeks, I came to Europe. We did it in LA, I did a couple more weeks. And then I went away again and then we finished it off in November–December, and mixed it in January.

Dave: And how much of the album features in the live set?

Ringo: Two, 'Love Me Do' of course, and 'La-De-Da', the single.

Dave: When you left the Beatles, you brought out two solo albums, one of songs you really liked from the past, and then a country 'n' western album. Then the third album came out and you said I'm going to do a bit more on this and really go for 'me'. This is a Ringo-kind-of-thing. And this album has three Top Tens, a couple of Number Ones. Were the other guys jealous?

Ringo: I don't think they were jealous, I think they were all shocked that I was the biggest seller at the time. That album just took off, you know, and it was good for me.

Dave: There was never the chance of having the other three on it?

Ringo: They were on it.

Dave: They were all on the album, but not at the same time.

Ringo: No, but that's the joy in my life. From that album that's the way I've tended to work, even with the All-Starrs live and all the albums since then. I've always had a lot of friends come on down and we have fun.

Dave: But all the albums since then, in between times you were making movies as well. Everything from *The Magic Christian* right up to *Caveman*. I've just mentioned two that got very good reviews for Ringo. Maybe the others didn't get as good reviews, but in other words you were Hollywood-ing, so did you ever think, I wouldn't mind this big Hollywood thing?

Ringo: Well I did try. I didn't say, I'm going to try Hollywood. I did think, well, maybe I'll make more movies and it didn't happen. I was just not invited to partake in anything real besides these two. I did a western in Spain called *Blindman* which was a lot of fun, and some TV spots like the Mae West Story, *Sextet*, with all small parts, so although I'd great hopes at that time ....I also did the David Essex movie, stuff like that, but it sort of faded out and that was the end of that. Now I really don't have that same interest that I had then. I'm more interested in what I'm doing now.

Dave: And that David Essex movie you mentioned, that was a huge success. Why didn't you do a number two of that?

Ringo: I didn't think it was as good. It was just about the guy who makes it and goes mad really and we all know that, so Adam Faith did it. He did a very nice job.

Dave: Ringo, you went a bit mad around that time. You were a big huge jet-setter, you spent a fortune gambling, drinking?

Ringo: I did. I did all that.

Dave: And did you enjoy it, while you were doing it?

Ringo: Well, you sort of do in the end. You think it's fun. It was fun at the time when you start, and suddenly that's all you're doing. They used to say I would go to any opening, even the opening of a letter ... and you just find yourself doing that, and you know it's a weird thing. It's a weird thing, but back to the movies, the last real movie I did was *Caveman*. At least I met Barbara on that so that was enough of that and we decided to get crazy together and you can see my whole career went downhill! I was too busy doing nothing really, making many plans but never getting up to actually doing anything about it till 1988, and I ended up in rehab and since then I'm working more and more and more.

It's like I was going downhill and now I'm running uphill.

Dave: And yeah, you have learned from it. You say 1988. In 1979 you were taken to hospital in Monte Carlo and you were like, in a bad way, and three months later you were back in it again?

Ringo: Yeah, well, you know, it's very difficult because it doesn't really matter what happens, or you know, you wake up in the morning and say 'never again'. I'm sure you've done that 'never again!'. I'm sure you have but you know it took a huge emotional, and, I feel, spiritual change for me to say 'that's that'. It's too crazy now. And you know I did seek help and got it.

Dave: Do you think you just had too much time on your hands?

Ringo: Well, I could have been busy, that's the deal. I mean I could have been busy, as you say, I could have put the energy into movies. I was putting some or very little energy into records and they all just dive-bombed, you know.

Dave: Just on the subject of drumming itself, you often said, 'All I want to do is be a drummer in a band.' I get the impression with this thing going on, it's the exact same thing. That's all you want to do?

Ringo: Well you know, it's interesting. From when I was thirteen and I only wanted to be a drummer, only wanted … didn't want to be a guitarist or an organ player, anything … and I was eighteen and a half and I got my first kit and that was it, that was the joy, the dream was starting to come true and then, like three months in, I only wanted to play with good players and then that dream came true, and you know that's still coming true in many ways. I'm still playing with these great people, so you know I have to look at the energy I have now and where I want to put it and I was so dissipated before, like all over, everywhere, but not doing anything that I'm focused on, just playing. This year of course we have the record, which we did last year, but mainly it's just playing.

Dave: Okay, well one of the things changing-wise for me was, like, when I saw a band change from A to B … [it] was with the single 'Rain' by the Beatles around '64, '65 … and the biggest change in that, the biggest noise, the biggest difference from what I'd heard before was your contribution. I mean, would you see 'Rain' up there as one of the greats in [the same way] that I would?

Ringo: I see it as one of the greats, but I also see it as one of the … for me, it's always when people say, 'What record did you like to drum on?' I always say, 'Rain', because I feel it was the first song I ever played like that. I mean it was a total style change for me and I've never really played like that since. You know what I mean, it's like one of those places in your life, you're off and then it happens and then it's over, and I'm still playing well, but I'm not playing like that.

Dave: There's another thing too. Like, I mean, take the Beatles 'thing' of the Ed Sullivan time. There was such a big thing. One of the things about you on the drums there was, and bands have said this since, that they saw you on TV and like you had the drums up high. Wow! And also you didn't have a chopstick in your hand, you were actually doing this [imitates banging down hard]. Were you ever aware of any of these things that you were doing, any of this?

Ringo: Well, I was really aware that, you know, I wanted to be part of the band and I had the smallest kit possible, so I would look … so you would see me. Do you know what I mean? And then we got the riser. That was just the best, I mean I was suddenly part of it and it is one of the few bands that was [like that] … John, Paul, George and Ringo. It wasn't Mick and Keith and the Stones. It wasn't so-and-so and them, but you know, at the time, I was conscious about the small drum kit. I held the sticks like that 'cos I didn't know any better, you know like front-loading like, that's how you hit things okay, and the riser, you know I can't honestly say I phoned up Ed Sullivan and said you got to put me on a big riser because that's how I like it. It was there and I got on it.

Dave: And have you been in love with the Ludwigs ever since?

Ringo: Oh, I've only ever played Ludwigs. I love them. I mean you know they're just … I feel I know them really well … and the sound I get from them is the sound I like. You know I changed once, I got another make and it didn't last weeks. I gave them to the kids. I just think they're, you know … they went through a patch … you know my early ones were really cool drums and they went through a patch where they weren't so good, but now, [in] the last sort of, five years, they've been making them well again, so I've been using them.

Dave: Okay! When people go and see you live on this tour and with the band, I mean people can hear everything now, modern technology … and it's the end of the millennium and all the rest. There's all sorts of things you can use, even though you can use click-tracks, but I know you don't?

Ringo: I can't play to click-tracks. I play with my soul, so … and I'm quite a good time-keeper you know, and I come from that school where we didn't have click-clack, it's like it gets in my way, so I can't really play, it gets me uptight really. Well my son, I mean it's nothing to him, and to the kids it's nothing.

Dave: Zak was in the band at one stage?

Ringo: He did two tours with me. That was great. 'How you doin' son? Fine Dad.' Ha, ha, ha.

Dave: When I mentioned that about all the technology that's there now and everybody in the auditorium can hear perfectly. There's one funny bit, like, say, the Shea Stadium thing. There you all are there. You're all just laughing at one stage?

Ringo: I think it's the hysterics of the crowd.

Dave: But can people hear anything?

Ringo: We didn't think they could hear too much because we knew we couldn't. So I'm always watching the front lines, foot-tapping or behind, bobbing, all the heads moving. Okay, we're up to that part. If they moved we're into harmonies, oh yeah, second chorus, you know what I mean. I couldn't really hear what was happening, so you sort of do it … [it] was sort of, you know, like braille out there for us. But it worked and I've always felt people never came to hear us in those days. They came just to see these people you know, these mop-tops.

Dave: Okay then. One of the things you keep talking about at the moment is fun, fun, fun, all the time at the moment, that the only reason to make this album *Vertical Man* – the only reason to be on stage is to have a good time and enjoy it?

Ringo: To play great music and have fun.

Dave: Now, one of the last ways for us to see you guys was on the *Let It Be* movie. You were having a crap time in the studio?

Ringo: Well yeah, we were breaking up and 'breaking up is hard to do!' It is ... we were going through this madness and, you know, everyone was growing up, you know. I didn't really want to be in the studio all the time anymore. I wanted to go and play with the kids and go on holiday, do stuff and, you know, the input from the major writers, John and Paul, wasn't close anymore, and John wanted to do his stuff. George just really wanted to be in India and Woodstock and if you look at Side Two of *Abbey Road*, they're all just short songs. It was like no one was finishing anything, so we finished. It was just time really. Eight years is a long time for any band to be together. I mean look at the bands today. You've seen bands that have been around four or five years, that's the end of it. They've had enough. It's hard to live with other people for that length of time.

Dave: Sure, but by the same token – seeing as you are out live now, doing it – if you take, for instance, the last gig the Beatles played officially. [It] was Candlestick Park in San Francisco in August '66 and that was, like, before Sgt Pepper and everything else. So then if you take '68, which is what we were talking about there – is there anyway at all you might have said, maybe, what we should do, is do a tour? Just because George says he doesn't want to tour again, maybe we just should, because going live brings you all together?

Ringo: I never said go on tour. I mean if we have had the options now, what sound we can put up there, you know all the technology maybe, but we still in, sort of, '65, we ended all that, w...ooh! What happened in '65 and '66, there really was not a lot of technology, it started later and suddenly I'd all these crazy things. Well let's give you a billion watts, let's give you a speaker as big as this room, but it was too late, we'd got in that studio mode and also it was pretty hectic and we'd no time for ourselves on the road, you know we would take a whole floor of a hotel and there'd be just the four of us: 'how you doin', not too bad thanks.'

Dave: So were you glad just to let it all go, when you see things like Yoko's double bed in the corner of the recording studio?

Ringo: It was very strange but ... eh! ...You know it was just very strange.

Dave: But it used to be just the five of you. George Martin and you guys?

Ringo: Or it used to be the five of us, but things changed, and any change it'd all get a bit crazy. Last question.

Dave: Okay ten albums, ten million albums. You've sold ten million solo albums.

Ringo: Have I? Is that all? Ha, ha, ha!

Dave: That's pretty good. Jeepers, what do you mean that's all?

Ringo: That must be just in Ireland. Ha, ha, ha!

Dave: Are you happy with a figure like that?

Ringo: Sure. I'd be happy with twenty. I'm only human.

Dave: Okay, then let's put it this way. You took a few years off then?

Ringo: No, I'm happy. I made albums. I'm not in control, I'm just blessed that, well, mainly the early ones, people love them as we've talked about before and you know you still make them and you put them out and you gotta see where it drops.

Dave: *The Anthology* album came out three years ago and you worked on that and did all the interviews for that and there was the videos, etcetera ... They've sold about twenty million copies and they tell us that ten million of those sales ...

Ringo: ... were sold to me!

Dave: No, or not in Ireland ... were sold to people between the ages of 12 and 25. Every single one of them not born when the Beatles had broken up?

Ringo: Isn't that great?

Dave: Yeah! I was just going to say that must make you feel great?

Ringo: Of all the stuff you talked about, the break up ... the this ... that ... the end result of the recording life of the Beatles still goes on. Kids are still buying it because it still holds up, so that's the bit I'm proud of, being involved with those three guys and kids today are still buying that.

Dave: Do you ever meet people who say, 'this is Ringo Starr', and they go, 'who'?

Ringo: Oh yeah!

Dave: ... and they say 'Thomas the Tank Engine'?

Ringo: Yeah! A lot of mothers show me little children, or show [me to] little children ... saying there he is ... and they're all saying, 'What do you mean Mum?' Really, you know ... and also they say, 'There's Ringo from the Beatles.' You know they don't really know. 'It's for me Mum!', that's the best one, 'The autograph, it's for me Mum.'

Dave: What do you like to do besides playing as a drummer?

Ringo: I like to paint. I like to paint, I like to cook.

Dave: And what do you mean by paint. What kind of painting?

Ringo: Naïve. Two lessons.

Dave: Have you heard The Chemical Brothers recently?

Ringo: No.

Dave: The Chemical Brothers have [recorded] 'Tomorrow Never Knows'.

Ringo: Oh!

Dave: You mean you didn't get any money for that, did you?

Ringo: I didn't write it.

Dave: Yeah! Of course that's true, because they have used that on one of their songs.

Ringo: It's a good song. I like it myself.

Dave: All right, I think we have to go.

Ringo: Yeah, we have to go.

Dave: Thanks very much. Mind yourself.

Ringo: Thank you Dave.

Dave: Thanks a million.

Ringo: Take care.

Dave: Fair play. Thank you.

Paul McCartney Interview with Tom Dunne, Today FM, 27 May 2003

According to Tom, 'I was in a meeting when Paul called, and Jedda Downey, my producer at the time, came in and said, "Paul McCartney is on the phone." The only thing I could say to her was, "He used to be in the Beatles you know." So we got everything to record the interview, DAT machines, tape recorders, you name it, just to make sure we got it recorded.'

Tom: Hello Paul.

Paul: Yeah! Hi, Tom.

Tom: How are you?

Paul: Loveleee ...

Tom: Very nice to talk to you, and very nice to welcome you to playing in Dublin again after so many years.

Paul: Ah! It's exciting for me man.

Tom: It's very exciting for the crowd and the audience as well. I have to say it's one of the most looked-forward-to gigs in ages. I just saw some of the stuff of the Red Square gig, which some people are comparing for atmosphere to Shea Stadium.

Paul: It was just something else. I mean you know, I've done, you know ... obviously we did 'Back In The USSR' in the show, so we were ready to do it, and I thought it's gonna go down well. But there's just no preparing yourself for actually being in Red Square and singing about Moscow girls and USSR and things like that to the *actual* people themselves. It was just phenomenonal ... you know, it was just like war. It was one of them ... you had to be there and you couldn't imagine it. I even couldn't imagine it you know, and suddenly I was like, I'm here, I'm doing it! They're there and we're in bloody Red Square. Unbelievable!

Tom: It's hard to believe that it still can get to you after all the gigs you've done and the amazing experiences you've had in your life. But I was in Barcelona, I saw the gig in Barcelona, what really struck me there was … I know you once said, 'All you need is love', but the amount of love at that gig, you know, how much love do you need?

Paul: Well, you need all you can get mate. I think we all do. You know, there's that much of it around … but, as you say, the gigs, we've been really lucky with this tour because we started off thinking, ah ya know, it's gonna be a nice tour, we've got a good band, we knew the numbers were good and we enjoyed our rehearsals. But once we started to get out there, and we started up in America, like you say. The sort of love in the audience like … whoa! … and it's feeding back to us and we start to react to that and, you know … just go, 'Whoa, God this is fantastic', you know! So this tour is built that way and it's just lovely for me to be bringing it home, you know, getting … getting it to the homeland, bringing it to the people who I want to show it off to.

Tom: And does it get to you, feeling all that love in the crowd and doing the songs, you see footage of yourself behind you. What kind of stuff goes through your mind?

Paul: Yeah! Well, you can't ask what goes through your mind because all sorts … you know, and it can really be anything from like, honestly like, the most crazy mundane things about something you were thinking that day and you're on autopilot, but mainly it does get to you, you know. I remember opening up on this tour, last year in Mexico, which was very passionate. Mexico City, big, big gig and they really know how to be an audience there.

They were crackers, you know, and normally it builds, you know, and we go to 'Hey Jude', or 'Let It Be', or something like that … [and then] they're really there, but this was from the word go! I just went, 'You say yes', 'Hello Goodbye' …and they were on it. They were jumping up and down and the noise was unbelievable.

Our roadies were all holding their ears and these guys are used to being in front of big stacks, you know, and we said, 'it's bloody deafening', you know. But it was fantastic, and even though the song wasn't an emotional one, just 'Hello Goodbye', it really choked me. I could barely get it out, gosh! You know you're doing this for me. It was like ... whoa, whoa ... that's lovely, little Mexicans ... ah! It was great.

Tom: So listen, tell me a little bit about Ireland. I know it has a special place in your heart and stuff, but what kind of special emotions will it have for you tonight to play here?

Paul: Well, you know, as you say, I've always loved the Irish people, coming from Liverpool you know – we consider that the capital of Ireland anyway – and yes, you know my family is Liverpool Irish. My mother came over from Co Monaghan when she was eleven and she became a nurse ... and sort of trained to be a nurse and a mid-wife and all of that in Liverpool ... I wasn't really conscious of that till much later in my life.

You just go, you know, it's your Mum and Dad in Liverpool. You don't think of all that stuff, but Heather and I got married here last year, in Castle Leslie, and that was just great you know. And it was really lovely to come home to my Mum's county and then to be with Irish people at that special moment, you know. So it's become, of late, a particular special place for us and ... I say we love the Irish people for their good fun, they've got big hearts – my kind of people.

Tom: Have you any surprises planned for tonight?

Paul: We're not really ... no. Oh! Wait a sec ... I'm looking at a copper here [looking out the window]. I'm looking at a copper there, he's in the motorcade here and he's ... big bits have just come off his bike ... it's hanging ...ha, ha, ha! Oh dear, the things that come up, he's pulled over. No, we're not thinking of any particular changes in numbers. I've mainly just wanted to bring the show home and bring it to all our sort of ... Liverpool [has] obviously been the main home town ... but places like Dublin, London, you know, all the places where we've been and have special attachment with ... so we're basically bringing a straight show home. We might wangle a couple of little things, you never know. We just sometimes might do that.

Tom: It's a fantastic show, Paul, and I'm absolutely dying to see it again. Would you go out again after this, seeing as you are enjoying yourself so much?

Paul: Oh yeah! Yeah! You know, I think people you know always ask, particularly as the years roll by, 'Is this your last tour?' It always takes me by surprise. Why would you think that? You know, of course, there is a reason why they would think it, but no, there's no thought in my mind and I don't even think when I'm 64 or 65 I'll be retiring.

Tom: I'm glad to hear that. Paul, it's been absolutely great talking to you and I hope you've a great show tonight and again, on behalf of all the fans in Ireland, you're very welcome and I hope you enjoy Ireland, and the gig, and you'll come back to us as soon as you can!

Paul: Alright man! Well, I know we will, and from me and Heather and the band and all our crew, we extend lots of love to you and all your listeners.

Tom: Paul, thanks very much.

Paul: See you Tom.

Tom: Thanks very much, bye now.

Paul: Ta-ta.

Tom: Bye.

Appendix 6

Irish Broadcasting and The Beatles

Once the madness of Beatlemania was over, Irish broadcasting organisations did not offer much in the way of Beatle-related programming until the late 1970s – and, even then, there was very little until after the death of John Lennon in 1980. The main purveyor of Beatle-related broadcasting in Ireland has been the Irish state broadcaster, Radio Telefís Éireann (RTÉ), but the wider Irish media, both licensed and unlicensed, has also provided programming and their activities are listed here. Location details for the broadcasts are given in a note at the end of the appendix. We have included only Irish radio and television programmes that have focused exclusively, and at length, on the group as a whole and on the subsequent activities of the group's individual members.

RTÉ, Dublin Airport. *In Town.* 7 November 1963

This was the date when the Irish media first met the Beatles face to face. On their arrival at Dublin Airport they were interviewed by RTÉ reporter, Frank Hall, for the RTÉ magazine television programme *In Town*. See Chapter 2 p 13 for a full transcript of the interview.

RTÉ (TV), *The Showband Show.* 7 November 1963

RTÉ's second interview of the day with the Beatles, this time conducted at the Gresham hotel. Paul Russell was the interviewer.

UTV. *Ulster News.* 8 November 1963

The opening shot of this one-minute interview conducted by Jimmy Robinson showed George Harrison trying to push John Lennon onto the Dublin–Belfast road just as a white van passed in the background. See Chapter 2, p 38 for the transcript of this interview.

BBC News, Belfast. *Six Ten.* 8 November 1963

The BBC's interviewer was Sally Ogle.

Granada Television. *Scene At 6.30.* 25 November 1963

See Appendix 5, p 158, for a full transcript of the dialogue between Gay Byrne and his special guests.

It was not until 1964, that the Irish media would have the opportunity to cover Beatle activities in Ireland again, when John, Cynthia, George and Pattie took their Easter break at Dromoland Castle.

RTÉ Radio 2. *The Lennon Tapes.* December 1981

In 1981 RTÉ began broadcasting this five-part BBC Radio series, featuring John Lennon's final interview with Andy Peebles. On Saturday 6 December 1980 John and Yoko gave a lengthy interview to Peebles. The session continued into the early hours of Sunday morning. The interview later became the radio series and also a book. The interview itself was later released in the UK on an official BBC CD, *John and Yoko: the Interview*. Pat Kenny introduced each RTÉ broadcast and parts of the series have since been used to supplement Irish Lennon and Beatles documentaries.

RTÉ Radio 2. *The B.P. Fallon Orchestra.* 1981–1987

B.P. Fallon is one of Ireland's most enduring and prolific Beatles programme makers. He began to appear on radio and TV programmes in Ireland in the 1960s and then moved to the UK where he became involved with a string of major music acts in the 1970s as a PR guru – most notably working for Led Zeppelin, Marc Bolan and Roy Harper. A brief connection with John and Yoko led to his appearance on *Top of the Pops* where he took part in a performance of 'Instant Karma'.

Fallon returned to Ireland in the 1980s and resumed broadcasting with RTÉ. During this period he produced the documentary *The Songs the Beatles Gave Away* for RTÉ Radio 2. The programme comprised a full run-down of songs the group had supplied to other artists – everything from 'Hello Little Girl' for Gerry and the Pacemakers to 'Penna' for Carlos Mendez.

His next major Beatles programme was *Mersey Beep, Liverpool 21 Years after the Beatles*. The programme was broadcast on 5 October 1984 and featured a series of location recordings made in Liverpool. During the course of the programme, Fallon took listeners on a walk in the footsteps of the Beatles' city: Beatle birthplaces and the now defunct Beatles Museum. The programme included an interview with Paul McCartney's brother, Mike.

By this time, B.P. Fallon's programmes were broadcast under the series title *The B.P. Fallon Orchestra* (*The BPFO*). Later programmes in the series featured interviews with one-time Wings guitarist Henry McCullough and session drummer Andy Newmark. McCullough gave a warts-and-all account of his life in the music business, including his time with Wings. Newmark gave a fascinating insight into the making of Lennon's last studio album, *Double Fantasy*. RTÉ Radio 2 broadcast this programme in late 1983. By the middle of the 1980s, B.P. Fallon had begun a series of programmes for RTÉ Radio entitled *Beep go the Beatles*. The format for the programmes included a good helping of Beatles music, lots of Beatles facts and a weekly guest. One guest (by telephone) was Bono, who told Fallon about childhood Christmases watching Beatles' movies such as *A Hard Day's Night* – as well as memories of hearing Lennon on BBC Radio singing Arthur Alexander's 'Anna' and 'Soldier of Love'.

The crowning glory for this phase of Fallon's programme-making was his interview with George Harrison. The programme, *Beep and the Beatle*, which was transmitted in two parts, was first broadcast on RTÉ Radio 2 on the evening of 6 December 1987. The interview topics ranged from Harrison's Beatle days to his spiritual beliefs, punk rock, the Concert for Bangladesh, film production and his recent chart comeback. The interview was recorded at the Knightsbridge headquarters of his Dark Horse Records company and was part of Harrison's promotion of his new album, *Cloud Nine*. The programme was subsequently re-broadcast by independent commercial radio station, Today FM, at Christmas 2002. As part of this re-broadcast, Fallon gave a brief summary of the original interview.

RTÉ Radio 1. *George Martin: The Fifth Beatle*. 9 December 1982

The Beatles' recording manager, George Martin, often dubbed the 'fifth Beatle', has made himself available for numerous interviews on Irish radio over the years. One of the earliest known was the interview on 9 December 1982 with broadcaster Myles Dungan, to mark the second anniversary of John Lennon's death in December 1982. The programme contained a mix of Beatles music and archive interviews, as well as a contemporary interview with Martin himself. Dungan's RTÉ colleague, Brendan Balfe, also produced a programme on the life and times of George Martin for his quick-moving *Profile in Sound* radio show. In May 1998, Martin was interviewed by RTÉ's rock guru, Dave Fanning. The interview was aired on his weekly music video show, *2TV*, which simultaneously broadcast on radio and television on Sunday mornings at that time.

Radio Nova. Beatles' Day. Easter Monday, 1984

On Easter Monday 1984, Radio Nova, the now defunct Dublin radio station, broadcast a day-long sequence of Beatles programmes presented by the station's bank of presenters. As part of the broadcast, Nova managed to persuade Allan Williams (the Beatles' former promoter) and Bob Wooler (former Cavern DJ) to take part in one slot. Sean Newman, who was a garage mechanic pal of Williams and the man who serviced the original vehicle for the Beatles' first journey to Hamburg, also took part.

RTÉ Radio 2. *Ringo's Yellow Submarine.* 1984

ABC Radio in America transmitted a 26-week series called *Ringo's Yellow Submarine: A Voyage Through the Beatles' Music*, featuring the former Beatle in the role of DJ reminiscing about the Beatles. The shows were all pre-taped at Ringo's London home in Tittenhurst Park during April and May 1983. Ringo narrated his recollections of the Beatles years to accompany the set list. RTÉ Radio 2 bought the series but reworked it, inserting chunks into its existing Saturday afternoon broadcasting schedule over the course of 1984. Irish audiences have never heard the full 26-week series on Irish radio.

RTÉ Radio 2. *Sgt Pepper's 21st Anniversary Special.* 6 June 1988

Mark Cagney marked the 21st anniversary of the release of *Sgt Pepper* by devoting a two-hour special to the making of the album. He played the album in its entirety and threw in many facts and figures, as well as playing 'Strawberry Fields Forever', 'Penny Lane' and 'Only A Northern Song', three tracks that were recorded at the time of the making of the album but did not make it onto the finished product.

RTÉ Radio 1. *The Arts Show.* 18 January 1990

This edition of the daily arts and entertainment show presented by Mike Murphy featured a report and review by RTÉ regular, Jimmy Greeley. The question-and-answer session between Murphy and Greeley was punctuated by a recording of a brief interview conducted with Paul McCartney the previous week, backstage at Wembley Arena in London during his 1989–1990 tour. During the course of the interview, McCartney gave a few bars of 'Give Ireland Back To The Irish'. Greeley went on to ask McCartney the age-old question, 'When are you going to play in Ireland?' McCartney answered by saying, 'It's up to the promoters, we don't have a date for Liverpool yet.'

RTÉ Radio 2. *McCartney On McCartney*. June 1990

On the first Saturday of June at 12 noon in 1990, RTÉ Radio 2 began broadcasting this special eight-part series, originally a BBC Radio 1 production. In the series, McCartney talks to the BBC DJ, Mike Read, about his career, from Beatlemania to the present day. Read had originally recorded the lengthy interview with Paul back in 1987 at the International Christian Community Studios in Eastbourne, Sussex. As well being aired on Irish radio, this interview was heard in the US and on the BBC World Service in sixteen half-hour episodes.

RTÉ Radio 1. *They were our Ecstasy*. 13 March 1993

RTÉ Radio 1 broadcast this 45-minute documentary focusing on the Beatles' Dublin visit of November 1963. During the course of the broadcast, people who were at the November 1963 concert were interviewed.

RTÉ Radio 1. *The Gay Byrne Show*. 7 November 1993

Broadcast on a daily basis, Gay's show was a legendary radio programme, which had already run for over 20 years by 1993. This broadcast was given over to mark the 30th anniversary of the Beatles' 1963 performance in Ireland. Numerous callers telephoned the show to give their memories of the group's visit.

Anna Livia FM. *City Limits*. 25 January 1994

This edition of the weekly Anna Livia radio show which aired every Saturday morning was partly given over to mark the 25th anniversary of the Beatles' Apple Rooftop performance back in January 1969. The Quarrymen, Ireland's only Beatles tribute band, played live from the rooftop of the Anna Livia radio station and the 45-minute set was broadcast live – but the session continued long after the broadcast came to an end at noon.

Anna Livia FM. *The Beatles' Christmas Day Show.* 25 December 1994
This one-hour broadcast made use of the Beatles' Christmas records that were sent out to the Beatles fan club members in the 1960s.

RTÉ Radio 2/ RTÉ Two (TV). *The Beatles Anthology.* October 1995
This simultaneous TV and radio broadcast was an hour-long visual press release from Apple Corps to promote the full version of the *Anthology*. It was headlined with these words: 'The definitive history of the Beatles will be told in the band's own words in a five-hour special.' The promo was packed with interviews and videos of all four members of the band – John's were taken from the Apple archives.

RTÉ TV broadcast the five-part version of *The Beatles Anthology* in full in November 1995. It was estimated that throughout the world there were 400 million people who watched the television series.

RTÉ One (TV). *Kenny Live.* Saturday 13 January 1996
On this broadcast, Pete Best revealed he had only visited Ireland twice since 1968. This trip was only to be a flying visit. In the course of the interview, Pat Kenny asked Best, 'What about the possibility of meeting up with the remaining Beatles?' Best went on to say, 'If you had asked me that question seven or eight years ago, I would have said "No way", but now it's becoming more likely.' He was also asked if he had any Irish roots himself. 'Yes,' said Best, 'my grandparents are Irish, but I'm not sure from which county – I think it's Limerick.'

RTÉ Radio 1. *Icons.* February 1997
February 1997 saw the start of a 13-part series in which the enduring rock guru, B.P. Fallon, profiled his favourite musicians. Fallon has met, at one stage or another, just about everybody who ever mattered in rock 'n' roll. John Lennon was featured in the series.

RTÉ 2FM. *Up-Beat.* 17 June 1997
RTÉ disc jockey, Gareth O'Callaghan, conducted a phone interview with Paul McCartney on the day before his 55th birthday. During the course of the interview, O'Callaghan and McCartney were joined on another line by Elvis Costello. The two artists had previously collaborated on McCartney's 1989 album *Flowers in the Dirt*. After a short chat with McCartney, Costello broke into a rendition

of 'Happy Birthday' in the style of Elvis Presley. O'Callaghan went on to ask McCartney the age-old question, yet again, 'When are you going to play in Ireland?' McCartney answered by saying, 'One day, I hope. I love coming to Ireland.'

RTÉ One (TV). *Kenny Live.* Saturday 23 May 1998
Surely a unique moment this, when Sir George Martin and Julian Lennon came together for an Irish television appearance with Pat Kenny. George talks about his Beatles years and Julian speaks of his 'distant' relationship with Yoko and his even more distant relationship with Sean Lennon. In a previous series Cynthia Lennon had also been interviewed by presenter Pat Kenny for the same show.

Sir George Martin and Julian Lennon come together for an Irish TV Appearance in 1998. *(Mick Lynch)*

Today FM. *Murray and Mackey.* 7 November 1998
As part of a morning show broadcast by Dublin-based Today FM, John Lennon's original Quarrymen (Rod Davis, Colin Hanton, Len Garry, Eric Griffiths and Pete Shotton) appeared with the Beatles' 'Mr Fixit', Alistair Taylor, to take part in an interview. The Beatles Fan Club (Beatles Ireland) had invited the six to take part in that year's Beatlemania weekend, which was held at the Castle Inn and Olympia Theatre.

During the interview, Pete Shotton told the audience about the time he flew by helicopter with John and Yoko to the remote island of Dorinish. The Quarrymen went on to play to a packed house at the Olympia Theatre that night.

RTÉ One (TV). *Open House.* 6 November 1999
On this occasion the host Marty Whelan interviewed Alf Bicknell, chauffeur to the Beatles. Bicknell told Whelan that he had joined the Beatles' team during their British tour late in 1964. He also mentioned that he was with the Beatles in August 1965 when they met Elvis Presley. 'He shook my hand and called me "Sir",' he recalled.

He was present at the group's last concert at Candlestick Park in San Francisco in 1966. After his appearance on this TV broadcast, Bicknell was to be the guest of the Beatles Ireland fan club as part of their Dublin Beatlemania weekend.

Anna Livia FM. *City Style.* 8 December 1999

On this day, Anna Livia broadcast programming dedicated to John Lennon and dubbed it 'John Lennon Day'. On the afternoon show, *City Style*, Harry Prytherch, former drummer with the Remo Four and leading authority on all things Mersey Beat spoke about the Beatles, John Lennon and Liverpool of the 1960s. Also taking part was the bass player with the Irish Beatles tribute band, the Quarrymen, Fran King, who spoke of his recent work with Sir George Martin at the National Concert Hall in Dublin.

On the telephone line from the UK was John Isherwood, a colourful folk singer credited with bringing humour to the folk scene in the sixties. The Beatles also signed Isherwood to Apple. Isherwood had actually received a royalty cheque from George Harrison dated 19 March 1970 for 1*s* 10*d* (just under 10p): Isherwood had never cashed the cheque. The last guest speaker was Pete Brennan, President of the Irish Beatles fan club, Beatles Ireland.

RTÉ 2FM. *Roots of Rock.* 8 December 1999

The programme featured Paul talking about some of his favourite songs by other artists and how they influenced his own music. The programme was recorded in Paul's home studio in Sussex and was first broadcast on the BBC World Service on 20 October 1999. This programme became a five-part series for the US and a special two-hour compilation of *Roots of Rock* was transmitted on BBC Radio 2 on Christmas Day in the UK. RTÉ only ever broadcast the 29-minute version.

RTÉ 2FM. *The Dave Fanning Show.* 8 December 1999

This day's transmission of Dave Fanning's late night show was RTÉ's penultimate programme in a day-long tribute to John Lennon and the Beatles. The state broadcaster had given a lot of airtime to the music of the Beatles over the course of the day to mark the 19th anniversary of the ex-Beatle's death.

Scott Maher and Fran King of The Classic Beatles with Sir George Martin at the National Concert Hall, Dublin, in 1999. *(Damian Smyth)*

For the first part of tonight's show, parts of the 'Beatles Tapes' by David Wigg, who had interviewed the band over the later part of the 1960s, were broadcast. Most of the music for this broadcast was taken from *The Beatles* (popularly known as *The White Album*) and *Revolver*. Fanning also used his interviews with Ringo, recorded at the Point Theatre just before his Dublin gig on 20 August 1998. (See Appendix 5, p 163, for the full transcript.)

RTÉ 2FM. *The Lennon Tapes*. 8–9 December 1999

From 11pm –1am, 2FM broadcast the whole of Andy Peebles' interview with Lennon. *The Lennon Tapes* had first been broadcast by RTÉ back in late 1981 (see entry on p 182).

RTÉ Radio 1. *A Night to Remember*. 20 December 1999

The show was an orchestral night of Beatles' music, conducted by Sir George Martin, and recorded in front of a live audience by RTÉ Radio at the National Concert Hall on 26 October 1999, but not broadcast until December of that year.

A week before the concert in Dublin, George Martin and his son Giles, who co-produced the show, were to take part with all involved in a week of rehearsals at The Factory, a rehearsal studio in Dublin's docklands area.

For this concert Martin was to call on home-grown Irish talent for his guest singers. All were première artists and respected in their own areas of music, such as Liam Ó Maonlaí, Brian Kennedy, Jimmy MacCarthy, Leslie Dowdall, Sean Keane, Eimear Quinn, and Fran King and Scott Maher of the Quarrymen. Strangely enough, Ireland was the second last country to see this orchestral production.

At the start of June, George Martin had taken his show to Israel. The country had missed out on Beatlemania in the 1960s as the government in power at the time was convinced that the raucous strains of the Beatles' music would corrupt their young.

RTÉ 2FM / RTÉ Two (TV). *2TV*. 9 November 2000

As part of a radio and television simulcast, RTÉ's Dave Fanning set aside part of his programme to the then recently released Beatles album of 27 Number One singles. The broadcast included interviews with Ringo, Paul and George Martin, as well as a few Beatles videos. At the top of the programme Fanning re-broadcast the 1963 interview by RTÉ's Frank Hall with the Beatles at Dublin Airport.

RTÉ Two (TV) / TG4 TV. *John Lennon Night.* 8 December 2000

To mark the 20th anniversary of Lennon's death, two Irish television stations, RTÉ Two and the Irish language station, TG4, presented a night of programming about the life and times of John Lennon.

Network 2 broadcast *Imagine*, an 81-minute colour film directed and produced by John and Yoko, released in 1972. Also broadcast was the 1969 'bed- in' and the 1972 concert 'John Lennon Live in New York City'. TG4 broadcast a programme called *Oíche Lennon* in which fourteen Irish artists sang some of Lennon's back-catalogue. Also broadcast by TG4 was the film *Yellow Submarine.*

UTV, Belfast. *The Kelly Show.* 30 November 2001

This chat show was an offering of the ITV network, serving Ulster and based in Belfast. On this occasion Alf Bicknell, the Beatles' chauffeur from the days of Beatlemania, was interviewed as part of a tribute to the late George Harrison, who had recently passed away. The promoter Trevor Kane who booked the Beatles for the King's Hall at the Royal Showgrounds, Balmoral, Belfast, on Monday 2 November 1964, was also a guest on the same show.

RTÉ 2FM. *Fanning and the Beatle.* 10–11 December 2001

For this programme, presenter Dave Fanning and producer Jim Lockhart travelled to London to conduct an interview with Paul McCartney in his MPL (McCartney Productions Limited) offices in Soho Square. As part of the broadcast McCartney talks to Fanning about life after Linda, 9/11, and the memories of his firefighter father, being 'lucky enough' to write with John Lennon and his new solo album, *Driving Rain.*

RTÉ 2FM. *Beatles Special.* 1 January 2002

This New Year's Day programme was a four-hour broadcast, featuring a mix of presenter Dave Fanning's own recorded interviews with Ringo and Paul. The programme also used parts of B.P. Fallon's interview with George Harrison and the Andy Peebles BBC interview with John and Yoko, recorded in New York in December 1980.

Anna Livia Radio FM. *Backbeat.* 23 February 2002

A George Harrison special, presented by DJ Ken Martin with guest speaker Pete Brennan. Also part of this programme, on the phone line from Liverpool, was Jacky Spencer, from the Liverpool Tourist Board. Jacky told the Anna Livia audience about a host of artists and bands who were to perform at a charity event the next night in Liverpool to mark what would have been the former Beatle's 59th birthday.

RTÉ 2FM. *The Dave Fanning Show.* 17 June 2002

Once again, RTÉ's rock guru Dave Fanning found time to honour Paul McCartney on his nightly radio programme the day before his 60th birthday. It was just over a week since Paul and Heather's wedding at Castle Leslie. As part of the tribute, Fanning first played the Beatles' song 'When I'm 64', followed by part of an interview that he had made with McCartney in London back in December 2001. Pete Brennan contributed a description of his meeting with Paul and Heather the day before their wedding at Castle Leslie.

RTÉ One (TV). *Open House.* 8 October 2002

Once again this afternoon chat boasted a Beatle-related guest. Allan Williams and his wife Beryl were in Dublin to help promote Irish actor Ronan Wilmot's stage musical based on the life of Williams himself. Both guests talked about the play and the formative years of the Beatles and their trip to Hamburg with the group in August 1960.

Alan Williams and wife Beryl on Irish TV in 2002. *(Pete Brennan)*

Tom Dunne, Paul McCartney and Dave Fanning. (*Bill Bernstein*)

Today FM. *Pet Sounds.* 27 May 2003

Tom Dunne conducted a short interview with Paul McCartney live on air, as Paul was driven from his Dublin hotel to that night's concert at the RDS Arena. This was Paul's only radio interview during his Irish visit. (See Appendix 5, p 177, for the full transcript)

RTÉ 2FM. *The Gerry Ryan Show.* 28 August 2003

Gerry Ryan interviewed former Beatle Pete Best by telephone from the Riverbank House Hotel in Wexford for his morning show. Best was in Ireland to take part in a show called *An Audience with Pete Best.* Much of the interview by Ryan was to cover the sacking of Best from the Beatles in August 1962 and how it still mystifies him to this day.

News Talk 106. 18 September 2003

Paul McCartney's long-standing press officer, Geoff Baker, was interviewed about the forthcoming re-issue of the Beatles album, *Let It Be (Naked).* Speaking from Paul's London office on behalf of Apple, he indicated that Apple was also about to release *Let It Be* on DVD.

Formerly, Baker had been a show-business writer for the London-based *Daily Star* and became Paul's press agent at the close of the 1980s, after writing a piece about Paul and Linda, which Paul liked. During August 2004, Geoff Baker stood down from this position and a new press officer was appointed.

RTÉ 2FM. *Let It Be (Naked) Special.* 17 November 2003

This broadcast consisted of the EMI press kit with which Dave Fanning had been supplied. His Beatles expertise and the additional 'fly-on-the-wall' bonus disc that came with the re-issued album proved invaluable. The bonus disc featured extracts from tapes made during the making of the film and original *Let It Be* album, giving a unique insight into the Beatles at work in rehearsal and in the studio during January 1969.

As is usual with this type of broadcast, the Beatle interview archives were put to good use. Fanning used an excerpt from an interview that Ringo had conducted from the back of his chauffeur-driven Mercedes during 1969. The last part of this special was given over to a few Beatles fans that rang the programme and gave their views on the album.

RTÉ 2FM. *The Dave Fanning Show.* 3 May 2004

A large part of this broadcast was given over to a promo recording featuring an interview with film director Richard Lester. In this recording, Lester talks about the making of the Beatles' 1964 film, *A Hard Day's Night*, which had recently become available on DVD.

RTÉ One (TV). *The Late Late Show.* Friday 7 May 2004

Yoko Ono was in Dublin for Amnesty International to open a major collection of art in aid of the organisation. Interviewed by Pat Kenny, Yoko was asked about her trip and her time with John Lennon.

RTÉ Radio 1. *The Ronan Collins Show.* 15 November 2004

Collin's programme normally plays a cross-section of music, but this show was dedicated to celebrating the release of the Beatles' US Capitol albums on CD, by playing 29 tracks from three of the four-album set. A further five tracks were played from the fourth album on the *Ronan Collins Show* the following day.

RTÉ 2FM. *The Dark Horse Years: Solo Years Special.* 29 November 2004

Dave Fanning was to mark the third anniversary of George Harrison's death by broadcasting a special programme based on George's Dark Horse titles. Fanning used the *Dark Horse* promo kit, which had been sent out to radio stations at the time of the issue of the *Dark Horse* boxed set.

Today FM. *Pet Sounds.* 27 January 2005

Normally presented by Tom Dunne, for this night Ann-Marie Kelly took the seat. This broadcast was billed as 'A John Lennon Special', but only the last hour of programme was given over to John Lennon. Today FM had obtained a copy of a WNEW-FM show that Lennon had recorded on Saturday 28 September 1974 in New York, available to Beatles fans for the last twenty years.

Back in 1974, While DJ Dennis Elsas was on the air, he had received a call that John was in the lobby of the radio station. It was around 3.30pm. He put on the longest record he could find, Chicago's *Ballet For a Girl in Buchanan*, which lasted more than fourteen minutes, and went to join John, who then came back with him to the studio. John joined Elsas on his Saturday afternoon show, introducing himself as Doctor Winston O'Boogie, and was on the air from 4–6pm. He and Elsas discussed his career from its earliest days, his relationship with the other three ex-Beatles, his immigration problems and the Rolling Stones.

During his stint on the show, John acts as the DJ, reads out the weather forecast and even delivers, in his own unique style, the various radio advertisements. This broadcast is now part of the American national radio archives.

RTÉ 2FM. *The Dave Fanning Show.* 22 March 2005

Dave Fanning interviewed Mark Edmonds of *The Sunday Times* magazine about a feature in the 20 March issue of the magazine, which told the story of the life of the Beatles' right-hand man, Mal Evans. Edmonds told Dave: 'As the Beatles' roadie for almost a decade, Mal Evans had a ticket to the greatest gig of them all. But he never knew it, and to his credit he never cashed in.'

RTÉ Two (TV). *John and Yoko's Year of Peace.* Easter Monday, 29 March 2005

This documentary was broadcast at 1am, as part of RTÉ's Easter weekend viewing, and records that now famous part of John and Yoko's 1969 honeymoon which they spent in a bed in Toronto. It also included rare footage from John and Yoko's wedding, the infamous bedside confrontation between John and conservative cartoonist Al Capp, Lennon debating with media expert, Marshall McLuhan, and meeting Canadian Prime Minister, Pierre Trudeau.

The newly married couple staged the notorious 'bed-in' at a Toronto hotel to promote their somewhat naïve, but sincere, campaign for world peace. They then moved on to Montreal, where 'Give Peace a Chance' was recorded in another hotel room, before returning to Toronto, where Lennon (accompanied by Eric Clapton and others) became the first Beatle to perform solo in concert. There is no film of that event on the 29 March programme, but there is a great deal of other Lennon footage, revealing him to be utterly honest, unpretentious, gentle and approachable. Ono and others who were there recall the events in interesting interviews conducted around the time of this 2000 documentary, but it is the scenes from 1969 that make this an invaluable document.

RTÉ One (TV) *Witness The Beatles*. Sunday 3 April 2005

This ten-minute broadcast started at 4.05pm and was part of a short series of history programmes produced by the BBC (BBC Worldwide) featuring eyewitness accounts of historic events. For this programme, entitled *The Beatles*, we were given a look at the band's first gig with the new line-up of John, Paul, George and Ringo, which took place on Saturday 18 August 1962. (Pete Best's final appearance with the Beatles had been on Wednesday 15 August.) The programme also showed footage of the present day Cavern and the venue of Ringo's first Beatles engagement, Hulme Hall, Port Sunlight, Birkenhead. This was the only Beatle-related subject in the BBC series.

Today FM. *The Essential Beatles*. 19 June 2005

Part one of this radio series focused on the Beatles, and *Essential* presenter Jim O'Neill spent an hour giving a potted history of the band, linking Beatles tracks in no particular order.

RTÉ 2FM. Paul McCartney Promo. Saturday 24 September 2005

An odd time and place for a Paul McCartney promo. Shortly after 7am on Saturday morning, Shane O'Donoghue broadcast the EMI promo for McCartney's new album, *Chaos and Creation in the Backyard*. It was a 55-minute mix of interview and songs in which McCartney talks about his new CD.

RTÉ 2FM. *The Dave Fanning Show*: The Cynthia Lennon Interview. 30 September 2005

Dave Fanning interviewed John Lennon's first wife, Cynthia Lennon, for his radio show and the interview was split into two parts. The second part was not broadcast until Monday 3 October. Cynthia was in the middle of a tour promoting her new book about her life and times with John Lennon. She had arrived in Dublin a few hours earlier from a book-signing in Liverpool. After her recording session in Dublin, Cynthia and her publicity team made their way to Belfast for an appearance on the UTV programme, *Kelly*.

UTV. *Kelly*. 30 September 2005

Cynthia Lennon joined Gerry Kelly to talk about her life with John, her current life, and her new book entitled, *John*. She told of the breakdown of their marriage and her relationship with Yoko Ono in more detail than ever before. The book was published in the same week as the broadcast.

Today FM. *Pet Sounds*: John Lennon Special. Monday 10 October 2005

Presented by Tom Dunne, the second part of this radio show, aired between 8pm and 9pm, was billed as a 'John Lennon Special' to mark what would have been Lennon's 65th birthday the day before.

The hour-long broadcast of music and, by now, familiar Lennon dialogue, kicks-off with 'Come Together'. This is followed by 'Ain't That A Shame', 'You've Got To Hide Your Love Away', 'Strawberry Fields Forever', 'And Your Bird Can Sing', 'Norwegian Wood (This Bird Has Flown)', 'Working Class Hero', 'Woman', '#9 Dream', 'Across the Universe', 'Two of Us', 'A Day in the Life' and 'Imagine'.

Choice FM. *Beatles Cover Show*. 6 November 2005

Choice FM, financed by Bay Broadcasting Ltd, was given a temporary service application to broadcast from 6 August – 13 November 2005 by the BCI (Broadcasting Commission of Ireland). On Sunday 6 November, the station broadcast a programme of Beatles cover songs presented by Eamon Carr, one time member of 'Horslips'.

RTÉ Two (TV). *The Last Broadcast*. 8 November 2005

This weekly late-night music show, presented by Dave Fanning, had a mix of live performances, interviews and videos. On this occasion, *The Last Broadcast* played a pre-taped interview with Paul McCartney as part of McCartney's promotion for his album *Chaos and Creation in the Backyard*. RTÉ broadcast seven minutes of the 30-minute, special edition DVD, which had come with the album. Viewers were treated to excerpts of two songs, the first single 'Fine Line' and 'Friends To Go'. Fanning also played the video for John Lennon's 1971 hit 'Jealous Guy' prior to the McCartney promo.

Today FM. *The Essential John Lennon*. 4 December 2005

This was the second Beatle-related broadcast in the series. Presented by Mark Cagney, this hour of classic tracks from Lennon was to mark the 25 years since Lennon was murdered. The broadcast kicks-off with 'Nobody Told Me' and continues with '(Just Like) Starting Over', 'Woman', 'Mind Games', 'Instant

Karma!', 'Jealous Guy', 'Working Glass Hero', 'Woman is the Nigger of the World', '#9 Dream', 'Imagine', 'Stand By Me' and 'Happy Xmas (War Is Over)'.

RTÉ 2FM. *The Gerry Ryan Show.* 7 December 2005

This airing of Gerry Ryan's show remembered John Lennon, marking his murder in New York some 25 years previously. Gerry Ryan interviews Eamon Carr about the life and times of John Lennon, in particular Lennon's post-Beatle life in New York right up to the day of his death in 1980. Carr gives an animated account of Lennon's last day. Listeners learn that it began at 7.30 am (local time) with breakfast at La Fortuna's, continuing at 9am with a visit to his local barber, where his hair was cut into a fifties style with a quiff, reminiscent of his Beatles days in Hamburg.

RTÉ Radio 1. *Liveline.* 7 December 2005

This afternoon phone-in show, presented by Joe Duffy, has a history of lively debate. This particular show went out on the eve of the controversial Channel 4 programme, *I Killed John Lennon*, a broadcast to mark the 25th anniversary of the ex-Beatle's death in 1980.

On the phone line from London was the producer of the Channel 4 programme, Irishman David Harvey, who found himself up against a barrage of abuse from disgusted Beatles fans. Amongst the contributors to the show are RTÉ's Dave Fanning, giving an overview on the subject, Richard Hall, who led the main objection to the Channel 4's programme, and Pete Brennan of Beatles Ireland, who all engaged in a very heated debate with Mr Harvey.

RTÉ 2FM.*The Dave Fanning Show.* 7 December 2005

Dave Fanning broadcast an interview, conducted in June of 2005, with Joe Eleo who was a tape operator for New York Radio station WNEW-FM. Eleo tells Fanning about the day that John Lennon made himself available to the New York station for a two-hour interview. This part of Fanning's show was an original piece of work. The rest of the broadcast was made up of substantial segments of the 1974 Elsas interview on WNEW-FM, which was run by Fanning on consecutive nights and ended on Friday 9 December. Despite reassurances by Fanning that what listeners were getting was new to Irish radio, the WNEW-FM recording had been made available to Dublin-based rival radio station, Today FM, in January 2005 (see p 193 for details).

Near FM 101.6. *The Beatles Bug.* 7 December 2005

This radio station was given a service application to broadcast some ten years earlier than 2005 by the BCI. DJ Mick Dunne kicked off his new weekly Beatles radio show *The Beatles Bug* at 9pm on Wednesday 7 December, the eve of the 25th anniversary of John Lennon's death. Dunne was to give the story of Lennon's last day in New York with tracks from *Double Fantasy* as well as some acoustic and pre-recorded interviews with John and Yoko.

RTÉ 2FM. *Breakfast Show*: Second Lennon Day. 8 December 2005

RTÉ opened its second day on all things Lennon on the breakfast show, with Shane O'Donoghue presenting. During the week leading up the 25th anniversary of Lennon's death, listeners to the show had been asked to send in a list of Lennon songs they would like to hear during the show.

East Coast FM. *The Morning Show.* 8 December 2005

Twenty-four hours after the *Liveline* debate, the controversial Channel 4 programme *I Killed John Lennon* (a broadcast to mark the 25th anniversary of Lennon's death) was discussed once again. Declan Meehan and Tracy Clifford managed to persuade David Harvey, the programme's Channel 4 producer, to talk about the documentary, which was to be shown that night.

Today FM. *Pet Sounds: John Lennon Special.* 8 December 2005

Presented by Tom Dunne, this broadcast was to mark the 25th anniversary of the ex-Beatle's death. The second part of the show was billed as yet another 'John Lennon Special', making good use of the Beatles' *Anthology* and its out-take versions of classic Lennon tracks.

A pre-recorded outside broadcast was provided by Dunne's colleague, Ann-Marie Kelly, who early in the day had ventured on to the streets of Dublin to ask the general public about their thoughts on the life and times of John Lennon. One told Kelly, 'Five bullets were fired and not one hit Yoko!'

The broadcast included Beatle interviews and the tracks 'Love', 'A Day In the Life', 'I Feel Fine', 'Girl', 'You've Got To Hide Your Love Away', 'Strawberry Fields Forever', 'Polythene Pam', 'She Said She Said', 'Step Inside Love' (John and Paul), 'Two of Us', 'Come Together', 'Working Class Hero' and 'Imagine'.

Near FM 101.6. *The Beatle Bug.* 14 December 2005
Mick Dunne presented the second edition of his weekly Beatles radio show. This time the 1966 album *Revolver* gets a one-hour special.

Near FM 101.6. *The Beatle Bug.* 20 December 2005
Mick Dunne presented a Christmas week edition of his weekly programme, kicking off with 'My Sweet Lord'. Dunne continued by making good use of the Beatles Fan Club Christmas records from the 1960s.

Near FM 101.6. *The Beatle Bug.* 28 December 2005
The fourth programme in the series *The Beatle Bug* was a Paul McCartney special. The show started with 'Jet', followed by 'Fine Line', 'Every Night', 'Pipes of Peace', 'Old Siam Sir', 'Give Ireland Back to the Irish', 'Junk', 'Maybe I'm Amazed', 'Nineteen Hundred and Eighty Five', 'Girls' School', 'Mull Of Kintyre', 'Flaming Pie', 'Riding To Vanity Fair', 'I'm Carrying' and 'Coming Up'.

Near FM 101.6. *The Beatle Bug.* 4 January 2006
By the fifth in the series, the programme had established itself into a steady routine and was set to continue for a long run. For this show, presenter Mick Dunne gave his hour-long broadcast over to 'Under the Covers', a programme dealing with Beatles' songs covered by a variety of artists from the sixties to the present day. More recent broadcasts in this series have included: 'A look at the life of John Lennon' (11 January 2006); 'Beatles Out-takes' (18 January 2006); '"Let It Be" Special' (25 January 2006); 'The Beatles and the Grammies' (8 February 2006); 'The Beatles' Love Songs' (15 February 2006); a George Harrison tribute (22 February 2006); and, for its final broadcast on 1 March 2006, 'Beatles Links'.

RTÉ One (TV). *Paul McCartney: Chaos And Creation Live At Abbey Road.* Thursday 5 January 2006
This TV broadcast had started life on BBC Radio 2 in September of 2005. Back in July 2005, Sir Paul returned to the Abbey Road studio to perform and reminisce before a small studio audience. During the beautifully filmed (not videotaped) documentary, Sir Paul explains the workings of the old Abbey Road recording equipment, demonstrates a variety of musical instruments, from various guitars

to Elvis Presley's bass and an early synthesiser, and sings a range of songs from all periods of his musical career. Viewers learn that Sir Paul is a Charles Dickens fan – that's where he borrowed the word 'peradventure' (meaning 'perhaps') for his song 'English Tea'. The show ends with a rousing improvisation he calls 'That's All For Now'.

RTÉ 2FM. *Larry Gogan.* Tuesday 17 January 2006

Veteran RTÉ broadcaster Larry Gogan, while presenting his daily afternoon programme, gave an hour of his broadcast time over to the Beatles. This part of the programme, known as 'The Golden Hour', gave his listeners a brief chart history of the group.

The playlist was 'She Loves You', 'Penny Lane', 'I Want To Hold Your Hand', 'Hey Jude', 'Can't Buy Me Love', 'Get Back', ' A Hard Day's Night', 'Something', 'Ticket To Ride', 'Hello, Goodbye', 'Yesterday', 'Lady Madonna', 'I Feel Fine', 'Let It Be' and 'All You Need Is Love'.

RTÉ 2FM. *The Dave Fanning Show.* 7 February 2006

Dave Fanning interviewed Róisín Ingle of *The Irish Times* about a new biography of Paul McCartney, written by Christopher Sandford, scheduled for release on 1 February.

The author has already published books on Mick Jagger and Sting and is a writer for *The New York Times* and Britain's *Daily Mail* and *Daily Telegraph*. Ms Ingle says Mr Sandford's biography is well written and well researched and is said to be unique in that it examines the final days of Linda, followed by a significant amount of material on Sir Paul's life after her death, with a special focus on his concerts and recordings. Mr Sandford's sources include court documents as well as interviews with Sir Paul's family members and colleagues.

As part of this feature, Fanning used parts of the interview he had done with Paul McCartney back in December 2001 (see p 190 for further details).

Today FM Radio. *The Essential Paul McCartney and Wings.* 24 April 2006

For the third Beatle-related broadcast in the *Essential* series, attention focused on Paul and his post-Beatles band, Wings.

RTÉ Radio 1. *Five Seven Live.* 16 May 2006

Earlier on this day, 16 May 2006, Paul and Heather had issued a statement to confirm that they were to split after almost four years of marriage. The announcement followed weeks of speculation in British newspapers about the state of the couple's relationship. Pete Brennan of Beatles Ireland was interviewed by Rachael English in a pre-recorded phone call about the breaking story and gave an Irish perspective on the breaking news.

RTÉ 2FM. *Marty in the Morning.* 1 November 2006

The *Marty In The Morning* team played a four-track sampler of the Beatles' new *Love* album, comprising 'Strawberry Fields Forever', 'Lady Madonna', 'Octopus's Garden', and 'While My Guitar Gently Weeps'. This was the first time that the sampler had been played on Irish radio.

Today FM. *Pet Sounds.* 2 November 2006

Sean Lennon appeared as a guest on this popular music show presented by Tom Dunne. As the son of John Lennon, perhaps the most beloved Beatle, and avant-garde musician Yoko Ono, Sean Lennon was a celebrity before he had even begun his recording career. That may be the reason why he did not choose straight-ahead pop as his musical vocation like his half-brother Julian. Instead, he cleverly positioned himself between pop and experimental. He was due to perform in The Village music venue in Dublin's Wexford Street. During his appearance on the show, Sean Lennon performed the Beach Boys' song,' God Only Knows'.

RTÉ One (TV). *Oileán.* 13 November 2006

This new series aimed to reveal hidden stories relating to islands off the coast of Ireland, and the first in the series looked at Dorinish, bought by John Lennon in 1967–68. (See Chapter 4 for the full story.)

RTÉ Radio 1. *The Dave Fanning Show.* 13 November 2006

RTÉ DJ Dave Fanning was reduced to one hour of broadcasting a night after his move from 2FM to RTÉ Radio 1. On 13 November he reviewed, with Eamonn Sweeney, the Beatles' then forthcoming album, *Love.* Also as part of this feature, Fanning played two tracks from an EMI sampler for the album, 'Strawberry Fields Forever' and 'While My Guitar Gently Weeps'.

RTÉ Radio 1. *The Radio 1 Music Collection.* 13 November 2006
'In Concert – Swingin' with the Beatles (Part One)' saw Brian Byrne and his Big Band perform new arrangements of Beatles songs. The concert had been recorded on 3 September at the National Concert Hall, Dublin, with guest singers Anne Bushnell and Colin Devlin. The show featured brand new 'Swingin'' arrangements of songs like 'Lucy In The Sky With Diamonds', 'Don't Let Me Down', 'Hey Jude', 'A Hard Day's Night', 'Penny Lane', 'Let It Be', 'Yesterday', 'Yellow Submarine', 'Long and Winding Road', 'God Only Knows', and 'Imagine'. Part two of this concert was broadcast one week later on Monday 20 November.

Today FM Radio. *Pet Sounds.* 16 November 2006
The second part of Tom Dunne's nightly radio show on this date was billed 'Love'. In fact DJ Dunne had been given the 'Love' press kit by EMI (Ireland), which he used in the broadcast. Dunne told his listeners about the fascinating re-working of numerous classic Beatles' recordings by the band's original producer, Sir George Martin, and his son Giles. 'Love' is also the title of the highly successful Cirque du Soleil show, a co-production with Apple Corps, featuring the music of the Beatles, which was wowing audiences in Las Vegas at the time of the broadcast. In creating the music for the show and for the album, George and Giles have created a continuous 'soundscape' – a series of well-known Beatles songs, augmented by additional instrumentation and vocals taken from their vast bank of original multi-track tapes. Dunne added:

> If you can imagine 'Strawberry Fields Forever', beginning with John's original demo, before going into an early take of the song and then climaxing in a musical collage, including the piano solo from 'In My Life' and the harpsichord pattern from 'Piggies', and lots, lots more – or 'Get Back', prefaced by the 'Hard Day's Night' opening guitar chord, the guitar and drum solos from 'The End', and segued into 'Glass Onion' – you will begin to get the picture. But hearing is believing! The guys have pushed back the boundaries and come up with a brand-new work that will add to the enduring legacy of the band. The result is an amazing album that only reinforces the timeless quality of the group's recordings.

At the end of Dunne's show, he tells his listeners that fans will have fun enjoying the roller-coaster experience of the album whilst trying to spot where all the pieces come from. It is also destined to open up a new legion of fans to the Beatles experience.

East Coast FM. *The Morning Show.* 29 January 2007

Broadcast on a daily basis and presented by Declan Meehan and Tracy Clifford, this show debated and discussed the issues of the day. Pop guru Mick Lynch was a guest (by telephone) on the 29 January programme to talk about the 38th anniversary of the Beatles' last live performance on the roof of their Apple offices in London in 1969.

RTÉ Radio 1. *The Dave Fanning Show.* 6 February 2007

Technology giant, Apple, reached a deal with the Beatles to end the dispute over the use of the Apple name. DJ Dave Fanning included a ten-minute interview with reporter Ken Sweeney from *Star Sunday*. Sweeney went on to tell Fanning the story about the two companies wrangling over the use of the Apple name and logo for more than 25 years.

The dispute dates back to 1980, when the late George Harrison noticed an advert for Apple computers in a magazine. He felt there was potential for trademark conflict with Apple Corps – set up by the Beatles in 1968 to release their songs and manage their creative affairs.

Fanning also played a very short segment of the interview he had conducted with Ringo Starr at Dublin's Point Depot and he played out with the Beatles' 1966 B-side, 'Rain'.

Today FM. *The Essential Album Collection.* 22 April 2007

The essential album for 22 April was *Sgt Pepper's Lonely Hearts Club Band* (1967) In fact this broadcast presented by Tom Dunne was also to mark the 40th anniversary of the album completion date of 21 April 1967.

Sgt Pepper's Lonely Hearts Club Band typifies the year of 1967 and, as such, must rank as a masterpiece as captures the time of its recording. For this radio broadcast, Tom Dunne played the complete album with the addition of 'Penny Lane' and 'Strawberry Fields Forever', two singles that were released prior to the album's release.

RTÉ 2FM, *The Gerry Ryan Show.* 25 May 2007

On this edition of his daily show, presenter Gerry Ryan played for the first time on Irish radio the new Paul McCartney single, 'Dance Tonight', from McCartney's forthcoming album *Memory Almost Full.* Presenter Ryan went on to give a favourable response on hearing the single for the first time.

RTÉ 2FM. *The Gerry Ryan Show.* 31 May 2007

During the course of his daily radio show, presenter Gerry Ryan paid homage and marked the 40th anniversary of the release of the Beatles' 1967 classic album *Sgt Pepper's Lonely Hearts Club Band*, by playing all the albums tracks during his three-hour broadcast.

Today FM. *Pet Sounds.* Thursday 31 May 2007

By far the best tribute to the Beatles on Irish radio for some time. Tom Dunne and his production team put together a three-hour extravaganza entitled, *Forty Years of Sgt Pepper*, which was split into three parts. The first covered the year before the Beatles recorded *Pepper*. Part two was given over to an in-depth look at the recording of the album, with contributions from all four Beatles as well as Sir George Martin. The final part of this broadcast looked at the influence the album has had on bands since 1967. With major contributions from the authors of this book, this programme went on to win a PPI (Phonographic Performance Ireland) Radio Award, towards the end of 2007.

East Coast FM. *The Morning Show.* 6 July 2007

On the 50th anniversary of the historic meeting between John Lennon and Paul McCartney at St Peter's Church, Woolton, Liverpool, on this day in 1957, East Coast Radio were the only Irish broadcasting organisation to show any recollection of this truly historic date. Pete Brennan of Beatles Ireland was interviewed by presenter Declan Meehan about the anniversary and the planned events in Liverpool over the coming weekend to mark the historic meeting.

Pete went on to tell Declan about John Lennon's band, the Quarrymen, and how they played during the afternoon on a makeshift stage in the field behind the church in Woolton. Brennan explained: 'It was while the Quarrymen were setting up their instruments in the church hall during the early evening that occasional tea-chest bass Quarryman, Ivan Vaughan, introduced to John and the others his classmate from Liverpool Institute, 15-year-old Paul McCartney.'

RTÉ Radio 1. *The Dave Fanning Show.* 4 October 2007

On the 4 October broadcast Dave Fanning interviewed, by telephone from London, Pattie Boyd about her new book *Wonderful Today*. The book was written with acclaimed biographer and journalist, Penny Junor. In it Boyd tells the story of her struggles against addiction, tragedy, infertility and her life with two of the twentieth century's greatest musical icons: her husbands George Harrison and Eric Clapton.

RTÉ 2FM. *The Gerry Ryan Show.* 9 October 2007

Presenter Gerry Ryan paid homage to John Lennon on what would have been his 67th birthday by playing two Lennon tracks, 'Working Class Hero' and 'Imagine'.

RTÉ Radio 1. *The Dave Fanning Show.* 18 October 2007

What collided in the cosmos to create such a force? Would you make the connection between the Beatles and writer John Osborne's 'Angry Young Man' movement? Well, one author has.

For the second part of the programme on 18 October, Dave Fanning interviewed, by telephone from New York, the author Jonathan Gould who discussed his new book *Can't Buy Me Love: The Beatles, Britain and America*. Jonathan Gould recounted some fascinating Beatles facts, including how the band saved the world from boredom. He expressed the opinion that (although ultimately the product of influences deeper than pop) the sixties, with their soaring optimism, were nowhere expressed more perfectly than in the music of the Beatles. The interview was punctuated with two Beatles songs, 'Paperback Writer' and 'Hello Goodbye'.

RTÉ Two (TV). *The Last Broadcast.* 31 October 2007

This weekly late-night music show, presented by Dave Fanning, had a mix of live performances, interviews and videos. On this occasion, *The Last Broadcast* played an EMI promo interview with Ringo Starr about his recently released album of greatest hits, named *Photograph*.

RTÉ Radio 1. *The Dave Fanning Show.* 27 November 2007

For the opening part of this show, Dave Fanning interviewed by telephone from Northern Ireland one-time Wings guitarist, Henry McCullough. It had been 40 years ago in Belfast that Jimi Hendrix had performed his one and only performance on an Irish stage on his 25th birthday. Support that night in 1967 came from McCullough.

RTÉ Radio 1. *The Dave Fanning Show.* 6 February 2008

For the opening part of the show, Dave Fanning interviewed by telephone the 1960s music icon, Donovan. He was asked to comment on the passing of the Maharishi Mahesh Yogi, a guru to the Beatles and the man who introduced the West to Transcendental Meditation. The Maharishi had died on Tuesday 5 February at his home in the Dutch town of Vlodrop, and was thought to be 91 years old. Fanning talked to Donovan about his time in Rishikesh in India in 1968 with the Maharishi and the Beatles. Donovan explained, 'The Maharishi's influence over the Beatles, as well as other western musicians, was at its peak [in 1968], and although their time with him was short, it had a marked impact on their lives and their music: we would not, for example, have had the *White Album* without him.' Fanning ended the piece by playing the Donovan song 'Hurdy Gurdy Man'.

RTÉ 2FM. *The Gerry Ryan Show.* 22 February 2008

For the second part of this edition of his daily show, presenter Gerry Ryan introduced Julia Baird, one of John Lennon's half-sisters, as studio guest. Julia was back in Ireland to promote her latest book *Imagine This*. The interview turned out to be a very informative and fascinating piece of broadcasting. Julia told the listeners that she was the first daughter of Julia Lennon and John Dykins, born in March 1947. Her parents didn't marry when they began to live together because her mother was not divorced from Freddie Lennon.

Her mother took her to see John perform for the first time when they were invited to watch the Quarrymen play at a street party in 1957. Julia remained in touch with John when he was in the Beatles until he moved to America. She never met Yoko Ono, although she talked to her on the telephone. Julia commented, 'She never seemed particularly anxious to let us share John with her. When John went to live with Yoko in America he lost touch with the entire family.' She had been completely out of touch with John for five years before his death.

The last time she had spoken to John was when she was in Ireland, having just given birth to her first child – John phoned to congratulate her.

East Coast FM. *The Morning Show.* 25 March 2008

Neil Aspinall, the confidant described as the 'Fifth Beatle', who became mastermind of the Fab Four's business empire, had died in New York the previous Sunday aged 66. Pete Brennan of Beatles Ireland was interviewed by presenter Declan Meehan to talk about the life and times of Aspinall. Brennan went on to tell the listeners that Sir Paul McCartney visited Aspinall in hospital days before he died from lung cancer, and how Aspinall had been a schoolfriend of both McCartney and George Harrison and had become guardian of the Beatles' shambolic business interests at Apple Corps in 1968, on the condition that he would do it 'only until they found someone else'. He quit the position in April 2007.

RTÉ Radio One. *The Dave Fanning Show.* 26 March 2008

Coming from a slightly different approach, presenter Fanning asked the question: who was the Fifth Beatle? referring to the recent death of Neil Aspinall. Once again Beatles Ireland's Pete Brennan was on hand to ponder the question put by Fanning. Brennan held the view that the Fifth Beatle was in fact Pete Best, one time Beatle drummer. Brennan went on to talk about Aspinall's formative years with the Beatles: 'Neil was in the same year at Liverpool Institute as Paul, and the year above George, asking him behind the bike shed, for a drag on his ciggie". Fanning then asked the question about Neil Aspinall having an affair with Mona, Pete's mother. Brennan went on to say: 'Aspinall had studied to become an accountant but came back into contact with Paul and George through his friendship with Pete Best. Neil was living at the house of Pete's mother, Mona, who ran the Casbah, the little club where the Beatles then played as the Quarrymen. Neil started working for them as a part-time roadie in 1961, running them to local gigs in an old van for five shillings per man per gig; £1 a night. What never came out at the time was Neil's affair with Mona. In fact they had a son who was born when Neil was only 19!' Towards the end of the interview with Fanning, Brennan added 'By 1962, Neil gave up his accountancy studies and joined the Beatles full-time. Later, when they had started national touring, he was joined by another roadie, Mal Evans. Mal was big and beefy and unflappable. Neil was lean, rather neurotic, always seemed worried. He was with them through all their years of fame. Neil was totally loyal and faithful to them and I think the Beatles were very fortunate to have him.'

East Coast FM. *The Morning Show.* 17 April 2008

To mark the 10th Anniversary of the death of Linda McCartney, Declan Meehan devoted some of his programme to talk to Pete Brennan of Beatles Ireland about her life, both prior to meeting Paul, while working as a freelance photographer, and her life with the Beatle as a photographer, musician, and devoted mother to their children, and her battle with cancer.

Liffey Sound FM. *The Beatles Generation.* 20 April 2008

A volunteer-run station based in west Dublin that was granted a broadcasting licence. Presenter Ken Martin had Beatles Ireland President Pete Brennan live in studio for the two-hour show to discuss everything from the Beatles Ireland fan club, to the recent death of Neil Aspinall, and the 10th Anniversary of the death of Linda McCartney, while playing some of the lesser-known Beatles recordings.

RTÉ Radio One. *The Dave Fanning Show.* 24 April 2008

Los Angeles-based journalist Lisa Derrick discusses the up-and-coming legal actions in the US by Yoko over the work of her late husband John Lennon. First case was taken against singer Lennon Murphy and her use of the 'Lennon' name as part of her recording career. The second action was with two New York-based film-makers and the use of the John Lennon hit 'Imagine' in a recently released film. The most interesting aspect of the interview was Yoko's legal action against her ex-husband Anthony Cox. Cox, an erstwhile film-maker, had shot hours of home-movie footage of both John and Yoko during the 1970s and over the last thirty years had attempted to profit from his work. Yoko had come to a financial agreement with Cox to buy all of the footage shot by him, but Cox had continued to offer the home movies to the highest bidder.

Today FM Radio. *Pet Sounds.* 28 April – 1 May 2008

'The Bluffer's Guide to John Lennon' formed a short part of this broadcast. Presenter Tom Dunne ran this item over the next few nights. Consisting of a few Lennon songs each night and a potted history of the man and his music, the

Legendary Irish DJ Declan Meehan, pictured here with Paul McCartney in 1986. *(Meehan Collection)*

item ended with a competition and an opportunity for Lennon fans to win the singer's back catalogue on CD of Japanese imports.

East Coast FM. *The Morning Show.* 18 June 2008

Pete Brennan, of the Irish Beatles fan club Beatles Ireland, was interviewed over the telephone by the programme's presenter Laura Wood about Paul McCartney's 66th birthday celebrations. Brennan was asked to give a brief overview of McCartney's career to date. Paul's recent concerts in front of 350,000 people in Kiev, Ukraine, on 14 June 2008 and his Liverpool concert on 1 June 2008 also came under the microscope, displaying the fact that, in spite of his advancing years, McCartney was still able to woo an audience.

RTÉ Radio One, *The Dave Fanning Show.* 18 June 2008

Paul McCartney turned 66 on 18 June 2008. Ringo Starr left him a phone message wishing him well and the one-time Beatles drummer would turn 68 on 7 July while he was out on tour with the latest edition of his All-Starr Band.

Dave Fanning marked McCartney's birthday with a few brief comments prompted by his listeners, who reminded him of the ex-Beatle's celebration. Fanning went on to play the McCartney 1970 hit 'Maybe I'm Amazed' to finish off this short segment of tonight's show.

RTÉ Radio 1. *The Dave Fanning Show*. 23 June 2008.
Tonight's show was presented by Eoin Sweeney. He talked to Gail Renard who discussed her encounter with John Lennon and how she got to own the handwritten lyrics to John Lennon's 'Give Peace a Chance' and hear the story of how they were given to her. In July the lyrics were to go under the hammer at Christie's in London.

East Coast FM. *The Morning Show*. 25 June 2008
The Morning Show had over the last few years developed a healthy interest in all things Beatles. So much so that its daily 'Do You Remember' slot would mention the group regularly, usually around a Beatle anniversary.

For today's edition, regular contributor Mick Lynch was on hand for a short question-and-answer session regarding the Beatles' 'Our World' appearance, which had been broadcast on Sunday 25 June 1967. Lynch went on to explain to presenter Declan Meehan about the Beatles' recording session for the BBC programme that, for the first time ever, linked five continents from EMI's Abbey Road studio, via the Early Bird 'space booster' satellite. The broadcast had taken the form of a party, with many of the group's friends sitting cross-legged on the studio floor, among them Mick Jagger, Marianne Faithfull and Eric Clapton to name but a few, all there to witness the world-premiere performance of 'All You Need is Love'.

East Coast FM. *The Morning Show*. 7 July 2008.
Remembering Ringo Starr's 68th birthday, Pete Brennan of Beatles Ireland gave an overall review of Ringo's life from being born in the poor part of Liverpool, his time with Rory Storm and his band and their time in Hamburg with the Beatles, replacing Pete Best, making films, his post-Beatle life and his concert in Dublin. He went on to mention the fact that Ringo is still touring with the All Starr bands and his son Zak is playing with the 1960s band, The Who.

Irish media cited in this chapter:

Anna Livia FM 103.2, 3 Grafton St, Dublin 2 (1994, 1999); *then* Griffith College, Dublin 8 (2002); *then* Docklands Innovation Park, East Wall Road, Dublin 3 (present day)

Choice FM 92.1 Marina House, Dun Laoghaire, Dublin

East Coast FM Bray, Co Wicklow

Granada Television Studio Four, Granada TV Centre, Manchester (Gay Byrne, November 1963)

Liffey Sound FM Lucan, Co Dublin

Near FM 101.6 North East Access Radio, Dublin 17

News Talk 106 Warrington House, Mount Street Crescent, Dublin 2

Radio Nova Herbert Sreet, Dublin 4 (closed in 1980s)

RTÉ (Radio Telefís Éireann) Donnybrook, Dublin 4

Today FM 124 Abbey St Upper, Dublin 1 *then* Marconi House, Digges Lane, Dublin 2 (present day)

TV4 TV Baile na hAbhann, Co na Gaillimhe

UTV Havelock House, Belfast Northern Ireland

Bibliography

Badman, Keith: *The Beatles After the Break-Up* (Omnibus Press, 1970–2001).
Miles, Barry: *The Beatles Diary Volume One* (Omnibus Press 2001).
Miles, Barry: *Paul McCartney: Many Years From Now* (Secker & Warburg 1997)
The Beatles: *Anthology*, (Cassell & Co, 2000).
Richard, Dilello: *The Longest Cocktail Party*, (Mojo Books, 2000).
Harrison, George: *I Me Mine*, (W H Allen, 1994).
Harry, Bill: *The Beatles Encyclopaedia*, (Virgin Books, 2000).
Lennon, Cynthia: *A Twist Of Lennon*, (Avon Books,1978 / Secker & Warburg, 1999).
Lewisohn, Mark: *The Complete Beatles Recording Sessions*, (Hamlyn, 1977).
Lewisohn, Mark: *The Complete Beatles Chronicle*, (Pyramid Books, 1989).
McDonald, Ian: *Revolution In the Head*, (Pimlico, 1994).
Reid, Eileen: *Eileen*, (Town and Country House, 1995)

Newspapers, Magazines and Journals

Beatles Ireland Magazine, *Beatles Monthly*, the *Belfast Telegraph*, the *Connaught Telegraph*, the *Daily Mail*, the *Daily Mirror*, the *Irish Independent*, the *Evening Herald*, the *Irish Sun*, *The Irish Times*, *The Mayo News*, *Mojo* Magazine, *Record Collector* Magazine.

Audio Visual Sources

Anna Livia, Dublin; BBC Northern Ireland; Century Radio, Dublin; East Coast FM, Wicklow; Granada Television; Radio Nova, Dublin; Radio Telefís Éireann; Today FM, Dublin; Ulster Television.

Websites

www.beatlesireland.info
www.maccareport.com

A bubble that is unlikely ever to burst

We are greatly indebted to the staff of Collins Press, who took on this project and were dedicated to creating a truly exceptional book and to tell one of the greatest success stories of the 1960s. Four hugely talented young men with Irish backgrounds produced music that was unique and timeless. The quality of their work is still held with respect and awe today. When the remaining two Beatles are gone, the afterglow will still live on and will never depart from the popular cultural scene. A bubble that is unlikely ever to burst.

Index